Reve… the Fourth Son

ROBERT G. BARBARIA

Enlighten Noah Publishing
3521 Ryder St.
Santa Clara, CA 95051

ISBN 1-929400-01-2

Printed in R.O.C.

First edition 2004

Contents

INTRODUCTION..........5

Foreword..........11

Chapter #1 The INHERITANCE..........19

Chapter #2 Spiritual Ascension..........33

Chapter #3 Spirit (Identity)..........41

Chapter #4 Soul (Purpose)..........51

Chapter #5 The ANGELS..........59

Chapter #6 Lucifer and his Fallen Regime..........69

Chapter #7 Speaking to the SPIRIT..........83

Chapter #8 The FOUR SONS of ***GOD***..........93

Chapter #9 EARTH Angels..........107

Chapter #10 Gender and Sexual Behavior..........115

Chapter #11 NUMBERS..........121

Chapter #12 MIRACLES..........133

Chapter #13 Welcome ***HOLY SPIRIT;*** THE ***DELIVERER 182***..........139

Chapter #14 Hardships..........161

Chapter #15 COMING DOWN with ***VENGEANCE***..........169

Chapter #16 ***GOD'S COMMANDMENTS*** and LAWS..........179

Chapter #17 The Survivors....................191

Chapter #18 LIFE within the CITY WALLS....................201

Chapter #19 The CONCLUSION....................213

Chapter #20 The SCRIBE & The GUARDIAN....................221

Chapter #21 JUDGMENT DAY!....................227

Chapter #22 HELL, an ETERNAL Reality....................235

Chapter #23 CYCLES....................241

Chapter #24 CREATION....................249

Chapter #25 Contradictions?....................263

INTRODUCTION

Shortly after ***THE LORD*** had come to me on the morning of October 13th 1997, I was told to write a BOOK. I was given the title of "REVELATION the FOURTH SON", and told that the BOOK would document the SPIRITUAL CHANGES I would undergo during my 26 month ASCENSION PERIOD. ***THE LORD*** said that on the 13th day of each month, starting on the 13th day of October in the year of 1997, I would spiritually ascend monthly to a next higher spiritual level; and, as I ascended my SPIRITUAL UNDERSTANDING and AWARENESS would increase exponentially for each of the succeeding levels. This ASCENSION PERIOD would continue on monthly until the 13th day of October 1999, and at that time I would be ***IMMANUEL*** (as ONE with ***GOD***).

I was also told that I would be given times and dates for certain EVENTS that were going to take place, and they as well were to be put into the BOOK. ALL the experiences I were to encounter were to be documented in the BOOK, along with some DETAILS on certain things that had taken place over the course of my life. Many of the things ***THE LORD*** had pointed out that had happened to ME I had never really given much thought to. However, after they were explained in DETAIL to ME, I could SEE how ***GOD*** had always been involved in ALL of my EXPERIENCES.

Many of the things occurring in MY LIFE that I had formerly thought were just circumstantial events, were not circumstantial at all, but rather the ***WILL of GOD. THE LORD*** PREPLANNED all these things in MY LIFE, such as; my Residence addresses, Drivers License and Social Security numbers, and even MY NAME.

However, once the BOOK had been completed and I asked if it should be published, ***GOD*** told ME the BOOK was not to be published, for it was much too revealing! ***HE*** said that ***HE*** only had ME write the BOOK for MY own EDIFICATION. Then a year or so later, ***GOD*** had ME write another BOOK for ***HIM,*** titled, "Revealing The Bible's Truth", and some of the first BOOK'S information was put into "Revealing The Bible's Truth" along with some Biblical

Scripture explanation.

After writing “Revealing The Bible’s Truth” for ***THE LORD*** and thinking it was the only BOOK I was intended to write, in November of 2002 ***GOD*** had ME write a third BOOK, and, its title is, “The ROD of IRON”. While writing “The ROD of IRON” I was told by ***THE LORD*** that the FIRST BOOK, “REVELATION the FOURTH SON” would also be published after it, but not in its current form. ***THE LORD*** said that ALL references given regarding TIMES and PLACES of KEY EVENTS were to be removed from the BOOK, for no one other than I could be told of these things. As a matter of fact, ***GOD*** had ME DESTROY all of the FIRST BOOK in its entirety, including the manuscript and computer files, and said, ***HE*** would give ME NEW WORDS to be put into the BOOK.

Once I had DESTROYED the manuscript and computer files for “REVELATION the FOURTH SON”, it was as though MY MEMORY had also been ERASED, for I could no longer recall the specific DATES and PLACES given in the BOOK regarding KEY EVENTS. However I still recall the MAJOR EVENTS that will soon take place throughout the world, even though the specific times and places for the EVENTS have been taken from my conscious memory.

THE LORD has told ME that each and everyday in this world should be viewed as the LAST DAY, for no one should know the time or day when they should meet their end. ***GOD*** says ALL should be PREPARED, for they know not the day when they should draw their LAST BREATH, whether it should be their LAST DAY, or the WORLD’S LAST DAY is irrelevant!

As of this time I cannot tell you what will be contained within the chapters of this BOOK, for I do not know. Unlike the other two BOOKS I have WRITTEN for ***THE LORD,*** where ***HE*** had given ME some advanced UNDERSTANDING of the contents of the BOOKS, ***HE*** will not do so with this BOOK! Even as I write this INTRODUCTION, the WORDS are being given to ME as I WRITE, and I cannot tell you what will even be in the very next paragraph. I BELIEVE ***THE LORD*** wants this BOOK to be FREE from any MINDFUL CONTAMINATION and WRITTEN ENTIRELY in the ***SPIRIT of GOD!***

In the PREVIOUS two BOOKS there have been WARNINGS given to the

CHURCH, but ***THE LORD*** says the time for WARNING has already come to pass, and NOW is the TIME for ACTIONS! Thus ***SAITH THE LORD of HOSTS, YOU HAVE BEEN WARNED AND HAVE DONE NOTHING TO REPENT OF YOUR WAYS, AND NOW I SHALL TAKE ACTION, AND WHO SHALL KEEP ME FROM IT!***

I SEE ALL THAT IS DONE IN THE CHURCHES, FOR NOTHING CAN BE KEPT FROM ME. THERE ARE THOSE OF YOU WHO BELIEVE YOU CAN DO AS YOU PLEASE AND GET AWAY WITH IT, BUT I TELL YOU, YOU HAVE GOTTEN AWAY WITH NOTHING; FOR I HAVE SEEN IT ALL WITH MINE OWN EYES AND AM DISGUSTED WITH YOU AND YOUR CHURCHES.

THE TIME OF MY WRATH IS UPON YOU AND THOSE OF YOUR FLOCK, FOR YOU HAVE BEEN WARNED AND HAVE REPENTED NOT. ONCE YOU HAVE SEEN MY GREAT POWER YOU WILL CRAWL INTO YOUR HOLES LIKE WORMS, BUT YOU CANNOT HIDE FROM ME, FOR I SEE AND KNOW ALL!

YOU HAVE MISLED MY PEOPLE FOR LONG ENOUGH, AND NOW I SHALL EXPOSE YOU AND ALL OF YOUR ABOMINATIONS. YOU HAVE TOLD MANY THAT YOU SPEAK IN THE NAME OF THE LORD, BUT I KNOW YOU NOT, FOR YOU SPEAK IN THE NAME OF SATAN, AND SIT IN HIS SEAT, AND FOLLOW AFTER HIS DETESTABLE ORDER. YOU CALL YOURSELVES PRIESTS, PASTORS, MINISTERS, AND PROPHETS, BUT I CALL YOU LIARS AND THIEVES.

TAKE HEED TO THE MESSAGE IN THIS BOOK AND REPENT, OR BEAR MY WRATH, FOR MY DAY OF VENGEANCE HAS COME UPON YOU. BEHOLD, YOU ARE NOTHING, AND YOUR WORK OF NAUGHT: AN ABOMINATION IS HE WHO CHOOSES TO FOLLOW AFTER YOU.

THE LORD has told ME that you are all looking for SIGNS of the END TIMES, but ***HE*** says the SIGNS are all before you, but you are TOO BLIND to SEE. JESUS spoke about EARTHQUAKES in divers places, and of WARS and rumors of WARS and these things have ALL come to PASS; but you yet still refuse to acknowledge that the TIME is NOW!

This BOOK will speak about THE ***DELIVERER*** and DELIVERANCE, however for many of you, who are just now reading this BOOK, the 1st RAPTURE has already taken place, and you are aware that YOU have been LEFT BEHIND. THE ***DELIVERER*** has left the EARTH with THE BRIDE of CHRIST, and the DEVIL has been cast down to RULE the EARTH for FORTY-TWO MONTHS; and will soon implement the "Mark of the Beast"! Your only HOPE is that you are included as one of the WEDDING GUESTS, and will RECEIVE RAPTURE along with the TRIBULATION SAINTS. Or, if you are of the EARTH and refuse to take the "Mark" and are beheaded for it, you may live again during the MILLENNIUM. Aside from these two possibilities, your only other HOPE is death and RESURRECTION for JUDGMENT, for your works do follow you!

Throughout the other two BOOKS, "Revealing The Bible's Truth" and "The ROD of IRON", it was explained how one must be BAPTIZED in THE ***HOLY SPIRIT*** to be SAVED. However after the 1st RAPTURE, THE ***HOLY SPIRIT*** has left the earth as THE ***DELIVERER,*** for THEY are ***ONE*** and the SAME, so NOW; YOU must PRAY that YOU RECEIVE the ***SEAL*** of the ***LIVING GOD*** for YOUR PROTECTION, for ***HOLY SPIRIT*** BAPTISM is no longer available.

After the 1st RAPTURE, place your TRUST in NO ONE! Not mother nor father, not sister nor brother, not husband nor wife, neither children nor friends, for you will know not who they really are! Except for the *WORD of* ***GOD*** be with YOU, YOU ARE ON YOUR OWN!

> ***Zechariah 12:12*** *And the land shall MOURN, every family apart; the family of the house of DAVID apart, and their wives apart; the family of the house of Nathan apart, and their wives apart;*
>
> ***Zechariah 12:13*** *The family of the house of Levi apart, and their wives apart; the family of Shim'-e-i apart, and their wives apart;*
>
> ***Zechariah 12:14*** *ALL THE FAMILIES THAT REMAIN, EVERY FAMILY APART, AND THEIR WIVES APART.*

Listen to no person claiming to preach the *WORD of* ***GOD*** who cites even a single word outside of the Scriptures given in the King James 1611 Authorized Version of the Holy Bible. Nor should YOU follow after the order of the doctrine given in the 22 Epistles included in the Canon, for they will be used by the

"False Prophet" to confuse your UNDERSTANDING of the *WORD of* ***GOD*** and to DECEIVE YOU.

Place not your confidence in the Church, for the TRUE CHURCH had left with the 1st RAPTURE, and the TRIBULATION SAINTS will not be part of the Church. They will PREACH independently and for the most part PREACH out of their own homes, meeting with small groups of people at a time in secrecy. Leaders of the Church will ban any of its members from attending those meetings.

Due to the number of people missing as a result of the RAPTURE being relatively small worldwide (10,400,000 people), the Church (led by the False Prophet) and the Antichrist who will rule over the government will come up with a clever explanation as to what had happened to the missing people. The family members LEFT BEHIND of them who had been taken in RAPTURE will be gathered up and interrogated, and those who refuse to cooperate in the "cover up story" will be tortured and killed.

Teaching outside of the Church will be outlawed, and anyone caught in attendance of the meetings being held by the TRIBULATION SAINTS will be prosecuted and incarcerated or killed. Then shortly after the preaching outside of the Church is made illegal, the personal owning of any Bible by someone outside of the Church will also be against the law. All Bibles will be removed from bookstores and any sale of a Bible will be punishable by death, and the common method of execution for any capital crime will be by decapitation.

> ***Amos 8:11*** *BEHOLD, the days come, saith* ***THE LORD GOD, THAT I WILL SEND A FAMINE IN THE LAND, NOT A FAMINE OF BREAD, NOR THE THIRST OF WATER, BUT OF HEARING THE WORDS OF THE LORD:***
>
> ***Amos 8:12 AND THEY SHALL WANDER FROM SEA TO SEA, AND FROM THE NORTH EVEN TO THE EAST, THEY SHALL RUN TO AND FRO TO SEEK THE WORD OF THE LORD, AND SHALL NOT FIND IT.***

THE LORD has told ME that all THREE of the BOOKS I have WRITTEN for ***HIM*** will also be BANNED by the Antichrist along with the Bible, for they verify the TRUTH in the *WORD of* ***GOD.***

Foreword

SPIRITUAL AWAKENING

In the BOOK titled, "The ROD of IRON", the various ASCENDABLE DIMENSIONS were talked about in the Chapter called "DIMENSIONS". WE explained how there are THIRTEEN ASCENDABLE VERTICAL DIMENSIONS existing within the UNIVERSE and also THIRTEEN ASCENDABLE VERTICAL DIMENSIONS existing in HEAVEN; all of which the SPIRIT of MAN can ASCEND to through BAPTISM in THE ***HOLY SPIRIT of GOD.*** These DIMENSIONS can only be realized through RAPTURE or when the ***GOD*** GIVEN SPIRIT separates from the body of flesh at the time of physical death. In this BOOK however WE shall talk about how the SPIRIT can also ASCEND through BAPTISM to various higher SPIRITUAL LEVELS while still remaining in the EARTH PLANE. This is what JESUS meant when HE PRAYED in the Seventeenth Chapter of the Gospel of John, saying, HIS Disciples were in the WORLD, but they were not of the WORLD. In HIS PRAYER HE SAID:

> ***John 17:14 I HAVE GIVEN THEM THY WORD; AND THE WORLD HATH HATED THEM, BECAUSE THEY ARE NOT OF THE WORLD, EVEN AS I AM NOT OF THE WORLD.***
>
> ***John 17:15 I PRAY NOT THAT THOU SHOULDEST TAKE THEM OUT OF THE WORLD, BUT THOU SHOULDEST KEEP THEM FROM THE EVIL.***
>
> ***John 17:16 THEY ARE NOT OF THE WORLD, EVEN AS I AM NOT OF THE WORLD.***

What JESUS refers to in the Scriptures is called SPIRITUAL ASCENSION. This is DIFFERENT than the ASCENDING of the SPIRIT through the various DIMENSIONS that can only occur during RAPTURE or SPIRIT SEPARATION from the body of flesh. SPIRITUAL ASCENSION is the RAISING of the SPIRITUAL INTELLECT and CONSCIOUSNESS while still remaining in the EARTH PLANE (the WORLD), whereas SPIRIT ASCENDING is a TRANSFIGURATION of the SPIRIT through DIMENSIONAL CHANGE.

This is the phenomenon I had experienced on the 13th day of October 1997, and had briefly described in the section called "About the Author" in the BOOK titled "Revealing The Bible's Truth". It was expressed in the BOOK that while I was experiencing the EVENT of SPIRITUAL ASCENSION on the morning of October 13th, it felt as though I was taken somewhere that was between this WORLD and someplace else. I was still in the WORLD but no longer of the WORLD, for I had been SEPARATED from it! This is the RAISING of SPIRITUAL INTELLECT and CONSCIOUSNESS through ***HOLY SPIRIT*** BAPTISM.

My experiencing this EVENT on that morning was not something that I had consciously wanted or even had remotely thought about, but it was rather the ***WILL of GOD*** that had PREDESTINED IT to be as it was on that very day! SPIRITUAL ASCENSION is called SPIRITUAL AWAKENING, and this is what the TWO WITNESSES and the TRIBULATION SAINTS spoken about in the Book of Revelation will ENDURE sometime prior to the beginning of the GREAT TRIBULATION.

Along with the RECEIVING of SPIRITUAL ASCENSION comes PROTECTION from EVIL, thus fulfilling the PRAYER of JESUS CHRIST. ***"I PRAY NOT THAT THOU SHOULDEST TAKE THEM OUT OF THE WORLD, BUT THAT THOU SHOULDEST KEEP THEM FROM THE EVIL" (John 17:15).*** The PROTECTION RECEIVED is physical protection and as well SPIRITUAL PROTECTION from any EVIL ACTION attempted against the PERSON in receipt of SPIRITUAL ASCENSION. The PROTECTION ONE RECEIVES by their ASCENSION is similar to being placed into a BUBBLE that is impervious to any outside forces and is called the ***SEAL of the LIVING GOD.***

> ***Revelation 7:2*** *And I saw another ANGEL ASCENDING from the EAST, having the* ***SEAL of the LIVING GOD:*** *and he cried with a LOUD VOICE to the FOUR ANGELS, to whom it was given to hurt the EARTH and the SEA,*

Revelation 7:3 *Saying, Hurt not the EARTH, neither the SEA, nor the trees, till we have SEALED the SERVANTS of OUR* ***GOD*** *in their FOREHEADS.*

The levels of SPIRITUAL ASCENSION for MAN will vary from LEVEL 6 through LEVEL 19, depending on their ANOINTING; however the TWO WITNESSES spoken of in the Book of Revelation will RECEIVE SPIRITUAL ASCENSION to LEVEL 21, for they are of the SERAPHIM. Regardless of what LEVEL of ASCENSION is achieved, PROTECTION is provided, however the TWO WITNESSES will experience DEATH even with the PROTECTION to fulfill the *DIVINE WILL of* ***GOD*** (Scripture).

Revelation 11:7 *And when they shall have finished their TESTIMONY, the BEAST that ASCENDETH out of the BOTTOMLESS PIT shall make war against THEM, and kill THEM.*

Revelation 11:8 *And their DEAD BODIES shall lie in the street of the GREAT CITY, which spiritually is called Sodom and Egypt, where also OUR LORD was CRUCIFIED.*

Revelation 11:9 *And they of the people and kindreds and tongues and nations shall see their DEAD BODIES three days and an half, and shall not suffer their DEAD BODIES to be put in graves.*

Revelation 11:10 *And they that dwell upon the earth shall rejoice over THEM, and make merry, and shall send gifts one to another; because these TWO PROPHETS tormented them that dwelt on the earth.*

Revelation 11:11 *And after THREE DAYS and an HALF the SPIRIT of LIFE from* ***GOD*** *entered into THEM, and THEY stood upon their feet; and great fear fell upon them which saw THEM.*

Revelation 11:12 *And they heard a GREAT VOICE from HEAVEN saying unto THEM,* ***COME UP HITHER.*** *And they ASCENDED up to HEAVEN in a CLOUD; and THEIR enemies beheld them.*

Revelation 11:13 *And the same hour was there a GREAT EARTHQUAKE, and the tenth part of the city fell, and in the EARTHQUAKE were slain of men SEVEN THOUSAND: and the remnant were affrighted, and gave GLORY to THE* ***GOD*** *of HEAVEN.*

Antichrist

The Antichrist is more than just one person and represents three, the DEVIL, the BEAST, and the FALSE PROPHET. In this BOOK WE will discuss the various descriptions of the Antichrist and show how they will try to mimic THE ***TRINITY (GODHEAD).*** The DEVIL (Lucifer) will portray himself as GOD, the BEAST will portray himself as CHRIST, and the FALSE PROPHET will claim he is the HOLY SPIRIT!

Many people will be DECEIVED by them and will believe they are who they have claimed themselves to be. By their cleverness, the whole world will be DECEIVED. However, the very ELECT, (the GUESTS of the WEDDING SUPPER) and the BLESSED, (the BEHEADED SOULS) will SEE through their disguises.

Matthew 24:24 FOR THERE SHALL ARISE FALSE CHRISTS, AND FALSE PROPHETS, AND SHALL SHOW GREAT SIGNS AND WONDERS; INSOMUCH THAT, IF IT WERE POSSIBLE, THEY SHALL DECEIVE THE VERY ELECT.

At first the three will appear to be Christian People, and they will start their mischief by cleverly distorting the *WORD of* ***GOD*** through the use of the Epistles of the Disciples. The Antichrist will implement a Religious Order creating many new laws of moral standards, and these NEW LAWS will appear to uphold that which the Church had previously taught; so for the most part, the Christians will see what they are doing as a good thing. However these new laws will deteriorate the personal rights of the people and give the Church and the Government complete control over them.

Once the new laws have been implemented, freedom to PRAY, read the HOLY BIBLE, and the ability to WORSHIP ***GOD*** will be denied to anyone wanting to do so outside of the Church; for the Church will be assuming the role of THE GREAT WHORE. The Church (THE GREAT WHORE) will then claim that ***GOD*** can only be WORSHIPPED in the Church, and anyone found doing so outside of the Church would be put to death for it. Then the "ABOMINATION that makes DESOLATE" (the IMAGE of the DEVIL) will be placed in all of the Churches, and the DEVIL will proclaim himself to be GOD.

DELIVERANCE

DELIVERANCE will be accomplished in several forms, and this BOOK will discuss those forms. WE will talk about DELIVERANCE prior to THE GREAT TRIBULATION, and how DELIVERANCE can be RECEIVED after THE ***DELIVERER*** (THE ***HOLY SPIRIT*** in the form of a MAN) has left the earth with THE BRIDE of CHRIST.

Although THE ***DELIVERER'S NAME*** cannot be given (as it was in the FIRST BOOK), a complete description will be given of ***HIM***, and ALL that ***HE*** shall do prior to ***HIS DEPARTURE*** with THE BRIDE. ***THE LORD*** expects ALL who shall be RECEIVED into HEAVEN KNOW who this ***PERSON*** is, for ***HIS*** NAME is given in ALL THREE of the BOOKS I have WRITTEN for ***THE LORD.***

Most of that, that the ***DELIVERER*** shall do, will be done in a COVERT MANNER, and ONLY THE BRIDE of CHRIST will know for certain who THE ***DELIVERER*** is; up until the time that the "ABOMINATION that makes DESOLATE" is setup in the TEMPLE in JERUSALEM and in all the Churches. Then by that time, THE ***DELIVERER'S NAME*** will be KNOWN throughout the world, for ***HE WILL HAVE RETURNED TO THE EARTH WITH HIS ANGELS,*** and THE TRIBULATION SAINTS will openly PREACH ***HIS NAME*** throughout the world.

RAPTURE

Even though RAPTURE has been explained in the other TWO BOOKS, further DETAILS on the RAPTURE will be given. WE will explain how the RAPTURE will occur and how ONE must be prepared for it, for it will COME in an INSTANT, and be GONE in the SAME.

WE will further discuss the various excuses that will be given by them who are LEFT BEHIND, who will try to explain to those who remain what had HAPPENED and why they had not been included. However they will deny that any RAPTURE had taken place, and will give a FALSE TESTIMONY of the EVENT! It will also be discussed how so many who had believed they had been SAVED by their participation in the Church were LEFT BEHIND, and how they will REFUSE to BELIEVE that the RAPTURE had occurred and they had not been taken with it!

DESTRUCTION of the EARTH

The BOOK will DETAIL some of the KEY EVENTS that will take place on the EARTH, thus DESTROYING ALL but a few people; who will remain alive to repopulate the EARTH during the MILLENNIUM. WE will discuss the living conditions for those who remain outside of the "CAMP of the SAINTS", NEW JERUSALEM, and what their life in this world will be like at the DAWNING of the LAST DAY!

It will be explained how both the NATURAL and SUPERNATURAL EVENTS will create a CHAOS that this world has never experienced from the time of its CREATION until that time. WE will also explain the circumstances surrounding the total DESTRUCTION of the WORLD that occurs at the CONCLUSION of the MILLENNIUM PERIOD.

HEAVEN on EARTH

A DETAILED DESCRIPTION of the NEW JERUSALEM will be given and the COMING of HEAVEN on EARTH will be explained, thus fulfilling THE LORD'S PRAYER. It will be explained how, while the EARTH sits in RUINS, the HOLY CITY, NEW JERUSALEM, displays a PLACE of PICTURESQUE landscape and MAGNIFICENT architectural BEAUTY, with an abundance of food and water, and all of the INGREDIENTS NECESSARY to make a place on EARTH in the SIMILITUDE of HEAVEN.

The BOOK will discuss the PURPOSE for the MILLENNIUM and the various activities that will take place during the MILLENNIUM. During that PERIOD, ***GOD'S*** CHILDREN will LEARN ***GOD'S WORD***, LIVE IN PEACE and HARMONY with EACH OTHER, and ENJOY the GARDEN of EDEN with ***THE LORD*** and the ANGELS as it was INTENDED to be in THE BEGINNING.

It will be explained how SOUL MATES will be joined in MARRIAGE during the MILLENNIUM and how the TWO will be UNITED throughout ETERNITY; this is the FIRST MARRIAGE. WE will also explain the SECOND MARRIAGE, the MARRIAGE to CHRIST. However, this MARRIAGE only applies to those of the BRIDE of CHRIST and not to the WEDDING GUESTS, as does also the THIRD MARRIAGE apply to only the BRIDE.

The THREE BOOKS

ALL THREE BOOKS, "Revealing The Bible's Truth", "The ROD of IRON", and "Revelation the FOURTH SON" should be treated as a SET, for they are inseparable and incomplete when any one of the THREE are MISSING. However, even as a SET, the THREE are incomplete without the inclusion of the King James 1611 Authorized Version of the HOLY BIBLE.

May the GRACE of ***GOD,*** the LOVE of JESUS CHRIST, and the FAITH given by THE ***HOLY SPIRIT*** be with YOU ALL. ***A-MEN'***

Chapter 1,
The INHERITANCE

There was a very SPECIFIC REASON as to why JESUS' MINISTRY did not start until HE had reached the age of 30 years old. Early in HEBREW tradition, the INHERITANCE was PASSED DOWN from the father to the eldest son nearing the time of the father's death. At that time the entire household and all of its belongings were handed over to the INHERITOR and he saw that the rightful portions of the INHERITANCE was shared amongst the other HEIRS, (his brothers). The daughters inherited nothing, and relied on a dowry from her parents for marriage and to share in their husbands INHERITANCE, whatever that might be. However, during the time of JESUS CHRIST, the Jews had changed the law thus making the eldest son eligible to receive his INHERITANCE at the age of THIRTY.

After the law had been changed and the son made eligible to receive his INHERITANCE at the early age of thirty, it was quite common for the INHERITOR (the eldest son) to put his parents out of the household and in general show very little regard for his parents' future well being. JESUS makes mention of this in the Scriptures:

> ***Matthew 15:3*** *But HE answered and said unto them,* ***WHY DO YE ALSO TRANSGRESS THE COMMANDMENT OF GOD BY YOUR TRADITION?***
>
> ***Matthew 15:4 FOR GOD COMMANDED, SAYING, HONOUR THY FATHER AND MOTHER; and, HE THAT CURSETH FATHER OR MOTHER, LET HIM DIE THE DEATH.***
>
> ***Matthew 15:5 BUT YE SAY, WHOSOEVER SHALL SAY TO HIS FATHER OR MOTHER, IT IS A GIFT, BY WHATSOEVER THOU MIGHTEST BE PROFITED BY ME;***

Matthew 15:6 AND HONOUR NOT HIS FATHER OR HIS MOTHER, HE SHALL BE FREE. THUS HAVE YE MADE THE COMMANDMENT OF GOD OF NONE EFFECT BY YOUR TRADITION.

NOTE: JESUS in the Scriptures is addressing the Pharisees and Scribes, telling them that by their changing the tradition of INHERITANCE, they were allowing the INHERITOR to do whatever had pleased him with his INHERITANCE, regardless of what grief his actions might cause his parents. In many cases the land that the parents had lived on was sold out from under them, leaving them with nothing, and no place to live. And, by the tradition of the Jews this was considered to be an acceptable act by the INHERITOR, thus having no regard for ***GOD'S FIFTH COMMANDMENT*** of HONORING THE FATHER AND MOTHER.

JESUS, being BORN in OCTOBER (and not in December as it is so celebrated), was THIRTY YEARS and SIX MONTHS OLD when HE was BAPTIZED in the ***SPIRIT of GOD*** and began HIS MINISTRY, for by tradition HE was of the ELIGIBLE AGE to RECEIVE HIS INHERITANCE, the EARTH. JESUS clearly UNDERSTOOD how the INHERITANCE was to be passed down from generation to generation, and MEANT by ***GOD*** to be SHARED amongst ALL of the CHILDREN and not just with a select few! HE saw how the Jews were corrupting the TRADITION of INHERITANCE by allowing the INHERITOR to do as he so selfishly had wanted to do with the INHERITANCE, and this troubled HIM.

In this Chapter WE will discuss WHO are the INHERITORS, and WHAT does the INHERITANCE consist of. But in order to properly UNDERSTAND these things, ONE must FIRST UNDERSTAND, HOW the INHERITANCE is PASSED DOWN and also HOW the INHERITANCE is ALLOCATED. WE will start with the EARTH, for the EARTH is the FIRST to be INHERITED!

Matthew 5:3 BLESSED ARE THE POOR IN SPIRIT: FOR THEIRS IS THE KINGDOM OF HEAVEN.

Matthew 5:4 BLESSED ARE THEY THAT MOURN: FOR THEY SHALL BE COMFORTED.

Matthew 5:5 BLESSED ARE THE MEEK: FOR THEY SHALL INHERIT THE EARTH.

These Scriptures taken from the 5th Chapter of the GOSPEL of Matthew list the GIFTS of INHERITANCE in a DESCENDING ORDER to the EARTH and then in an ASCENDING ORDER back to HEAVEN. The REASON JESUS PREACHED the sermon in this ORDER is because this is the ORDER in which the INHERITANCE is RECEIVED. If you READ the entire 5th Chapter of Matthew, YOU might take note of the SEQUENCE in which the INHERITANCE is RECEIVED!

The INHERITANCE FIRST comes down from HEAVEN, and the RIGHTFUL INHERITORS are PERSECUTED for being HEIRS to it; then through the ASCENSION of SPIRIT, the HEIRS RECEIVE their INHERITANCE of the EARTH for ONE THOUSAND YEARS (the MILLENNIUM), for the EARTH is not ETERNAL and is governed by TIME. Then during the MILLENNIUM the SPIRIT ASCENDS to become a BODY of LIGHT:

> ***Matthew 5:14 YE ARE THE LIGHT OF THE WORLD. A CITY THAT IS SET ON A HILL CANNOT BE HID.***

NOTE: In the TWELFTH LAYER of the previous Scripture, JESUS so NOTES how the CHILDREN of ***GOD*** will take on the FORM of a BODY of LIGHT. Also, the CITY referred to in the Scripture so notes the CITY of NEW JERUSALEM that the CHILDREN of ***GOD*** will LIVE in during the MILLENNIUM. It also speaks of the CITY of NEW JERUSALEM that will COME for the BRIDE and the WEDDING GUESTS for them to ASCEND in and LIVE in HEAVEN, throughout ETERNITY, and become PERFECT, as ***GOD IS PERFECT, THUS TAKING ON THE LIKENESS OF THE FATHER.*** This is the closing verse in the 5th Chapter of the GOSPEL of Matthew:

> ***Matthew 5:48 BE YE THEREFORE PERFECT, EVEN AS YOUR FATHER WHICH IS IN HEAVEN IS PERFECT.***

GIFTS of INHERITANCE

Although the GIFTS of INHERITANCE cannot be NUMBERED, for they are MANY, nor can most of them be MINDFULLY comprehended, WE will therefore only discuss the SEVEN COMPREHENDIBLE GIFTS in the ORDER of their RECEIPT from ***GOD.*** The following is a list of the SEVEN COMPREHENDIBLE GIFTS RECEIVED through INHERITANCE:

1. The GIFT of the EARTH.

2. The GIFT of ABSOLUTE FREEDOM.
3. The GIFT of UNDERSTANDING and KNOWLEDGE.
4. The GIFT of ETERNAL LIGHT (LIFE).
5. The GIFT of ETERNAL COMFORT.
6. The GIFT of TOTAL WISDOM.
7. The GIFT of HEAVENLY DOMAIN.

WE will discuss each one of the SEVEN COMPREHENDIBLE GIFTS GIVEN through INHERITANCE to ***GOD'S*** CHILDREN, for they apply to both THE BRIDE of CHRIST and to the GUESTS of the WEDDING SUPPER.

The GIFT of the EARTH

In the 5th Chapter, and in the 5th verse of Matthew, when JESUS says that the MEEK will INHERIT the EARTH, HE MEANS IT MOST LITERALLY and not figuratively. In the BOOK, "The ROD of IRON", Chapter 5 titled, "The Significance of NUMBERS", it is said that the NUMBER 5 and the triplicate FIVES (555) represent The CHURCH. It is not by coincidence that Matthew 5:5 says that the MEEK will INHERIT the EARTH, for the CHURCH (GOD'S PEOPLE, ISRAEL) will partake in the INHERITANCE of the EARTH.

At the CONCLUSION of the GREAT TRIBULATION, ***THE CREATOR,*** THE ***HOLY SPIRIT of GOD,*** for ***GOD,*** will CREATE a CITY, and the CITY will be called "NEW JERUSALEM". This CITY will be in the SIMILITUDE of the CITY of JERUSALEM in HEAVEN, however it will be on a much smaller scale and it will be COMPOSED of PHYSICAL MATERIALS, whereas the JERUSALEM in HEAVEN is made of HEAVENLY MATERIALS. The CITY will be in size more like an entire country rather than a city, and will provide ample space to accommodate the SIX BILLION PEOPLE and the ONE BILLION ANGELS who will partake in the MILLENNIUM by RAPTURE.

After the GREAT TRIBULATION when the Devil, Lucifer is cast down into the PIT and sealed, there will only be 104,000,000 people left alive upon the earth. However, ***GOD'S*** FOUR BILLION CHILDREN, ONE BILLION ANGELS, and the two billion Beheaded SOULS will partake in the MILLENNIUM by RAPTURE. All SEVEN BILLION will live within the WALLS of the GREAT CITY of NEW JERUSALEM. The 104,000,000 people that survived the GREAT TRIBULATION will live outside of the CITY and be scattered throughout the regions that survived the GREAT WAR; for the balance of the EARTH will be unsuitable to sustain human life. The 104,000,000 people will live out normal life spans and repopulate the EARTH over the ONE THOU-

SAND-YEAR MILLENNIUM PERIOD. At the CONCLUSION of the LAST DAY (the end of the MILLENNIUM PERIOD), the population of the 104,000,000 will have increased to 7,000,000,000 people.

It may also be noted that the FOUR BILLION of ***GOD'S*** CHILDREN living in NEW JERUSALEM will consist of TWO BILLION who had RECEIVED RAPTURE from the EARTH, and TWO BILLION who had RECEIVED RAPTURE from PARADISE. The same equal split applies to the EARTH Angels who will partake in the MILLENNIUM. However, ALL of the BEHEADED SOULS will come from people living during the time of the GREAT TRIBULATION. These are the people that had martyred themselves by refusing to denounce ***GOD*** and take the "Mark of the Beast".

During the MILLENNIUM, JESUS CHRIST will RULE over the entire EARTH. The growing population of the 104,000,000 people (the survivors of the GREAT TRIBULATION) will be made to come into the CITY on certain HOLY and FEAST DAYS to WORSHIP ***GOD.*** There will be a CURSE put upon anyone who does not HONOR ***THE LORD of HOSTS*** on the FESTIVE DAYS. The CURSE can come in the form of HARDSHIPS for an individual or an entire CLAN or nation that consist of famines and draughts. The CURSE can also cause them not HONORING ***THE LORD*** to physically endure bodily CONSUMPTION and death, by the IMMEDIATE CONSUMPTION of their flesh from off their bones.

This period of time on EARTH, after the time of the Battle at Armageddon (Me-gid'-don), is explained in the 14th Chapter of the Book of the Prophet Zechariah. WE shall list a few of the KEY SCRIPTURES relating to that TIME, however the 14th Chapter of Zechariah should be read in its entirety.

> ***Zechariah 14:9*** *And THE LORD shall be KING over ALL the EARTH: in that DAY shall there be ONE LORD, and HIS NAME ONE.*
>
> ***Zechariah 14:10*** *All the land shall be turned as a plain from Ge'-ba to Rim'-mon south of JERUSALEM: and it shall be LIFTED UP, and inhabited in HER PLACE, from Benjamin's gate unto the place of the FIRST GATE, unto the corner gate, and from the Tower of Ha-nan'-e-el unto the KING'S WINEPRESSES.*
>
> ***Zechariah 14:11*** *And men shall dwell in it, and there shall be no more UTTER DESTRUCTION; but JERUSALEM shall be SAFELY INHABITED.*

NOTE: The Scriptures of 14:9 through 14:11 speak of how THE LORD, JESUS CHRIST will RULE over the entire world, and also how the CITY of NEW JERUSALEM will be LIFTED UP (RECREATED) and INHABITED with ***GOD'S*** PEOPLE. It also speaks of how it will be a time of PEACE on EARTH (no more UTTER DESTRUCTION) for ALL them living within the GATES of NEW JERUSALEM will live in PEACE. However for them living outside of NEW JERUSALEM there will be NO PEACE for them ***SAITH THE LORD,*** but rather a CURSE (a PLAGUE).

> ***Zechariah 14:12*** *And this shall be the PLAGUE wherewith* ***THE LORD*** *will smite ALL the people that have fought against JERUSALEM; Their FLESH shall CONSUME away while they stand upon their feet, and their EYES shall CONSUME away in their holes, and their TONGUE shall CONSUME away in their MOUTH.*

> ***Zechariah 14:13*** *And it shall come to pass in that DAY, that a GREAT TUMULT from* ***THE LORD*** *shall be among them; and they shall lay hold every one on the hand of his neighbour, and his hand shall rise up against the hand of his neighbour.*

NOTE: These last two Scriptures tell that while there will be PEACE within the GATES of NEW JERUSALEM, outside of the GATES there will be infighting amongst them who survived the GREAT TRIBULATION. They will fight over the land and over the wealth of the world that was left by them who had died in the BATTLE of ARMAGEDDON. The next Scripture speaks of how the Jews (those of Judaism who have been CONVERTED to CHRIST) will fight against the Antichrist at the time of the DAWNING of the LAST DAY.

> ***Zechariah 14:14*** *And Judah also shall fight at JERUSALEM; and the WEALTH of all the HEATHEN round about shall be gathered together, gold and silver, and apparel, in great abundance.*

> ***Zechariah 14:15*** *And so shall be the PLAGUE of the horse, of the mule, of the camel, and of the ass, and all these beasts that shall be in these tents, as this PLAGUE.*

NOTE: These Scriptures speak of how all the WEALTH of the EARTH will be gathered up and given to ***GOD'S*** CHILDREN. It also says that the CURSE (the PLAGUE) will not only apply to the people, but it shall also apply to EVERYTHING LIVING within the camp of the CLAN or nation that has been CURSED!

> ***Zechariah 14:16*** *And it shall come to pass, that every one that is left of ALL the nations which came against JERUSALEM shall even go up from year to year to WORSHIP the KING,* ***THE LORD of HOSTS,*** *and keep the FEAST of TABERNACLES.*

> ***Zechariah 14:17*** *And it shall be, that whoso will not come up of ALL the families of the EARTH unto JERUSALEM to WORSHIP the KING,* ***THE LORD of HOSTS,*** *even upon them shall be no rain.*

> ***Zechariah 14:18*** *And if the family of Egypt go not up, and come not, that have no rain; there shall be the PLAGUE, wherewith* ***THE LORD*** *will smite the heathen that come not up to keep the FEAST of TABERNACLES.*

NOTE 1*:** What these last three Scriptures are saying is, any nation or any family who refuses to come up to NEW JERUSALEM and WORSHIP on ***THE LORD*'S** HOLY DAYS, will be PUNISHED. For their FIRST OFFENSE, they will receive DROUGHT and FAMINE; and if they still refuse to come and WORSHIP on the HOLY DAYS, their FLESH will be CONSUMED ***SAITH THE LORD of HOSTS. It may also be noted, when the Scripture makes reference to the KING, it refers to JESUS CHRIST, and when it makes reference to ***THE LORD of HOSTS,*** it refers to THE ***HOLY SPIRIT,*** THE ***DELIVERER,*** for it is ***HE*** who returns to the EARTH on ALL of the SABBATHS.

NOTE 2: Of the 104,000,000 people that survive the GREAT TRIBULATION, some are of the DAMNED SEED (the Canaanite). Prior to the completion of the MILLENNIUM (the LAST DAY) ALL of the Canaanite that had survived will suffer the "CURSE of CONSUMMATION", ***SAITH THE LORD of HOSTS.***

> **Zechariah 14:21** *Yea, every POT in JERUSALEM and in Judah shall be HOLINESS unto* ***THE LORD of HOSTS:*** *and ALL they that SACRIFICE shall come and take of them, and seethe therein: and in that DAY there* ***<u>shall be no more the Canaanite</u>*** *in the HOUSE of* ***THE LORD of HOSTS.***

The GIFT of ABSOLUTE FREEDOM

During the MILLENNIUM ALL of ***GOD'S*** CHILDREN will RECEIVE the GIFT of ABSOLUTE FREEDOM. This freedom will allow ***GOD'S*** CHILDREN to move about within the CONFINES of the CITY to where so ever they may choose. The EARTHLY version of the CITY of NEW JERUSALEM will be in the likeness of the HEAVENLY CITY of NEW JERUSALEM, thus making it so on EARTH, as it is in HEAVEN.

Outside of the CITY there will be both day and night, as it is now; however in the CITY there will be only DAYLIGHT, for it will never darken in the CITY over the ONE THOUSAND-YEAR MILLENNIUM PERIOD. This is because the CITY will take on the likeness of HEAVEN where there is ALWAYS LIGHT.

All of the DWELLING PLACES will have doors without locks, and over the course of the ONE THOUSAND YEARS anyone may ENTER another's household without the need of an invitation, although a PERSON'S PRIVACY will never be VIOLATED; and ALL GUESTS welcomed.

The MILLENNIUM will be a TIME of LEARNING, and whatever interests ONE may have regarding what they are to learn, will be of each individual's own FREE choosing. However, ALL will be taught the *WORD of* ***GOD,*** for there is a MANDATE that ALL ENTERING into HEAVEN must be capable of UNDERSTANDING as a minimum, FOUR LAYERS of Scripture DEPTH. The ONE BILLION ANGELS in the MILLENNIUM will see to the maintenance, cleanliness, and the upkeep of the CITY, and they will also ACT as INSTRUCTORS, GUIDES, and TEACHERS of ALL HEAVENLY THINGS. As they are the HOSTS in HEAVEN, so shall they be on EARTH. ALL FOUR BILLION of ***GOD'S*** CHILDREN will be GIVEN a SKILL, and that SKILL shall CONTINUE ON THROUGHOUT ETERNITY. The SKILL GIVEN will be viewed by the CRAFTSMAN as a HOBBY, more so than a job; for the CRAFTSMAN will have GREAT PLEASURE in demonstrating and sharing in the use of his or her SKILLS with others.

Each SKILL GIVEN will be UNIQUE to that INDIVIDUAL, with no TWO SKILLS being the SAME; for INDIVIDUALITY is the SPICE of LIFE! For instance, if TWO INDIVIDUALS were both SCULPTORS, each ONE would have UNIQUENESS in STYLE and in CONCEPT. And, even though they might SCULPT the same object with both achieving a MASTERPIECE, there would be subtle differences in the SCULPTING, differentiating the TWO works of art.

The MESSAGE here is, that the KEY INGREDIENT to ABSOLUTE FREEDOM, is in the ability for ONE to demonstrate and express HIS or HER own INDIVIDUALITY without restriction or constraint. ***GOD*** has given each of ***HIS*** CHILDREN a UNIQUE PERSONALITY, and during the MILLENNIUM you will LEARN how to PROPERLY and FREELY express that PERSONALITY.

> ***Matthew 5:16 LET YOUR LIGHT SO SHINE BEFORE MEN, THAT THEY MAY SEE YOUR GOOD WORKS, AND GLORIFY YOUR FATHER WHICH IS IN HEAVEN.***

The GIFT of UNDERSTANDING and KNOWLEDGE

This is ONE of the MARVELOUS GIFTS of INHERITANCE that ONE cannot come to fully appreciate until AFTER its RECEIPT. This is the ability to both LEARN and RETAIN that which has been TAUGHT to YOU, on any subject, and then take it a STEP further by YOUR ability to IMPROVE upon it. The IMPROVEMENT comes by CONTINUAL LEARNING through the GIFT of UNDERSTANDING and KNOWLEDGE of any subject TAUGHT. There is not anything achieved by MAN that cannot be IMPROVED on by the process of UNDERSTANDING and KNOWLEDGE.

THE LORD has TOLD ME that when ONE believes that they have LEARNED all there is to be LEARNED, they have then either BECOME ***GOD,*** or have died, for LEARNING stops at death. ***GOD*** has given each of ***HIS*** CHILDREN an ETERNAL LIFE, therefore things can be LEARNED each and every MOMENT of it! It should be the GOAL of each CHILD to ACHIEVE the GREATNESS of their ***FATHER,*** and one cannot achieve that GREATNESS if they have not the GIFT of UNDERSTANDING and KNOWLEDGE.

GOD hasn't the need for UNDERSTANDING and KNOWLEDGE for ***HE KNOWS ALL THERE IS TO KNOW,*** so ***GOD*** passes down through INHERITANCE this GIFT to ***HIS*** CHILDREN so they might become as ***HE IS, ALL KNOWING.***

The GIFT of ETERNAL LIGHT (LIFE)

It has been said in ALL of the BOOKS that I have WRITTEN for ***THE LORD,*** that LIGHT is LIFE, TRUTH and SERENITY, for all that exists has come from LIGHT. At the CONCLUSION of the LAST DAY (the end of the

MILLENNIUM) the ONE BILLION ANGELS and the FOUR BILLION of ***GOD'S*** CHILDREN (THE BRIDE and the WEDDING GUESTS) will SPIRITUALLY ASCEND into a BODY of LIGHT. JESUS demonstrated this TRANSFIGURING into LIGHT while in the presence of three of HIS Disciples, Peter and the brothers, James, and John.

> ***Matthew 17:1*** *And after six days JESUS taketh Peter, James, and John his brother, and bringeth them up into an high mountain apart,*

> ***Matthew 17:2*** *And was TRANSFIGURED before them: and HIS FACE did shine as the SUN, and HIS raiment was WHITE as the LIGHT.*

As explained in the BOOK "The ROD of IRON", in the Chapter titled "DIMENSIONS", there are THIRTEEN ASCENDABLE DIMENSIONS within the UNIVERSE, with the THIRTEENTH DIMENSION being that of LIGHT. Then there are THIRTEEN more DIMENSIONS in HEAVEN that are ALL LIGHT DIMENSIONS. Therefore anyone entering into HEAVEN must be in the FORM of LIGHT, and at the CONCLUSION of the MILLENNIUM ALL that are to ASCEND to HEAVEN must take on the FORM of LIGHT! This is the ability to be in the LIKENESS and SPIRIT of ***GOD,*** and this comes through the INHERITANCE of the GIFT of ETERNAL LIGHT.

The GIFT of ETERNAL COMFORT

> ***Matthew 5:4 BLESSED ARE THEY THAT MOURN: FOR THEY SHALL BE COMFORTED.***

At the BEGINNING of the MILLENNIUM, there will be many who will have had lost their LOVED ONES, for they were not worthy to RECEIVE SAVING GRACE and ETERNITY. Sorrow will run deep for them leaving LOVED ONES behind, but they shall be COMFORTED ***SAITH THE LORD of HOSTS.*** THE ***DELIVERER,*** being THE ***HOLY SPIRIT of GOD*** in the FORM of a MAN, will COMFORT them and explain as to why those who are missed had been LEFT BEHIND, and them being COMFORTED will UNDERSTAND!

At the CONCLUSION of the MILLENNIUM the WORLD will be brought to its END and the WHITE THRONE JUDGMENT will be held, and many shall be cast into HELL or back to the DUST of the EARTH for their JUDGMENT. This will also be a time of sorrow, for ALL will WITNESS the JUDGMENT of ***GOD*** against those who would not SERVE ***HIM. THE LORD of HOSTS***, THE ***HOLY SPIRIT of GOD***, will again provide COMFORT to ***GOD'S*** CHILDREN.

> ***Revelation 21:3*** *And I heard a GREAT VOICE out of HEAVEN saying, BEHOLD, the TABERNACLE of* **GOD** *is with MEN, and* **HE** *will dwell with them, and they shall be* **HIS** *PEOPLE, and* **GOD HIMSELF** *shall be with them, and be their* **GOD.**

> ***Revelation 21:4*** *And* **GOD** *shall wipe away all TEARS from their eyes; and there shall be no more DEATH, neither SORROW, nor CRYING, neither shall there be any more PAIN: for the former things are PASSED AWAY.*

> ***Revelation 21:5*** *And* **HE** *that sat upon the THRONE said, BEHOLD,* ***I MAKE ALL THINGS NEW,*** *and* **HE** *said unto me, WRITE: FOR THESE WORDS ARE TRUE AND FAITHFUL.*

> ***Revelation 21:6*** *And* **HE** *said unto me,* ***IT IS DONE. I AM ALPHA AND OMEGA, THE BEGINNING AND THE END. I WILL GIVE UNTO HIM THAT IS ATHIRST OF THE FOUNTAIN OF THE WATER OF LIFE FREELY.***

> ***Revelation 21:7 HE THAT OVERCOMETH SHALL INHERIT ALL THINGS; AND I WILL BE HIS GOD, AND HE SHALL BE MY SON.***

The GIFT of TOTAL WISDOM

The GIFT of TOTAL WISDOM is the means in which ONE can properly and soundly apply UNDERSTANDING and KNOWLEDGE to achieve a POSITIVE end result. WISDOM is KEY to apply that, which has been learned in a PRODUCTIVE and POSITIVE manner.

In a carnal state, WISDOM increases with time, whereas in a SPIRITUAL STATE when time is irrelevant, WISDOM need not depend on time or PRAGMATISM (previous experience) to be functional. In a carnal state WISDOM relies on experience, however when given the GIFT of TOTAL WISDOM certain things become KNOWN without ever having to have experienced them; and this GIFT applies to either the Carnal Being or to the SPIRITUAL PERSON who is in RECEIPT of the GIFT.

The GIFT of UNDERSTANDING and KNOWLEDGE would be WORTHLESS without the GIFT of TOTAL WISDOM; for if the ONE with the UNDERSTANDING and KNOWLEDGE did not know how to apply it, what PURPOSE would the UNDERSTANDING and KNOWLEDGE serve? ***THE LORD*** purposely limits ONE'S WISDOM while on EARTH, because Life on EARTH would be unbearable to the WISE. KING SOLOMON said that once HE had been GIVEN GREAT WISDOM, with that WISDOM came much GRIEF.

> ***Ecclesiastes 1:17*** *And I gave MY HEART to know WISDOM, and to KNOW madness and folly: I perceived that this also is vexation of the SPIRIT.*

> ***Ecclesiastes 1:18*** *For in MUCH WISDOM is MUCH GRIEF: and he that increaseth KNOWLEDGE increaseth SORROW.*

NOTE: What SOLOMON is saying in the Scriptures is, once HE started to look at this world through WISE EYES, HE had a very difficult time enduring life in this world. And, the more WISER HE became, the more difficult HIS existence in the world became. This is because life in this world to the UNWISE appears to be wonderful, whereas to the WISE, due to TIME CONSTRAINTS, it appears to be TROUBLING and a VEXATION to the ***GOD*** GIVEN SPIRIT, who is the ETERNAL (TIMELESS) PERSON in this world.

This is why this part of YOUR INHERITANCE is not given until after the START of the MILLENNIUM when there will be a TIME of HEAVEN on EARTH; for TOTAL WISDOM is TIMELESS, and for them within the CONFINES of NEW JERUSALEM, TIME will be held CONSTANT! At the initial SOUNDING of the SEVENTH TRUMPET, TIME WILL CEASE FOR THE SAVED (***GOD'S*** CHILDREN) AND FOR THE BLESSED (the BEHEADED SOULS), but it will continue on for the remnant of the people left on earth.

> ***Revelation 10:5*** *And the ANGEL which I saw stand upon the SEA and upon the EARTH lifted up* ***HIS HAND*** *to HEAVEN,*

> ***Revelation 10:6*** *And SWEAR by* ***HIM*** *that liveth for ever and ever, who CREATED HEAVEN, and the things that therein are, and the*

EARTH, and the things that therein are, and the SEA, and the things which are therein, that there should be TIME no longer.

NOTE: These Scriptures taken from the 10th Chapter of the Book of Revelation speak of the EVENT of TIME being held CONSTANT at the initial SOUNDING of the SEVENTH TRUMPET. The SEVENTH TRUMPET will SOUND TWICE, once at the BEGINNING of the MILLENNIUM and again at THE END of the LAST DAY (the END of the MILLENNIUM).

The GIFT of HEAVENLY DOMAIN

This is the GREATEST GIFT of INHERITANCE, for this ENABLES the RECIPIENT to SPIRITUALLY ASCEND into their RIGHTFUL PLACE in HEAVEN and DWELL where ***GOD DWELLS.*** As explained in the BOOK titled "The ROD of IRON", the ***GOD*** GIVEN SPIRIT has the ability to DIMENSIONALLY ASCEND beyond the "EARTH PLANE", and can achieve ABSOLUTE CONSCIOUSNESS (ETERNAL LIFE) in a LIGHT FORM. The METHOD in which this TRANSFIGURATION is ACHIEVED is called RAPTURE, because the FEELING of TRANSFIGURATION is ECSTASY!

The RIGHTFUL HEIR

ALL things are given to JESUS CHRIST for ***HE*** is the RIGHTFUL HEIR to ALL BELONGING to ***THE FATHER.*** However unlike the Jews, JESUS CHRIST SHARES ALL that is GIVEN to HIM with ALL of ***GOD'S*** CHILDREN. The Scripture describing the SAVIOR, MESSIAH, tells of how HE will divide ALL that is GIVEN to ***HIM*** with the WORTHY (called the STRONG in the Scripture).

> ***Isaiah 53:12*** *Therefore will **I** divide HIM a portion with **THE GREAT,** and HE shall divide the spoil with the STRONG; because HE hath POURED OUT HIS SOUL unto DEATH: and HE was numbered with the transgressors; and HE bare the SIN of MANY, and made INTERCESSION for the TRANSGRESSORS.*

NOTE: This last Scripture tells of how JESUS CHRIST is GIVEN a PLACE within ***THE GODHEAD, as YESHUA,*** (called in the Scripture, "a portion with the GREAT") and how ALL the riches of the world (the SPOIL) is GIVEN to

HIM for HIS GIVING HIS LIFE for the WORLD (HIS DYING on the CROSS for the sins of the world). It also says that HE will divide those RICHES with the WORTHY (those of CHRIST, called in the Scripture, “the STRONG”).

> ***John 16:15 ALL THINGS THAT THE FATHER HATH ARE MINE: THEREFORE SAID I, THAT HE SHALL TAKE OF MINE, AND SHALL SHEW IT UNTO YOU.***

ONLY THROUGH JESUS CHRIST CAN ONE BECOME HEIR TO THE ***PROMISE of THE FATHER***.

Chapter 2
SPIRITUAL ASCENSION

It was briefly explained in the FOREWORD of this BOOK how there is a difference between SPIRITUAL ASCENSION and SPIRITUAL ASCENDING. Whereas SPIRITUAL ASCENDING is achieved by DIMENSIONAL CHANGE and TRANSFIGURATION, and can only come by RAPTURE or the SEPARATION of the SPIRIT from the BODY of FLESH; SPIRITUAL ASCENSION occurs without DIMENSIONAL CHANGE and while the SPIRIT remains within the PHYSICAL BODY. This is to say, the SPIRIT remains within the "EARTH PLANE" and in the PHYSICAL WORLD while it yet ASCENDS in INTELLECT and AWARENESS, thus RAISING SPIRITUAL CONSCIOUSNESS and this is called SPIRITUAL AWAKENING.

SPIRITUAL AWAKENING (REBIRTH)

SPIRITUAL AWAKENING occurs AFTER ***HOLY SPIRIT*** BAPTISM has been PERFORMED; or, it can also occur after ONE has RECEIVED the ***SEAL of THE LIVING GOD.*** However the latter CONDITION, RECEIVING the ***SEAL of THE LIVING GOD,*** acts only as an alternate to BAPTISM when there isn't the PRESENCE of THE ***HOLY SPIRIT of GOD*** to PERFORM the BAPTISM; such as it will be during the GREAT TRIBULATION.

The TWO CONDITIONS should not be CONFUSED for there are significant differences between them. Whereas with ***HOLY SPIRIT*** BAPTISM, the RECIPIENT RECEIVES both PROTECTION and ONE or MORE of the NINE GIFTS GIVEN by THE ***HOLY SPIRIT,*** with SPIRITUAL ***SEALING,*** the RECIPIENT only RECEIVES PROTECTION. Also, whereas only THE ***HOLY SPIRIT of GOD*** can PERFORM ***HOLY SPIRIT*** BAPTISM, SPIRITUAL ***SEALING*** can be PERFORMED by any ONE of the SEVENTH LEVEL ANGELS or by any ONE of the TWELVE HIGHER HEAVENLY ORDER BEINGS. The TWELVE are: the FOUR METATRON, the FOUR COVENANT ANGELS, and the FOUR SERAPHIM. Another difference between the TWO is that BAPTISM is ETERNAL, whereas being ***SEALED*** for PROTECTION has only a TEMPORARY status.

It may also be noted that when ONE is ***SEALED*** as opposed to being BAPTIZED, the GIFT of FAITH is not GIVEN, and this allows that person's own faith to be open to CHALLENGING by the DEVIL. However the challenging of ONE'S faith can only go on for TEN DAYS after their REPENTANCE, and if their faith does not falter or fail during those TEN DAYS, ***THE LORD*** will not allow the Devil to further challenge that INDIVIDUAL'S faith. This is called the "TRIAL and TRIBULATION PERIOD" and is spoken about in the Book of Revelation. This TRIAL and TRIBULATION PERIOD applies to those called the "WEDDING GUESTS" and it occurs both prior to and during the GREAT TRIBULATION. Prior to the GREAT TRIBULATION, the TRIAL and TRIBULATION PERIOD lasts for FORTY DAYS after RECEIVING BAPTISM. However, during the GREAT TRIBULATION, when BAPTISM is no longer available and ***SEALING*** is used as an alternate to BAPTISM, the TIME of TRIAL and TRIBULATION is shortened to TEN DAYS after the REPENTANCE of SIN. Once the TEN DAYS are successfully completed, then the PERSON who had REPENTED of their SIN to ***GOD*** will RECEIVE the ***SEAL of the LIVING GOD,*** and their faith can no longer be CHALLENGED.

As explained in "The ROD of IRON", when the BRIDE of CHRIST RECEIVES ***HOLY SPIRIT*** BAPTISM, their NAMES are immediately ENTERED into the REGISTER in HEAVEN and they RECEIVE the GIFTS GIVEN by THE ***HOLY SPIRIT***. However for the WEDDING GUESTS, there is a FORTY-DAY lag between the time of their BAPTISM and the time when their NAMES have been put into the GUESTS REGISTER in HEAVEN. It isn't until after their NAMES are entered into the REGISTER that the WEDDING GUESTS RECEIVE the GIFTS GIVEN by THE ***HOLY SPIRIT.*** Once THE ***HOLY SPIRIT*** leaves the EARTH, and BAPTISM is no longer available and ***SEALING*** is used as an alternate to BAPTISM, then the TRIAL and TRIBULATION PERIOD is shortened to TEN DAYS.

> ***Revelation 2:10 FEAR NONE OF THOSE THINGS WHICH THOU SHALT SUFFER: BEHOLD, THE DEVIL SHALL CAST SOME OF YOU INTO PRISON, THAT YE MAY BE TRIED; AND YE SHALL HAVE TRIBULATION TEN DAYS: BE THOU FAITHFUL UNTO DEATH, AND I WILL GIVE THEE A CROWN OF LIFE.***

It may be noted from the last Scripture that the ONES who must be FAITHFUL until DEATH, refers to the BEHEADED SOULS who will not RECEIVE the ***SEAL of THE LIVING GOD*** for their PROTECTION, and this does not apply to them who are called the WEDDING GUESTS. But it must also be noted that the ***SEALING*** comes TEN DAYS after REPENTANCE, and even for the WEDDING GUESTS, if their faith should falter or fail during those TEN DAYS, they shall not be SAVED, ***SAITH THE LORD of HOSTS.***

Once ONE has either RECEIVED BAPTISM (before THE GREAT TRIBULATION PERIOD) or ***SEALING*** (after THE GREAT TRIBULATION has begun), SPIRITUAL ASCENSION will COMMENCE. This AWAKENING of the SPIRIT is called SPIRITUAL REBIRTH, or as the Scripture refers to it as, the BRINGING FORTH OF THE MAN CHILD.

> ***Revelation 12:5*** *And SHE brought forth a MAN CHILD, who was to RULE all nations with a ROD of IRON: and HER CHILD was caught up unto* ***GOD,*** *and to* ***HIS*** *THRONE.*

Every person RECEIVING either BAPTISM or ***SEALING*** will have their SPIRITUAL INTELLECT RAISED to at least the SIXTH LEVEL of CONSCIOUSNESS, and this will enable them to both SEE and FEEL (BEHOLD) the Spiritual Presence of both GOOD and EVIL! During THE GREAT TRIBULATION, it will be the RESPONSIBILITY of those who are ***SEALED*** to WARN those who have not yet been ***SEALED*** of any Spiritual Entity threatening their safety. Those who will LEAD the effort in SPIRITUAL GUIDANCE are called the TRIBULATION SAINTS, and all of them will be the DESCENDANTS of the HEBREW PEOPLE (the TWELVE TRIBES of ISRAEL) that have been CONVERTED to CHRISTIANITY and ***SEALED*** at the TIME the DEVIL is cast down to the EARTH. For them, their ***SEALING*** will be INSTANTANEOUS, and there will not be a TEN-DAY lag in their ***SEALING*** as it will be for the others. There will be ONE HUNDRED AND FORTY-FOUR THOUSAND of the TRIBULATION SAINTS throughout the WORLD, and not ONE will FALTER or FAIL, ***SAITH THE LORD!***

> ***Revelation 7:4*** *And I heard the NUMBER of THEM which were* ***SEALED:*** *and there were* ***SEALED*** *an HUNDRED and FORTY and FOUR THOUSAND of ALL the Tribes of the CHILDREN of ISRAEL.*

PROTECTION

Once ***SEALED,*** the PERSON RECEIVING the ***SEALING*** is ENCAPSULATED in a SPIRITUAL BUBBLE, and this BUBBLE will be VISIBLE only to that INDIVIDUAL. The BUBBLE will appear to look like TRANSPARENT moving images or wavy lines before the EYES, and when first looking through them they will be somewhat distracting; for at times they will appear to be obstacles, and can startle the ***SEALED*** who are looking through the BUBBLE.

However the BUBBLE (the ***SEAL***) will be also VISIBLE to the ANGELS, or any Spiritual Entity, and will PROVIDE both PHYSICAL and SPIRITUAL PROTECTION. ***THE LORD*** has told ME that even a NUCLEAR EXPLOSION cannot penetrate the ***SEAL,*** for it is impervious to any external forces, and ONLY ***GOD*** can break through it or remove it. A person having the ***SEAL*** can be standing in the midst of TURMOIL and not be affected by it. And, if anyone tries to cause harm to ONE who has been ***SEALED,*** they themselves in the SAME MANNER will be harmed, ***SAITH THE LORD of HOSTS.***

> ***Revelation 11:5*** *And if any man will hurt them, fire proceedeth out of THEIR MOUTH, and devoureth their enemies: and if any man will hurt them, he must in THIS MANNER be killed.*

Neither the DEVIL nor will any Spiritual Entity attempt to attack ONE having the ***SEAL of the LIVING GOD.*** However the ***SEAL*** will not be evident to the common person, and those having been corrupted by EVIL will certainly try to hurt them with the ***SEAL.*** However, ALL EFFORTS tried to HARM ONE with the ***SEAL*** will FAIL, and whatsoever HARM they intended to cause to the ONE ***SEALED*** will FALL UPON THEM who had perpetrated the HARM!

Ascension Plateaus

Each LEVEL of ASCENSION is called a PLATEAU, and each PLATEAU has a NAME assigned to it. There are TWENTY-SIX PLATEAUS in total, however MAN can only achieve ASCENSION to the NINETEENTH PLATEAU, which is the LEVEL of the SAINT and the PROPHET. This represents a LEVEL of SPIRITUAL AWARENESS equivalent to that of the SIXTH LEVEL INHABITANT in HEAVEN. After BAPTISM or ***SEALING,*** the RECIPIENT will undergo SPIRITUAL ASCENSION to at least the SIXTH PLATEAU, and this process will begin as soon as that PERSON'S NAME has been

REGISTERED in HEAVEN as either "THE BRIDE", or ONE of the "GUESTS of the WEDDING SUPPER". The PROCESS of ASCENSION will take place over a SIX to NINETEEN MONTH period of time, reaching only ONE PLATEAU of ELEVATION per every THIRTY-DAY PERIOD of TIME.

For the PERSON RECEIVING the SIXTH PLATEAU of SPIRITUAL AWARENESS, it will take SIX MONTHS of ASCENSION, commencing on the DAY of their REBIRTH (BAPTISM or ***SEALING***) and continuing on until the SIX-MONTH ANNIVERSARY of their REBIRTH. For the SEVENTH PLATEAU, it will continue on until the SEVEN-MONTH ANNIVERSARY, and so on up to the NINETEEN-MONTH ANNIVERSARY for them RECEIVING the NINETEENTH PLATEAU. It should be noted that NONE of the WEDDING GUESTS will RECEIVE ASCENSION above the THIRTEENTH PLATEAU. Therefore, after the GREAT TRIBULATION has begun, only the TRIBULATION SAINTS and the TWO WITNESSES will have SPIRITUAL AWARENESS above the THIRTEENTH LEVEL. It should also be noted that the SPIRITUAL BUBBLE will only be detectable by that INDIVIDUAL after they have RECEIVED ASCENSION to the SIXTH PLATEAU, albeit the PROTECTION provided by the ***SEAL*** is IMMEDIATE.

There is a specific reason as to why ONE cannot DETECT the BUBBLE prior to their ASCENSION to the SIXTH PLATEAU of AWARENESS. This is because the BUBBLE is SPIRIT, and ONE cannot detect SPIRIT until they have reached the SIXTH PLATEAU of AWARENESS. It was explained in the BOOK titled "The ROD of IRON", in the Chapter called "DIMENSIONS", that the SIXTH DIMENSION is the DIMENSION of "SPIRIT". And, although the ONE RECEIVING the ASCENSION has not ASCENDED to that DIMENSIONAL LEVEL, they have through SPIRITUAL ASCENSION, the AWARENESS of that DIMENSION and can DETECT SPIRIT by the RAISING of their SPIRITUAL INTELLECT to that LEVEL of AWARENESS!

It should start becoming obvious to YOU that the NAMES of the ASCENSION PLATEAUS are the SAME as the NAMES of the DIMENSIONS discussed in the BOOK titled, "The ROD of IRON. In the "EARTH PLANE", there are FOUR PHYSICAL DIMENSIONS, and they are called, LENGTH, WIDTH, HEIGHT, and TIME. Without any ASCENSION whatsoever, ONE has the AWARENESS of all FOUR of these DIMENSIONS. For ONE to RAISE their SPIRITUAL INTELLECT to AWARENESS above the "EARTH PLANE", they must be RAISED to a LEVEL of AWARENESS above the "GAP" which is the FIFTH PLATEAU to the SIXTH PLATEAU, which is that of the SPIRIT LEVEL! ONE must be in SPIRITUAL AWARENESS to COMPREHEND and DETECT SPIRITUAL MATTER. The following is a list of the

THIRTEEN ASCENSION PLATEAUS within the UNIVERSE that WE have discussed thus far:

1. The Length Plateau
2. The Width Plateau
3. The Height Plateau
4. The Time Plateau
5. The GAP PLATEAU
6. The SPIRITUAL PLATEAU
7. The SOUL PLATEAU
8. The CATALYTIC PLATEAU
9. The CONTAINMENT PLATEAU
10. The INERTIA PLATEAU
11. The ACCELERATION PLATEAU
12. The RESONANCE PLATEAU
13. The LIGHT PLATEAU

The THIRTEEN HEAVENLY PLATEAUS will not be listed nor discussed in this BOOK, because they can only be UNDERSTOOD by them having already ACHIEVED an INTELLECT of the FOURTEENTH PLATEAU or GREATER. At this point in time, there are only a handful of people on the EARTH with this level of AWARENESS, so it would be meaningless to try to EXPLAIN the HEAVENLY PLATEAUS of AWARENESS.

The THIRTY STEPS

As it was explained a bit earlier in this Chapter, each level of ASCENSION occurs over a THIRTY-DAY PERIOD of TIME. Each DAY of ASCENSION can be viewed as a STEP of ELEVATION, likening to a STAIRCASE having THIRTY STAIRS with a DOOR at the TOP of it. ***THE LORD*** views each month as having THIRTY DAYS, therefore on the months that have fewer or greater days than THIRTY, the THIRTY STEPS of ASCENSION will occur over the span of that month, being completed on the ANNIVERSARY DAY of that month, whether it is shorter or longer than thirty days.

Once all THIRTY STEPS have been ASCENDED and YOU have reached the top of the STAIRCASE, the door will be opened to YOU allowing YOUR access to the next STAIRCASE. This will continue on until each PREDETERMINED LEVEL of ASCENSION has been achieved. Although the feelings that ONE will EXPERIENCE as they ASCEND will vary amongst INDIVIDUALS, some CONFUSION will be EXPERIENCED, and this is NORMAL. As ASCENSION occurs, the LEVEL of AWARENESS INCREASES, thus causing those ASCENDING to start questioning things in life and about themselves that had previously been overlooked by them. When this phenomenon occurs, it will cause that INDIVIDUAL to question his or her own MENTAL STATE of INTEGRITY, and a common question one will ask them self is; "AM I GOING CRAZY"?

The reason for this type of CONFUSION is that the ASCENSION causes the AWARENESS to elevate and the NATURAL STATE of MIND will try to EVALUATE the CHANGE in AWARENESS. It will initially appear to the MIND that the CHANGES are of an EXTERNAL INFLUENCE and it will be uncertain as to whether the CHANGES are of a POSITIVE or NEGATIVE INFLUENCE. However, as the ASCENSION continues on, the MIND will submit to the SPIRIT and ACCEPT the CHANGES as being POSITIVE, after the ASCENSION has BRIDGED the GAP PLATEAU. In other WORDS, the first FIVE MONTHS of ASCENSION are the most difficult to COMPREHEND, and during that period of time it would be GOOD for that INDIVIDUAL to have someone around them who had already EXPERIENCED the first FIVE LEVELS of ASCENSION.

ASCENSION will take place on its own without the need of assistance, and all the PERSON who is EXPERIENCING it will need to do is to TRUST IN ***GOD.*** YOUR SPIRIT will immediately ACCEPT the CHANGE in AWARENESS as being GOOD, while YOUR MIND will remain skeptical and be uncertain about it. However, the SPIRIT will always achieve its GOAL, and the MIND will become submissive to the SPIRIT as the LEVEL of ASCENSION PROGRESSES.

Due to the MIND being a product of the EARTH, and the EARTH being under the control of the DEVIL, prior to the MIND'S submission to the SPIRIT it will retaliate against the SPIRIT. The MIND will try to play tricks to FOOL YOU into believing YOU are not of a sound state of MIND. However all tactics used by the MIND will fail, for YOUR SPIRIT cannot FAIL because it has RECEIVED BAPTISM or ***SEALING,*** and with that BAPTISM or ***SEALING*** comes ***SAVING GRACE!***

BAPTISM and SEALING

A person of the EARTH can PERFORM neither BAPTISM nor SEALING, because NEITHER BAPTISM or ***SEALING*** is from the EARTH. Any person claiming that he or she has the ability to BAPTIZE or provide ONE with the

SEAL of the LIVING GOD, is but a FOOL. And, anyone believing they have been BAPTIZED or ***SEALED*** as such, is all the more a FOOL!

BAPTISM can only be PERFORMED by THE ***HOLY SPIRIT of GOD,*** and ***SEALING*** can be the only ALTERNATE to BAPTISM, and the ONE PERFORMING the ***SEALING*** MUST BE OF THE SEVENTH ORDER LEVEL OR HIGHER IN HEAVEN, and EMPOWERED BY ***GOD*** TO DO SO. This NONSENSE being taught by the Church that a Water Baptism performed by a Priest, Minister, or Pastor will save a person's SOUL, is both a LIE and a DECEPTION.

BAPTISM and or ***SEALING*** COMES only after a REPENTANCE to ***GOD*** has been made by an INDIVIDUAL and that REPENTANCE has been ACCEPTED by ***GOD.*** This is BETWEEN YOU and ***HE,*** and <u>NO ONE ELSE</u> ***SAITH THE LORD of HOSTS! THE LORD*** says that only YOU and YOU alone can either LOSE YOUR SOUL or SAVE IT, and NO ONE ELSE can do that for YOU or be BLAMED for it! If YOU FAIL to REPENT and to SERVE ***GOD,*** that is YOUR CHOICE, or if YOU REPENT and try to SERVE ***GOD,*** that is also between YOU and ***HE.*** Therefore, if either of the TWO OUTCOMES is a result of MUTUAL TRUST or DISTRUST between YOU and ***GOD,*** where is the NEED for a third person's INVOLVEMENT?

THIS NONSENSE OF THE NEED OF A THIRD PERSON HAS TROUBLED THE CHURCH FROM ITS BEGINNING. I AM BOTH THE WAY AND THE MEANS SAITH THE LORD, AND NO MAN CAN DO WHAT I CAN DO, SO THEREFORE THEY CANNOT DO IT FOR ME! YOUR RELATIONSHIP WITH ME IS BETWEEN THE TWO OF US AND NO ONE ELSE, AND WHAT WE DO TOGETHER, WE DO IN SECRET!

> ***Matthew 6:5 AND WHEN THOU PRAYEST, THOU SHALT NOT BE AS THE HYPOCRITES ARE: FOR THEY LOVE TO PRAY STANDING IN THE SYNAGOGUES AND IN THE CORNERS OF THE STREETS, THAT THEY MAY BE SEEN OF MEN. VERILY I SAY UNTO YOU, THEY HAVE THEIR REWARD.***

> ***Matthew 6:6 BUT THOU, WHEN THOU PRAYEST, ENTER INTO THY CLOSET, AND WHEN THOU HAST SHUT THY DOOR, PRAY TO THY FATHER WHICH IS IN SECRET; AND THY FATHER WHICH SEETH IN SECRET SHALL REWARD THEE OPENLY.***

Chapter 3,
SPIRIT (IDENTITY)

On October 14th 1997, the day after ***THE LORD*** had initially come to ME, ***HE*** explained the differences between the Spirit and the SOUL. The English Dictionary defines the Spirit as being the "Life Giving Force", and this is true; for the Spirit is the ESSENCE of Life. However, the Spirit is more than just the ESSENCE of LIFE, it is the SPIRIT who PERSONIFIES LIFE by giving the LIFE FORM an IDENTITY.

THE LORD told ME on that day, MY SPIRIT provided MY IDENTITY, and MY SOUL provided MY PURPOSE in life. AT first I wasn't exactly sure what ***HE*** had meant by this, but after I had meditated on the subject for quite some time, it started to make SENSE to ME. I had always seen my physical makeup as my identity, because I believed the physical image I viewed in a mirror represented the person I am. However, ***THE LORD*** explained if that were true, then a blind person would not be aware of their own identity, because they would not be able to see their own physical image.

It was also explained to ME how the SPIRIT provides ONE with a PERSONALITY and also INDIVIDUALITY, and this is why there isn't any two persons on earth that are alike. After JESUS' RESURRECTION, HE only appeared as HE had looked before to HIS Disciples on two occasions. Whereas all the other times HE had appeared after HIS RESURRECTION, HE appeared as a STRANGER to them. But after they had spoken to the STRANGER for a short period of time, they then KNEW the STRANGER was JESUS CHRIST.

When HE had appeared as a STRANGER, JESUS never once told them who HE was, but yet the Disciples still KNEW it was JESUS. So one might ask, how could they have known that the PERSON to whom they were speaking was JESUS CHRIST, for HE had taken on an entirely different physical appearance? The answer to this QUESTION is actually quite simple; the Disciples had come to KNOW JESUS CHRIST SPIRITUALLY, and because they knew JESUS in the SPIRIT, they could DISCERN that the SPIRIT of the STRANGER was that of JESUS CHRIST.

In this Chapter WE want to TEACH YOU about the SPIRIT and its IDEN-

TITY, and how the SPIRIT PERSONIFIES the PERSON of the SPIRIT. WE want to explain how when ONE SPIRIT comes to LOVE another, it is the PERSON of the SPIRIT who is LOVED and not the Person of the Flesh. The same is also TRUE in regard to a relationship of HATRED, for it is the Spiritual person that is hated by the other Spirit and not the person of the flesh. WE will explain as to why you can never come to truly know another individual, until you have come to KNOW that person SPIRITUALLY, and that SPIRITUAL RELATIONSHIPS are the only TRUTHFUL RELATIONSHIPS that are neither bound to TIME nor to PHYSICAL APPEARANCE.

A Spiritual Relationship can be either a GOOD RELATIONSHIP or an EVIL one, and both of these SCENARIOS will be discussed in this Chapter. A GOOD SPIRITUAL RELATIONSHIP is one of PARTNERING and FRIENDSHIP. However the EVIL Spiritual relationship is one of TORMENT and DECEPTION. And, whereas the GOOD SPIRITUAL RELATIONSHIP thrives on the SUCCESS of it, the EVIL one looks towards its FAILURE and DEMISE.

Types of Spirits

On EARTH there are THREE TYPES of Spirits, the Spirit of the EARTH, that is given by the EARTH, the Spirit of the DAMNED that is given by the DEVIL, and the SPIRIT of MAN that is GIVEN by ***GOD.*** This relates to the THREE DIFFERENT TYPES of PEOPLE WE had talked about in the other two BOOKS, "Revealing The Bible's Truth" and "The ROD of IRON". The EARTH given Spirit is that of the "GENTILE", the Spirit of the "DAMNED" is that of the "CANAANITE", and the ***GOD*** GIVEN SPIRIT is that of "ADAM", the "BLESSED", the MAN with a SOUL.

Every living person on the EARTH has an EARTH given Spirit, whether they are of the "DAMNED Spirit" (the Canaanite) or of the "BLESSED SPIRIT" (ADAM), and, the EARTH given Spirit RESIDES in the same body of flesh, as does either the "DAMNED" or the "BLESSED SPIRIT". This is why it is IMPOSSIBLE without the GIFT of SPIRITUAL DISCERNMENT, GIVEN by THE ***HOLY SPIRIT of GOD,*** to spiritually differentiate as to, who is who, spiritually. The COMMON Spirit, the Spirit of the EARTH remains to be the PRIMARY identity of the person until they are either POSSESSED by the DEVIL or REBORN in the SPIRIT of ***GOD.*** And, until either one of these two conditions prevail it is the EARTH given Spirit that is the dominant Spirit. Then all the while the EARTH given Spirit dominates the body of flesh it MASKS the person's TRUE SPIRITUAL IDENTITY.

As the TIME grows NEAR to the TIME of the END, YOU will SEE just how intermingled the SPIRIT of the GOOD and the Spirit of the Evil are, for at that TIME ALL SPIRITUAL IDENTITY will be EXPOSED. YOU are going to be SHOCKED when YOU SEE exactly who is EVIL and WHO is GOOD in the WORLD, for many whom you had thought to be GOOD, are really EVIL, and, visa versa. There will be sons and daughters, mothers and fathers, sisters and brothers, aunts, uncles, and cousins, with some being GOOD and some being EVIL within the SAME FAMILY; and this will be made vividly clear once their TRUE IDENTITIES are EXPOSED. JESUS talks about this separation of the GOOD and the EVIL at the TIME of the END.

> ***Matthew 25:32 AND BEFORE HIM SHALL BE GATHERED ALL NATIONS: AND HE SHALL SEPARATE THEM ONE FROM ANOTHER, AS A SHEPHERD DIVIDETH HIS SHEEP FROM THE GOATS:***

> ***Matthew 25:33 AND HE SHALL SET THE SHEEP ON HIS RIGHT HAND, BUT THE GOATS ON THE LEFT.***

JESUS also referred to the GOOD and the EVIL as the WHEAT and the TARES among the WHEAT. The WHEAT is the GOOD and the TARES are the EVIL. The following Scriptures tell of how the seed of the DEVIL (the TARES) have been intermingled with the SEED of the GOOD (the WHEAT).

> ***Matthew 13:24 Another PARABLE put HE forth unto them, saying, THE KINGDOM OF HEAVEN IS LIKENED UNTO A MAN WHICH SOWED GOOD SEED IN HIS FIELD:***

> ***Matthew 13:25 BUT WHILE MEN SLEPT, HIS ENEMY CAME AND SOWED TARES AMONG THE WHEAT, AND WENT HIS WAY.***

> ***Matthew 13:26 BUT WHEN THE BLADE WAS SPRUNG UP, AND BROUGHT FORTH FRUIT, THEN APPEARED THE TARES ALSO.***

> ***Matthew 13:27 SO THE SERVANTS OF THE HOUSEHOLDER CAME AND SAID UNTO HIM, SIR, DIDST NOT***

THOU SOW GOOD SEED IN THY FIELD? FROM WHENCE THEN HATH IT TARES?

Matthew 13:28 HE SAID UNTO THEM, AN ENEMY HATH DONE THIS. THE SERVANTS SAID UNTO HIM, WILT THOU THEN THAT WE GO AND GATHER THEM UP?

Matthew 13:29 BUT HE SAID, NAY; LEST WHILE YE GATHER UP THE TARES, YE ROOT UP ALSO THE WHEAT WITH THEM.

Matthew 13:30 LET BOTH GROW TOGETHER UNTIL THE HARVEST: AND IN THE TIME OF THE HARVEST I WILL SAY TO THE REAPERS, GATHER YE FIRST TOGETHER THE TARES, AND BIND THEM IN BUNDLES TO BURN THEM: BUT GATHER THE WHEAT INTO MY BARN.

NOTE: The GOOD SEED referred to in the Scriptures is that of ADAM, the BLESSED SEED, and the TARES spoken about is the DAMNED SEED, that of CAIN, the Son of the DEVIL. The ENEMY referred to is the DEVIL, who also impregnated EVE who gave birth to the DEVIL'S SEED, CAIN. The FIELD spoken of in the Scripture is the EARTH and the HOUSEHOLDER is ***GOD***. The TIME of the HARVEST is the TIME of the END, and the REAPERS are the ANGELS. The TARES that are to be gathered, bundled, and BURNED, are the EVIL who are to be cast into HELL, and the WHEAT gathered and put into the BARN, are the GOOD SEED who are DESTINED for HEAVEN.

These WARNINGS are posted throughout the HOLY BIBLE; to BEWARE at the TIME of the END, to NOT TRUST IN ANYONE; for YOU WILL NOT KNOW, who, they really are! The Evil are so intermixed amongst the GOOD, and are so well hidden, that an Evil Mate could be either a husband or wife of many years, with the other being unaware of it. This also applies to any family member or friend you may think to be TRUSTWORTHY, for EVIL lives amidst you!

Matthew 24:8 ALL THESE THINGS ARE THE BEGINNING OF SORROWS.

Matthew 24:9 THEN SHALL THEY DELIVER YOU UP TO BE AFFLICTED, AND SHALL KILL YOU: AND YE SHALL BE HATED FOR MY NAME'S SAKE.

Matthew 24:10 AND THEN SHALL MANY BE OFFENDED, AND SHALL BETRAY ONE ANOTHER, AND SHALL HATE ONE ANOTHER.

Mark 13:12 NOW THE BROTHER SHALL BETRAY THE BROTHER TO DEATH, AND THE FATHER THE SON; AND THE CHILDREN SHALL RISE UP AGAINST THEIR PARENTS, AND SHALL CAUSE THEM TO BE PUT TO DEATH.

Luke 21:16 AND YE SHALL BE BETRAYED BOTH BY PARENTS, AND BRETHREN, AND KINSFOLKS, AND FRIENDS; AND SOME OF YOU SHALL THEY CAUSE TO BE PUT TO DEATH.

Micah 7:5 *Trust ye not in a friend, put ye no confidence in a guide: keep the doors of thy mouth from her that lieth in thy bosom.*

Micah 7:6 *For the son dishonoureth the father, the daughter riseth up against her mother, the daughter in law against her mother in law; a man's enemies are the men of his own house.*

Spiritual DECEPTION

Shortly after my initial meeting with ***GOD***, I was told by ***THE LORD*** that a man was going to be sent to ME, and this man was the Spirit of one of the original TWELVE Disciples that had walked with JESUS CHRIST. Sure enough, just as ***THE LORD*** had told ME, on the very next day I received a call from one of my Mother's friends who she had known from Church. She had him call ME because she was concerned about MY SPIRITUAL well being; for she did not UNDERSTAND and was CONFUSED about the CHANGES that were taking place in ME as a result of MY CONVERSION.

Over a period of more than FIVE YEARS I befriended this man who was sent to ME, and placed MY solemn TRUST in him, for I had believed he was the Spirit of the Apostle Peter. However, after the publishing of "Revealing The

Bible's Truth", ***THE LORD*** exposed this man's TRUE IDENTITY to ME.

All the while I had been talking with this person and placing MY TRUST in him, he had been talking out of both sides of his mouth, and telling my Mother exactly the opposite of that which he had been telling ME. As soon as ***THE LORD*** had made ME aware that this man had betrayed MY TRUST, I confronted him on the matter. And, as it is with ALL EVIL, once they have been EXPOSED, they will say or do anything to HIDE their IDENTITY again. The man then in desperation made a TRAGIC MISTAKE; after I had asked if he would swear to ***GOD*** against his SOUL, if he were wrong in his words and actions, he said, "in a minute he would do so and commit his soul to HELL, if he were to be wrong about the matter", and further said, it was I who was wrong and had ERRED.

On the very next morning, ***THE LORD*** told ME that I was never to SPEAK to this man again, and that his soul had already been taken from him, for he had been PREDESTINED to HELL, even before his CONCEPTION! But I reminded ***THE LORD*** that ***HE*** had told ME that this man was the Spirit of one of the original TWELVE Disciples, and I had believed he was the Spirit of the Apostle PETER, so how could he have been PREDESTINED for HELL? But ***THE LORD*** told ME that ***HE*** had never given me the Disciple's NAME, and that the man whom I had entrusted wasn't Peter, but rather Judas Iscariot, the Disciple that had BETRAYED JESUS CHRIST!

As I pondered over what ***GOD*** had told ME about the man, and how he was the Spirit of Judas Iscariot, the BETRAYER, I wondered how I had become so easily fooled into believing he was a good person, even to the point of thinking he was the Spirit of the Apostle Peter. As I pondered on the subject, I recalled that this man was a Deacon at the Church, and also a volunteer worker for the Salvation Army. He was also a very close friend to both of my parents, and had all the credentials of a person who was serving ***GOD***. I then asked myself during this time of confusion, why no one other than I could see this man's TRUE IDENTITY, and that he REEKED of EVIL?

But ***THE LORD*** cleared up the MATTER for ME and said, that even the man himself KNEW NOT who he was, and believes himself to be a good person, ALBEIT HE IS THE SON of PERDITION! ***GOD*** also told ME that MY DECEPTION by the EVIL was to be WRITTEN in this BOOK, for it is MEANT to be a WARNING to the people, to BEWARE of those whom they place their TRUST in; for EVIL can disguise itself in such a way it cannot be detected by MAN. I BELIEVE that there isn't a person on the EARTH CLOSER to ***GOD*** than ***I AM,*** and if I can be FOOLED, anyone can be FOOLED, SO BEWARE!

Spiritual MASKING and DISGUISE

As previously explained, the Spirit provides one with their IDENTITY, and for the GOOD this is a BLESSING, but for the EVIL this is a CURSE. The GOOD wants ALL to come to KNOW him or her SPIRITUALLY, because they are PROUD to be a CHILD of ***GOD.*** However, EVIL is aware that it is EVIL, and a SON of PERDITION (product of the Devil) wants to hide its IDENTITY. The EVIL refuses to EXPOSE them self to another, not even to another EVIL Entity. Whereas the GOOD flourish in the LIGHT, the EVIL lurks in DARKNESS, for in the LIGHT they become EXPOSED. EVIL only gathers together in a TIME of MISCHIEF.

> ***Luke 11:34 THE LIGHT OF THE BODY IS THE EYE: THEREFORE WHEN THINE EYE IS SINGLE, THY WHOLE BODY ALSO IS FULL OF LIGHT; BUT WHEN THINE EYE IS EVIL, THY BODY ALSO IS FULL OF DARKNESS.***
>
> ***Luke 11:35 TAKE HEED THEREFORE THAT THE LIGHT WHICH IS IN THEE BE NOT DARKNESS.***
>
> ***Luke 11:36 IF THY WHOLE BODY THEREFORE BE FULL OF LIGHT, HAVING NO PART DARK, THE WHOLE SHALL BE FULL OF LIGHT, AS WHEN THE BRIGHT SHINING OF A CANDLE DOTH GIVE THEE LIGHT.***

In these last Scriptures taken from the GOSPEL of Luke, JESUS CHRIST is SPEAKING to the EARTH given Spirit of MAN, who can either be the HOST to the GOOD or to the EVIL. HE WARNS them to beware of the SECONDARY Spirit within them, and gives a methodology for them to check themselves of what Spiritual Matter they might consist of. The reason JESUS WARNS them is because the GENTILE (one with only the earth given Spirit) can be SAVED, and be included as a GUEST of the WEDDING SUPPER, if the EVIL within them is cast out.

You have been told in the BOOK titled, "The ROD of IRON", that TWO BILLION people with a SOUL will lose them, and some of those SOULS will be given to the GENTILES. If ***GOD*** accepts a GENTILE'S REPENTANCE of SIN, they too can be SAVED and REBORN in CHRIST. At the time of their REBIRTH and REGISTRY in HEAVEN as a GUEST of the WEDDING SUP-

PER, they are GIVEN a SOUL. The SOUL they are GIVEN is ONE that had been taken from another person, for ***GOD'S PURPOSE WILL BE SERVED!***

When an EVIL Entity resides within a person, they hide behind the Spirit (IDENTITY) of the GENTILE, which is the Spirit of the EARTH that all MANKIND possess. One of the tell tale signs of a person being POSSESSED by a DEMONIC Spirit, is that person's unwillingness to maintain an EYE CONTACT with anyone. The EYE is the PORTAL to the SOUL, and when a CHILD of ***GOD*** looks through the EYE and into the SOUL of one being DEMON POSSESSED**,** the SPIRIT of ***GOD*** within the CHILD will DETECT the Soul of the DAMNED, therefore EXPOSING them!

Being very CLEVER in their DISGUISES, the POSSESSED will nearly always portray them self as being ***GOD*** SERVING individuals, and will rarely ever blow their cover by doing something that could be OBSERVED by another as being EVIL. The bulk of them will proclaim themselves to be Christians, for they want to infiltrate the Church and be ready to take control of it, once Lucifer is cast down to the earth. Unlike the Charles Manson types, the WORST of the lot will be strong supporters of the Church, and will be people who have authority and prestigious jobs. These will be people who are viewed by the General Public and the Church Congregation as being upstanding Citizens, who are admired for their accomplishments and considered trustworthy.

One of the KEY functions of the TRIBULATION SAINTS will be to IDENTIFY the EVIL ONES and WARN them who are yet to be SAVED about them. This is one of the reasons why the TRIBULATION SAINTS are both MARKED and SEALED with the ***SEAL of the LIVING GOD*** immediately, and do not undergo the TEN-DAY delay. At the SOUNDING of the FIRST TRUMPET and the casting down of Lucifer to the earth, ALL of the EVIL ONES will be in POSITION to rapidly take control. They at that time will most diligently move to CORRUPT and DECEIVE as many as possible, and only the TRIBULATION SAINTS will know who these people are!

Once EVIL begins to ABOUND it will grow like CANCER, and there will be no stopping it! Many of the GOOD PEOPLE still in power, will move towards changing the world for the good of the people, but they will be accused of being traitors, fail in their efforts, and be incarcerated and killed by the Antichrist. The Government will take on the form of the Roman Empire and will make public spectacles of those who are captured and killed. These EVENTS will be televised throughout the world and a fear instilled in the people so that each and every person on the earth who is not SAVED, will willingly turn in a family member to save their own life. Regardless of whether it is a mother or father, a daughter or son, a sister or brother, a husband or wife, if those around them suspect any family member or friend is breaking the law set by the Antichrist, they will turn them in to the Authorities to protect themselves.

GOOD RELATIONSHIPS versus Evil Ones

It is very easy to CONFUSE a LOVING RELATIONSHIP or a FRIENDLY RELATIONSHIP with an Evil Relationship. This is because the EVIL within a person can be so well hidden and disguised, one partner in the relationship can never really know who the other partner is, regardless of their time spent together. This is why JESUS said that YOU should LOVE one another, because LOVE is what SEPARATES GOOD from EVIL, for EVIL cannot LOVE in any way.

THE LORD tells ME that people CONFUSE acquaintances with LOVED ONES and FRIENDS, and it is these Acquaintanceships that allow the EVIL to commingle with the GOOD. LOVE is spontaneous and knows no boundaries of time, whereas Acquaintanceships are temporary, void of LOVE, and are governed by time.

The reason that TIME is the governing element in an Acquaintanceship is because once the EVIL is exposed in the Acquaintanceship, it ENDS, whereas a TRUE LOVING RELATIONSHIP never ENDS! YOU must not try to LOVE another person, for if YOU have to try to LOVE there isn't any LOVE PRESENT. YOU cannot learn to LOVE another, as you have been more than likely taught; YOU either LOVE them or YOU DON'T. There isn't any TIME element in a LOVING RELATIONSHIP or FRIENDSHIP, and if either appears to deteriorate with TIME, the element of LOVE is not PRESENT in the RELATIONSHIP, nor has it ever been. LOVE can only grow and can never diminish, and if it appears that the Relationship is diminishing, then EVIL is within it.

Neither the Spirit of the Canaanite or the Spirit of the GENTILE can either LOVE or be LOVED, for only the ***GOD*** GIVEN SPIRIT to MAN can RECEIVE the GIFT of LOVE. The Canaanite cannot LOVE because they bear the Soul of the DAMNED, and the GENTILE cannot LOVE because they have not a SOUL, and the LOVE of ***GOD*** comes in the FORM of a SOUL. Therefore, the GENTILE can be either the HOST to the ***GOD*** GIVEN SPIRIT of MAN who can LOVE, or host to the Spirit of the DAMNED who can only HATE. The GENTILE can be a host to multiple Spirits of the Canaanite at the same time, whereas the GENTILE (the Spirit of the EARTH) can only be a HOST to a SINGLE ***GOD*** GIVEN SPIRIT.

Summary

Let US summarize that which WE have covered thus far in this Chapter. Every living person on EARTH has the EARTH given Spirit of the GENTILE. This is an animal Spirit that is given by the EARTH to the higher intellectual order mammal allowing them the thought process and also providing them with individuality and an identity. This is all part of carnal life, which allows the carnal man to have dominion over all the other animals of the world. However, the GENTILE'S thought process, individuality and identity all cease at the time of their death, and the Spirit of the GENTILE returns to the EARTH who had given it.

Now enters into the carnal world, TWO other SPIRITUAL ORDERS of LIFE, ONE that is BLESSED by ***GOD,*** called the GOOD, and one that is DAMNED by ***GOD*** called the EVIL. Due to both SPIRITUAL LIFE FORMS being Spirit only, they must too, in order to inhabit the carnal world, have a body of flesh. It is the GENTILE who provides that body of flesh and acts as a carnal living host to either type of Spirit while in the carnal world.

The THREE SPIRITUAL SEEDS, that of the BLESSED, that of the DAMNED, and that of the CARNAL Man (the GENTILE) were all separated from one another up until the TIME of JESUS CHRIST, the COMING of the MESSIAH. Prior to JESUS, being different races of people separated the THREE SPIRITUAL TYPES, and these were the HEBREW (the BLESSED), the Canaanite (the DAMNED), and the GENTILE (***GOD'S*** SIXTH DAY CREATION, carnal man). The HEBREW was WARNED by ***GOD*** to only MARRY within their own RACE, whereas at that time, the Canaanite and the GENTILE intermarried, and this intermarrying started with CAIN.

However, for the past two thousand years, intermarriage between ALL THREE SPIRITUAL TYPES have been ongoing, thus making differentiating between the THREE impossible for anyone other than ***GOD.*** In many families throughout the WORLD today, all THREE TYPES of SPIRITS exist in the SAME FAMILY, making the FAMILY UNIT only bound by human genetics, and not by SPIRIT, and this is the sowing of the TARES in with the WHEAT spoken of in the Scriptures.

GOD will soon separate the THREE AGAIN, and the DAMNED will be cast into HELL, the CARNAL (the GENTILE) will be returned to the DUST of the EARTH, and the GOOD will be ***DELIVERED*** to HEAVEN, ***SAITH THE LORD of HOSTS! A-MEN'***

Chapter 4
SOUL (PURPOSE)

Whereas the SPIRIT provides the ESSENCE of LIFE and your IDENTITY, the SOUL PROVIDES your PURPOSE in LIFE and your ETERNITY. MAN cannot enter HEAVEN without a SOUL, and it is the ***GOD*** GIVEN SOUL that allows MAN to ASCEND beyond the "EARTH PLANE", for with the SOUL comes EMOTION and the ability to differentiate between GOOD and EVIL. The EARTH given Spirit of the GENTILE receives a CONSCIENCE in lieu of a SOUL, and a CONSCIENCE should not be confused with a SOUL, because the two are quite different.

A CONSCIENCE is received along with the ability to think (the thought process) and acts as an INTERROGATOR, but the SOUL acts as a JUDGE. Whereas the INTERROGATOR analyzes based on moral conduct, the JUDGE (the SOUL) JUDGES actions based on TRUTH through EMOTIONAL FEELING. This is to say, the CONSCIENCE evaluates moral actions based on LAWS, whereas the SOUL justifies SPIRITUAL ACTIONS based on TRUTH.

THE ***HOLY SPIRIT of GOD*** comes to only those who have a ***GOD*** GIVEN SOUL, and this is why JESUS CHRIST refers to THE ***HOLY SPIRIT*** as THE ***SPIRIT of TRUTH (John 16:13),*** and it is through the SOUL that THE ***HOLY SPIRIT*** SPEAKS to a CHILD of ***GOD***. It is the VOICE of THE ***HOLY SPIRIT*** that SPEAKS through the SOUL and provides the GUIDANCE to the SPIRIT of MAN, enabling the MAN to DIFFERENTIATE between RIGHTEOUS WORKS and EVIL ACTIONS. The SOUL then provides the FEEDBACK to the PERSON as to whether the actions taken by the SPIRIT are RIGHTEOUS or UNRIGHTEOUS by way of FEELINGS (EMOTION), and these FEELINGS provided by the SOUL in turn act as a GUIDE.

When ONE'S ACTIONS are within the TRUE PURPOSE of the SOUL, the EMOTION generated by the ACTIONS made by the SPIRIT is one of ACCOMPLISHMENT and the FULFILLMENT of PURPOSE. This gives the SPIRIT a FEELING of GREAT PLEASURE. However, if the actions taken by the SPIRIT deviate from the SOULS TRUE PURPOSE, then the JUDGE (the SOUL) sees the actions of the SPIRIT as UNRIGHTEOUS, and the SOUL will then GENERATE an EMOTION of Self-Disapproval and REMORSE. The SPIRIT in turn SEES this DISPLEASURE of its OWN ACTIONS as a FAILURE in PURPOSE, thus causing the SPIRIT to want to make REPENTANCE to ***GOD*** for its actions! Once made, the REPENTANCE of the ACTIONS are then RECEIVED by ***GOD*** and are either ACCEPTED or REJECTED by ***HIM,*** depending on the severity of the SIN and the SINCERITY of the REPENTANCE. If ***GOD*** GRANTS forgiveness, then ATONEMENT is made for the SOUL and the SIN is removed and FORGOTTEN, as though it had never happened!

Every SOUL serves a PURPOSE in ***GOD,*** and a CHILD of ***GOD'S*** PURPOSE is always RIGHTEOUS, because ***GOD*** is RIGHTEOUS. Even the Soul of the DAMNED serves a PURPOSE in ***GOD,*** for ***GOD*** CREATED both the GOOD and the EVIL. And, even though the EVIL perpetrates EVIL actions to fulfill their own selfish desires, the ***GOD*** GIVEN PURPOSE of their actions will EVENTUALLY fulfill a RIGHTEOUS PURPOSE! For ***GOD*** is RIGHTEOUS in ALL that ***HE*** does, even though at times it may appear to be otherwise!

The Gentile and the BEGINNING

The GENTILE was the first to walk upon the EARTH, and is referred to as ***GOD'S*** SIXTH DAY CREATION. This Man is a product of the EARTH, having all of his or her biological features coming from the EARTH. This person was made in the likeness of ***GOD,*** albeit the GENTILE lacks a SOUL. This is to say that the GENTILE, although being in appearance the SIMILITUDE of ***GOD***, lacks in ***GODLY QUALITIES,*** for the GENTILE cannot differentiate between GOOD and EVIL, that of which is a MANDATE for a PERSON being GRANTED ACCESS to HEAVEN.

It wasn't until after the CREATION of ADAM and EVE, when they had made their choice of CARNAL LIFE over SPIRITUAL LIFE and SINNED against ***GOD,*** that anyone other than the ***GODLY*** could DIFFERENTIATE between GOOD and EVIL. However, the GARDEN of EDEN was made in the SIMILITUDE of HEAVEN, thus forbidding SIN to be in it, and the MAN (ADAM) and his wife (EVE) were cast out of the GARDEN for their SINNING. By the TWO (ADAM and EVE) experiencing the exposure to SIN, and willingly SINNING against ***GOD***, if the TWO were then to EAT of the TREE of LIFE after their SINNING, they would have RECEIVED ETERNITY. This was because they then had taken on the ***GODLIKE QUALITIES*** of knowing the DIFFERENCE between GOOD and EVIL, even though their choice was that of EVIL. However their ETERNITY would not be an ETERNAL PLACE in HEAVEN, but rather an eternal place in HELL, for the TWO had made the CHOICE of EVIL over GOOD, and had placed SIN upon their SOUL. ***GOD*** cast both ADAM and EVE out of the GARDEN, for if they had remained and ATE of the TREE of LIFE, their eternity would have been one of DAMNATION. THEREFORE, ***GOD*** removed ADAM and EVE from the GARDEN for their own PROTECTION against eternal DAMNATION.

Having a CARNAL BODY of FLESH and looking like the GENTILE, once removed from the GARDEN of EDEN, both ADAM and EVE hid themselves in the thicket. They no longer had the PROTECTION from the GENTILE as they had had while they were in the GARDEN, and hid themselves out of FEAR of the GENTILE, who was known to kill any intruder in the vicinity of his immediate family. So ***GOD*** kept the GENTILE away from ADAM and EVE, the ONE'S ***HE*** had GIVEN a SOUL, and allowed them to live near, but not in, the GARDEN of EDEN. So ADAM and EVE set up a camp near to the EAST GATE of EDEN, and there they lived out the days of their life.

> ***Genesis 3:22*** *And* ***THE LORD GOD*** *said, BEHOLD, the MAN has become as ONE of* ***US,*** *to KNOW GOOD and EVIL: and now, lest he put forth his hand, and take also of the TREE of LIFE, and EAT, and live FOR EVER:*
>
> ***Genesis 3:23*** *Therefore* ***THE LORD GOD*** *sent him forth from the GARDEN of EDEN, to till the ground from whence he was taken.*
>
> ***Genesis 3:24*** *So* ***HE*** *drove out the MAN; and* ***HE*** *placed at the EAST of the GARDEN of EDEN CHER'-U-BIMS, and a FLAMING SWORD which turned every way, to keep the way of the TREE of LIFE.*

NOTE: The last three Scriptures tell you that ADAM'S body of FLESH came forth from the EARTH, and therefore CARNALLY; ADAM was exactly the same as the GENTILE; with the only difference between ADAM and the GENTILE being, ADAM had a SOUL. However, the SOUL is TRANSPARENT, and cannot be seen CARNALLY with the HUMAN EYE, and this gave ADAM the appearance of the GENTILE. To keep ADAM and EVE away from the TREE of LIFE and eternal DAMNATION, ***GOD*** placed an ANGEL at the EAST GATE of EDEN to prevent their ENTRY into the GARDEN. As it is in HEAVEN so was it with the GARDEN of EDEN, with the only entry into it being the EAST GATE.

At this point in time in the Life Cycle of the EARTH, there were only two types of people existing, the GENTILE, who hadn't a SOUL, and ADAM and EVE who had a SOUL. However, both her HUSBAND ADAM and Lucifer the Devil, while in the GARDEN had impregnated EVE, and she gave birth to TWIN BROTHERS from the TWO DIFFERENT fathers. The FIRSTBORN she named CAIN, who was the offspring of Lucifer (the DEVIL), and the SECOND SON she delivered was named ABEL, who was the OFFSPRING of ADAM.

After the BIRTH of the TWINS, CAIN and ABEL, there were now THREE TYPES of people existing on the EARTH. The three types were, the GENTILE (the carnal man of flesh without a SOUL), the BLESSED (ADAM and HIS OFFSPRING having a SOUL), and the DAMNED (Lucifer and his offspring bearing a Soul of SIN). These THREE types of PEOPLE lived together for a period of 8224 years, and then due to the overwhelming EVIL existing in the world, ***GOD*** DESTROYED IT with a GREAT FLOOD, leaving only NOAH and his wife Me'-a-te'-rah and NOAH'S THREE SONS, Shem, Ham, and Japheth, and their three wives alive after the GREAT FLOOD. It was through the THREE SONS of NOAH that the THREE SEEDS of LIFE continued. Through SHEM came the OFFSPRING of ADAM (the BLESSED SEED), through HAM came the offspring of the DEVIL (the DAMNED, the Canaanite), and through NOAH'S son Japheth came the GENTILE, ***GOD'S*** SIXTH DAY CREATION.

GOD meticulously separated the THREE types of PEOPLE by races, and whereas the GENTILE and the CANAANITE over a course of time intermarried, the BLESSED SEED, the HEBREW was FORBIDDEN by ***GOD*** to intermarry, up until the COMING of JESUS CHRIST. Therefore up until the TIME of JESUS, the GENTILE could only receive the Soul of the DAMNED, by way of marriage to the Canaanite, and having offspring with them.

After the COMING of JESUS CHRIST and HIS RESURRECTION, the LAW prohibiting intermarriage for the HEBREW was abandoned, and the THREE SEEDS of LIFE intermarried throughout the world. The GENTILE then became the HOST of the BLESSED SOUL and the DAMNED Soul, and continued as well as the SOULLESS person of ***GOD'S*** SIXTH DAY CREATION.

All THREE types of PEOPLE are now present within family groups. A father can be BLESSED while the wife is of the GENTILE or of the DAMNED, and visa versa, allowing their offspring to be any one of the combination of the THREE types of PEOPLE, leaving only ***GOD*** knowing who is who! WE covered this subject while discussing the variations in SPIRIT, and the same scenario applies to the SOUL. This is why JESUS was so adamant in WARNING against JUDGING one another, for you know not who, you may be JUDGING. You may be of the SOULLESS or the DAMNED, and CONDEMNING a PERSON with a SOUL because their actions appear to be unrighteous, and all the time you are CONDEMNING them, they are DESTINED for HEAVEN, and YOU will return to either the DUST of the EARTH, or are DESTINED for HELL! JUDGE only YOURSELF and not another, leave JUDGMENT to ***THE LORD of HOSTS!***

QUALITIES of the SOUL

A SOUL is RECEIVED through the LINEAGE of ONE'S ancestry and can be passed down from either of the PARENTS or BOTH, to their OFFSPRING. If both PARENTS are of the BLESSED SEED, then ALL of their offspring will be of the BLESSED SEED and RECEIVE a SOUL at the time of their physical birth. In the EYES of ***GOD,*** BIRTH takes place at the time of CONCEPTION, when the SPERM UNITES with the EGG. ***GOD*** refers to the UNITING of the SPERM and the EGG as "THE FIRST PHYSICAL MARRIAGE" for the TWO become as ONE in the WOMB, with the EGG representing the BRIDE and the SPERM representing the GROOM. GENDER isn't determined for the CHILD until after it has received its SPIRIT and its SOUL, for the SPIRIT determines the GENDER. For the EARTH given Spirit the Gender is solely determined biologically, however with the ***GOD*** GIVEN SPIRIT the GENDER is PREDETERMINED and the Biological Gender will match that PREDETERMINATION.

If only ONE of the Parents are of the BLESSED SEED, then the offspring of the TWO can be any combination of the TWO types of SEEDS. Furthermore, with there being THREE types of SEEDS on the EARTH, and the GENTILE being the COMMON HOST of the other two types along with their own type, then the offspring can be of any of the permeations and combinations of the THREE types of SEEDS.

On the other hand, if both of the Parents are of the DAMNED SEED, then ALL of their offspring will be of the DAMNED SEED, and these offspring are referred to as the SONS of PERDITION. These children of the DAMNED are PREDESTINED for HELL and there isn't anything that anybody can do to CHANGE their DESTINY. However, NOTHING is IMPOSSIBLE for ***GOD,*** and if ***HE*** so decides to change ONE'S DESTINY, ***HE WILL!*** This is to say ***GOD CAN EVEN GIVE HOPE TO THE HOPELESS.***

ALL RECEIVING a SOUL, even if it is a DAMNED Soul, receive the ability to experience EMOTION; however for the DAMNED Soul, the EMOTION of LOVE is OMITTED from it. As explained in "The ROD of IRON", it is through the ability to experience EMOTION that the SPIRIT can DIMENSIONALLY ASCEND to HEAVEN. With LOVE being the GREATEST EMOTIONAL FEELING, it is the KEY to ASCENDING and to the ASCENSION PROCESS. The SOUL can be looked at like a BLADDER that is filled in its entirety with EMOTION, and with the DAMNED Soul being VOID of LOVE a DOUBLE portion of HATRED is given to it, to maintain its fullness and proper size.

A CHILD of ***GOD*** experiences ALL EMOTION, and it is NOT until the CHILD has EXPERIENCED EVIL EMOTION and has CAST it OUT of their SOUL, that they can RECEIVE ETERNITY. This EXPERIENCING and CASTING OUT of the EVIL from the SOUL can only be done on the EARTH and while the CHILD of ***GOD*** is in a CARNAL FORM of life. After CASTING OUT the EVIL, ***GOD*** then replaces that which had been CAST OUT with LOVE to keep the BLADDER in its FULLNESS and proper size.

The BLADDER (the SOUL) can be viewed as a HOT AIR BALLOON that cannot ASCEND because it carries too much weight. EVIL EMOTION can be viewed as LEAD, that which is very HEAVY, while LOVE can be VIEWED as a FEATHER, which is very LIGHT. As the LEAD (EVIL) is removed from the HOT AIR BALLOON, and replaced with FEATHERS (LOVE), it starts to ASCEND in FLIGHT. Whereas EVIL EMOTION within the SOUL weights it down to the EARTH, the EMOTION of LOVE within the SOUL allows the SOUL to ASCEND.

To illustrate the HOT AIR BALLOON scenario WE have just used in the EXPLANATION of LOVE versus EVIL EMOTION, WE will use some Scriptures taken from the Book of Zechariah. These same Scriptures were used in "The ROD of IRON" to explain the whereabouts of the ARK of the COVENANT during ISRAEL'S captivity. However in this case, WE want YOU to see the E'-PHAH spoken of in the Scriptures as a BASKET, that is suspended below a HOT AIR BALLOON. And, WE want YOU to SEE the WOMAN who is put into the BASKET (the E'-PHAH) as EVIL EMOTION overwhelming a SOUL, thus making it too heavy to ASCEND in FLIGHT. We also want YOU to SEE the land of SHI'-NAR spoken of in the Scripture, as being a PLACE far from the PRESENCE of ***GOD.***

Zechariah 5:5 *Then the ANGEL that talked with me went forth, and said unto me, LIFT UP NOW THINE EYES, AND SEE WHAT IS THIS THAT GOETH FORTH.*

Zechariah 5:6 *And I said, What is it? And HE said, THIS IS AN E'-PHAH THAT GOETH FORTH. HE said moreover, THIS IS THEIR RESEMBLANCE THROUGH ALL THE EARTH.*

Zechariah 5:7 *And, BEHOLD, there was lifted up a talent of LEAD: and this is a WOMAN that sitteth in the MIDST of the E'-PHAH.*

Zechariah 5:8 *And HE said, THIS IS WICKEDNESS. And HE CAST it into the MIDST of the E'-PHAH; and HE cast a weight of LEAD upon the mouth thereof.*

Zechariah 5:9 *Then lifted up I mine eyes, and looked, and, BEHOLD, there came out TWO WOMEN, and the wind was in their WINGS; for they had WINGS like the wings of a stork: and they LIFTED UP the E'-PHAH between the EARTH and the HEAVEN.*

Zechariah 5:10 *Then said I to the ANGEL that talked with me, Whither do these BEAR the E'-PHAH?*

Zechariah 5:11 *And HE said unto me, TO BUILD IT A HOUSE IN THE LAND OF SHI'-NAR: AND IT SHALL BE ESTABLISHED, AND SET THERE UPON HER OWN BASE.*

NOTE: The BASKET (the E'-PHAH) that the WOMAN was put into can be viewed as a basket being suspended below a HOT AIR BALLOON. Once the WOMAN'S MOUTH had been sealed with a talent of lead, the BALLOON could no longer ASCEND because it was too heavy and needed TWO ANGELS (the WOMEN with WINGS like a STORK) to carry it to its permanent resting place. The place where the BASKET (the E'-PHAH) was taken to was the Land of SHI'-NAR. This was the City that NIMROD (a direct descendant of Lucifer) had established and also where the Tower of Babel had been constructed. SHI'-NAR was considered to be an EVIL PLACE and a PLACE of ***GOD'S*** CON-

DEMNATION, for it was at Babel where ***GOD*** took from MAN, his ability to COMMUNICATE in the SPIRIT.

The E'-PHAH and the TALENT of LEAD is used in the Scripture in the SAME manner as WE had used the HOT AIR BALLOON and BASKET, to illustrate the WEIGHT of SIN upon the SOUL, and how the EVIL within the SOUL will prevent it from ASCENDING. The Scripture further tells of the outcome of the SOUL that cannot ASCEND on its OWN; the ANGELS bring it to a PLACE of CONDEMNATION, where the Spirit can no longer COMMUNICATE, a PLACE that JESUS calls OUTER DARKNESS (Matthew 8:12).

SPIRIT and SOUL

The HOT AIR BALLOON can also be used to illustrate a COMPLETE PERSON bearing a SPIRIT and a SOUL. ALL ***GOD*** given SPIRITS can be viewed in the likeness of the HOT AIR BALLOON that on its own can ascend. However this wouldn't serve any PURPOSE, for without the BASKET attached to it, the BALLOON carries NOTHING.

The BASKET being suspended by the BALLOON can be viewed as being the SOUL of a PERSON. Once the BASKET (the SOUL) is attached to the BALLOON, then the BALLOON SERVES a PURPOSE, for now when it ASCENDS it CARRIES with it the SOUL of the SPIRITUAL PERSON, which is the PURPOSE of the SPIRITUAL PERSON.

It should be somewhat obvious to YOU by now that those bearing the Souls of the DAMNED can NEVER ascend, for a Soul without LOVE and filled with EVIL is much too heavy for flight. Everyone in HEAVEN SERVES A PURPOSE, and that PURPOSE is LOVE, and LOVE comes only by way of a ***GOD*** GIVEN SOUL, for ***GOD*** is LOVE.

In summary, this describes the outcome of the THREE TYPES of PEOPLE on the EARTH. The BLESSED, being full of LOVE and VOID of EVIL will ASCEND up to HEAVEN. The GENTILE, being void of a Soul serves only a purpose on earth, and at the termination of the GENTILE'S life, they simply return to the DUST of the EARTH and are forgotten forever. The DAMNED, having a Soul that is too heavy to ascend, for it is filled with EVIL, also serves only a purpose on earth, for only the EARTH can be HOST to both the GOOD and the EVIL. However, because the DAMNED bear a Soul, at the time of their death the burden of weight on their Soul causes them to DESCEND into the bowels of HELL, "SHI'-NAR", a place established by EVIL and far from the PRESENCE of ***GOD.***

Chapter 5
The ANGELS

When ***THE LORD*** had first come to ME I spoke only to ***HIM, (THE ALMIGHTY GOD)*** and it wasn't until three or four months after MY CONVERSION that I started speaking with JESUS CHRIST. JESUS informed ME that this was not the normal method of CONVERSION but it was rather a UNIQUE PROCESS I was going through; for after JESUS' RESURRECTION, ALL coming to know ***THE LORD*** MUST speak first with JESUS CHRIST! ***GOD*** normally sends JESUS FIRST to the PERSON destined for BAPTISM, and then after their BAPTISM and RECEIPT of THE ***HOLY SPIRIT***, CONVERSATIONS with ***GOD*** can take place; PROVIDING the ONE BAPTIZED has RECEIVED the GIFT of TONGUES (HEBREWAH).

I was TOLD that MY speaking to ***GOD*** and ***HIS ANSWERING*** ME in the COMMON LANGUAGE (in this case English) was really quite UNIQUE, because in the NEW COVENANT, ***GOD*** no longer SPEAKS in the COMMON LANGUAGE. The COMMON LANGUAGE refers to any earthly language spoken by man, when the thought process is required to speak. In the NEW COVENANT, SPIRITUAL BAPTISM is a REQUIREMENT, and NOW, only in the SPIRIT can one SPEAK to and WORSHIP ***THE LORD***, for ***GOD IS A SPIRIT!***

> ***John 4:23 BUT THE HOUR COMETH, AND NOW IS, WHEN THE TRUE WORSHIPPERS SHALL WORSHIP THE FATHER IN SPIRIT AND IN TRUTH: FOR THE FATHER SEEKETH SUCH TO WORSHIP HIM.***

> ***John 4:24 GOD IS A SPIRIT: AND THEY THAT WORSHIP HIM MUST WORSHIP HIM IN SPIRIT AND IN TRUTH.***

Prior to MY CONVERSION and MY reading of the HOLY BIBLE, I hadn't really given any thought at all to the ANGELS, and I wasn't exactly certain whether or not they were real, or merely a religious myth. This confusion I had about the ANGELS was mostly due to the lack of teaching about them in the churches. As a child attending Sunday school, the Angels were rarely spoken about, and although at times were mentioned, nothing of substance describing who they were or what they were about had ever been discussed.

In the SEVENTH MONTH after MY CONVERSION, the ANGELS were introduced to ME. JESUS introduced some of the ANGELS, while others introduced themselves, and WE have had many CONVERSATIONS covering a whole host of subjects. Most of OUR CONVERSATIONS consist of their teaching ME, but our RELATIONSHIPS have grown to a point where I can CONFIDE in them on some very personal matters, and they both direct and COUNSEL ME on those matters. There is not a person on this EARTH that I TRUST in more than the ANGELS, and if it weren't for them being always with ME, I suppose by now with all the CHANGES taking place in MY LIFE I would have lost MY sanity.

The FIRST ANGEL I had met INTRODUCED HERSELF to ME, and SHE said HER NAME was ***JAEL.*** SHE told ME shortly after HER INTRODUCTION that SHE was my GUARDIAN ANGEL and had been with ME in SPIRIT from MY time of BIRTH to look after MY every move. ***JAEL*** brought ME back through MY childhood and showed ME when and where SHE had INTERVENED during MY LIFE, and how SHE had kept bad situations I had gotten MYSELF into, from getting worse.

One such situation and INTERVENTION occurred during MY third marriage, just prior to the birth of MY youngest DAUGHTER. During this marriage I had gotten quite involved with drugs, specifically amphetamines, called "crank", and I was routinely taking crank for well over a year. Then suddenly a woman came into my life, and the way we had met was quite odd, for she was a recent hire of one of my largest customers and was given my account to manage. At that time I was the Vice President of Sales and Marketing for an electronics firm, and because this particular customer represented a very large portion of the company's business, I personally handled the account.

Having routine meetings to discuss the status on various projects the two companies were jointly working on, at one of these meetings I met this woman who now MANAGED our account. At OUR first meeting, both SHE and I made some sort of a SPIRITUAL CONNECTION and WE both FELT the CONNECTION but said nothing about it. Neither of US understood at that time as to why WE were so ATTRACTED to each other, and although WE both knew WE had never met before, it was as though WE had at some time in the PAST been INTIMATELY CLOSE to one another. While WE both tried to keep OUR relationship on a professional basis, it seemed as though our two companies were doing everything possible to bring us closer together. Every opportunity was given to US to get to know one another, and although it seemed by chance, WE both knew it was something GREATER than chance that was PULLING US TOGETHER!

This Young Lady was really quite classy and would never consider dating a married man, and my marriage was in its very early stages and I certainly wasn't looking to have an affair. But the more WE tried to avoid each other, something of a business nature would always come up causing US to meet. I could literally feel this woman's PRESENCE, and SHE could FEEL MINE. Even when WE were apart, WE could SPEAK to one another SPIRITUALLY and discuss later what had transpired in OUR SPIRITUAL CONVERSATIONS. I know that this seems crazy, but it is the ABSOLUTE TRUTH.

In a very short period of time (about six weeks or so) the TWO of US could no longer resist each other, and WE fell deeply in LOVE causing ME to separate from my wife. Being at that time pregnant with my child, my wife could not understand what had happened to cause our marriage to collapse, for we were not having any problems or so it seemed. Other than my drug addiction, that of which no one other than myself was aware of at that time, nothing seemed to be wrong in the marriage, and even I couldn't understand why we were splitting up. However, when looking back at the situation, my source of supply for the drugs was coming from both my wife, and her brother-in-law, and this was why ***THE LORD*** was separating me from them.

When I was with this woman the thought of drugs never once entered MY MIND, and I was totally overwhelmed by the SPIRITUAL FEELING of EUPHORIA I RECEIVED when in HER PRESENCE; and this FEELING by far surpassed any "high" I had experienced while on drugs. Then, shortly after MY DAUGHTER was born, the SPIRITUAL CONNECTION between the TWO of US seemed to diminish, and neither of US could UNDERSTAND why, but the relationship shortly thereafter ended.

Then after being separated and off drugs for more than a year, I started dating my wife again; and although we had nearly completed our divorce proceedings, we put them on hold and eventually got back together. I have never again been even remotely interested in taking drugs of any sorts, and have had the opportunity on several occasions to take them, but declined. Then several years after getting back with my wife we decided to call it quits and completed our divorce. But this time we did it in a peaceful manner through a notary, rather than through lawyers and the court system. Even to this very day we both still LOVE each other, albeit not as husband and wife, but more like FATHER and DAUGHTER, for she is quite a bit younger than I. We talk almost daily with one another, and together share in our daughter's life. We even at times celebrate certain occasions together, however our LOVE is not one of an intimate relationship but rather one of a close FRIENDSHIP.

JAEL explained to ME what had happened to cause my marriage to temporarily split. SHE said, ***THE LORD*** was concerned about MY drug problem, and wanted ME off the drugs. So ***GOD*** put HER SPIRIT into the WOMAN that I had been so attracted to, causing ME to leave MY wife; for it was ***JAEL*** whom I had seen SPIRITUALLY within the WOMAN. ***JAEL*** said that once I had become weaned off the drugs, SHE was made to leave the woman and return to HER post as my GUARDIAN, and once ***JAEL'S*** SPIRIT had left her, there was no longer a SPIRITUAL CONNECTION between the woman and I. This caused the two of us to move away from one another and resume our lives as they had been prior to our meeting. ***JAEL*** also asked ME, didn't I find it a bit odd, that after going back to my wife, the woman seemingly disappeared from all facets of MY LIFE, leaving not a trace of her whereabouts behind? I have neither seen nor heard a single word about this woman since my wife and I got back together, and that was nearly twenty years ago!

The SWITCHING of GUARDIANS

After MEETING ***JAEL***, I was INTRODUCED by HER and JESUS to several other ANGELS, all being ANGELS of the SEVENTH LEVEL. I first met GABRIEL, and then RAPHAEL, MOR'-PHI-ET, and DARIUS, and they all had DIFFERENT PERSONALITIES. It took awhile, but after some period of time, I could recognize their VOICES when they were not visible and would SPEAK to ME. But during the short-term I would ask, which one of them was SPEAKING, and whoever was SPEAKING would very politely give ME their NAME.

I was TOLD by ***GOD*** MY NAME in HEAVEN, and when the ANGELS would address ME they called ME by my FIRST NAME "ROBERT" and then followed the name "ROBERT" with MY HEAVENLY NAME. This method of ADDRESSING ME continued on for well over a year, and then somewhere along the line, the NAME "ROBERT" was dropped, and they ALL call ME now by only my HEAVENLY NAME. During that year, I was TOLD by ***JAEL*** that the other FOUR ANGELS were going to TRADE places with HER for some period of time and be MY GUARDIAN, but JESUS would be HER first replacement, and only after HE had filled HER POST, could the others assume the ROLE as MY GUARDIAN.

It was rather an ODD FEELING when these changes in GUARDIAN took place. I could literally FEEL the ONE step out of ME, and the other step in, even though the changing of GUARDIANS took place in an INSTANT. When ONE would step out, it seemed as though a gust of wind blew through the very essence of my BEING, and as the OTHER replaced the ONE that had left ME, I could FEEL the essence of their BEING within ME, and for each ONE that FEELING was different.

When the change was made between ***JAEL*** and JESUS, it was a very SUBTLE CHANGE, and there wasn't any feeling of significance caused by the CHANGE. I could tell the CHANGE had taken place and was forewarned of it, and with JESUS as MY GUARDIAN I never felt any uneasiness as was felt with some of the OTHERS. I was always forewarned of the CHANGES just prior to the occurrence, and when the CHANGE was made to DARIUS I felt the STRENGTH of the PRESENCE of his PERSONALITY and was for a short period of time subdued by it. However, after a day or two I felt COMFORTABLE with DARIUS as MY GUARDIAN ANGEL.

The timeframe spent with each ONE of the GUARDIANS varied. I was with JESUS the longest, and with MOR'-PHI-ET the least amount of time, but the durations with the various GUARDIANS was never shorter than a two week period. Although the LOVE expressed by all FOUR GUARDIANS (GABRIEL, RAPHAEL, MOR'-PHI-ET, and DARIUS) was quite moving, I found that only MOR'-PHI-ET was as COMFORTABLE with ME as ***JAEL*** and JESUS was. It was explained to ME by the ANGELS, that MOR'-PHI-ET and I have KNOWN each other for a VERY LONG TIME, and he is a very close FRIEND of MINE, and this is why I felt so COMFORTABLE with him, and he with ME. Then after I was told about MY past RELATIONSHIP with MOR'-PHI-ET, I IMMEDIATELY remembered the LOVING FRIENDSHIP WE had had in the past with one another.

After about a one year period of HOSTING a NEW GUARDIAN, ***JAEL*** returned to HER original POST of being MY GUARDIAN, and even when I HOSTED the OTHERS, SHE was always PRESENT and never left MY side. At times I felt as though SHE were MY MOTHER looking after ME and not trusting anyone else with that responsibility. But OUR RELATIONSHIP is really quite INTIMATE, and even when SHE assumed the role of a MOTHER, I never saw HER as a MOTHER, but rather as a CONCERNED WIFE.

SPIRITUAL IDENTIFICATION

The ANGELS continually aid in the Spiritual Identification of certain people involved with MY life. As was previously discussed in this BOOK, Spiritual Identities even amongst family members can vary immensely. I was just recently informed, FIRST by ***THE LORD*** and again by the ANGELS about the Spiritual makeup of the members in MY own earthly family. I was SURPRISED, but not shocked to find out that MY own earthly mother is of the CANAANITE, and MY SEED had come through MY earthly FATHER who is of the BLESSED SEED, as did MY older brother's SEED come through him as well. MY two half-sisters, neither of which is of the BLESSED SEED, are each from a different LINEAGE, with the eldest being of the GENTILE, and the youngest being as her mother, of the SEED of CAIN (the CANAANITE).

If you knew my earthly mother and her two daughters you would refuse to believe that any of them could be of the SEED of CAIN or the GENTILE, because all three are regular church goers and believe they are SAVED. MY mother has even told ME that she has spoken in TONGUES (HEBREWAH). However, I have never heard her do so, and if she is of the LINEAGE of CAIN, she cannot be BAPTIZED in the ***SPIRIT of GOD*** and RECEIVE the GIFT of TONGUES.

THE LORD has told ME that MY earthly mother's first husband was of the GENTILE, and that is why his offspring is BOTH of the SEED of CAIN (through the mother) and of the GENTILE (through the father). My earthly mother has kept the secret of her two daughters being from someone other than my FATHER from all of her friends, even those whom she is most close to. ***THE LORD*** says, so is it with the CANAANITE to LIE about most personal matters if they might appear to be degrading to one's self-proclaimed righteous nature, or, when they feel it will intrude upon or REVEAL their TRUE SPIRITUAL CHARACTER.

I have been TOLD that the BLESSED SEED had come down from my GRANDMOTHER'S side of the FAMILY, to MY FATHER, and then down to his two sons, MY brother and I. I have been GIVEN the TRUE Spiritual IDENTITIES of ALL of MY earthly family members, and their offspring, as to WHO is WHO, Spiritually. It was most interesting to find out that the younger of MY two biological half-sisters, the one who is of the CANAANITE, married ONE of the BLESSED SEED, and all three of their children are of the BLESSED SEED. Whereas the eldest half-sister married another GENTILE, and both of their offspring is of the GENTILE.

I was TOLD that only one of my FOUR former WIVES was of the BLESSED SEED, and SHE is the only one that I had maintained a RELATIONSHIP with after the divorcement. However, both of MY CHILDREN are of the BLESSED SEED, and although the eldest of the two has yet to come to KNOW ***THE LORD,*** she will come around in the not so distant future!

The GIFT of SPIRITUAL DISCERNMENT at times can be most troubling, for many of the people I in the past have had great regard for, have since turned out to be spiritually unworthy people, not deserving of any type of relationship with ME. But ***THE LORD*** does not DISCLOSE the unworthy to ME until after ***HE*** has EXPOSED their CHARACTER through their EVIL ACTS, and does this on a very gradual basis.

After publishing "Revealing The Bible's Truth", a Reviewer's Copy of the BOOK was given to MY biological mother. After reading the BOOK, the one issue she wanted to make clear to ME, was her REFUSAL to BELIEVE that CAIN was the SEED and the OFFSPRING of the DEVIL. The ANGELS have told ME that her REFUSAL to believe in this TRUTH is due to her knowing spiritually that she is of the LINEAGE of CAIN. For if she submits to the TRUTH, she submits to being of the DAMNED, even though she is not conscious of why she so strongly refuses to accept it as being the TRUTH! Another thing made obvious to ME about the CANAANITE LINEAGE, is the continual judgment by the CANAANITE of other people, and their always using themselves as being an example of the good versus the evil of them who they are judging.

They do this because their father is the "King over the children of Pride" and although they can always find fault in others, they see themselves as being righteous and good in all that they do. You will find with the CANAANITE, they enjoy talking badly about others, while boasting of themselves, and can do so for hours on end, when another person is available to listen to them. They will always make their remarks about the one they are judging in such a way that it will appear to be constructive criticism. However they will only confront the one who they have judged on the matter, after being caught in their actions by them, and made to justify their words.

The ANGEL versus MAN

The ANGEL is a CREATION of ***GOD*** whereas MAN is a DESCENDANT of ***GOD,*** by way of the SERAPHIM. The ANGEL however is SPIRITUALLY SUPERIOR to MAN, and in HEAVEN the ANGEL is above MAN up to the SEVENTH LEVEL, even though there is an equivalency in SPIRITUAL

GIFTS of the ANGEL and the MAN of the SIXTH LEVEL.

At the EIGHTH LEVEL in HEAVEN, the ANGEL and the BRIDE become UNIFIED in CHRIST, and then become EQUIVALENT to one another through MARRIAGE. The ANGEL goes into CHRIST through the COVENANT ANGEL, whereas the MAN is RECEIVED into CHRIST through JESUS CHRIST and ***HOLY SPIRIT*** BAPTISM. Therefore, only the BRIDE of CHRIST can ASCEND to the LEVEL EQUIVALENT to that of the ANGEL. This is why in the Book of Revelation the Apostle John sees each of the FOUR SERAPHIM as having SIX WINGS, for the WINGS represent the ANGEL, and the NUMBER SIX represents MAN, thus symbolically indicating that CHRIST brings both the ANGEL and MAN SPIRITUALLY TOGETHER as ONE in HEAVEN.

The ANGEL having been with ***GOD*** and SERVED ***HIM*** long before the CREATION of the HEAVENS and the EARTH resides ABOVE MAN outside of CHRIST. The majority of PEOPLE in HEAVEN are CALLED the GUESTS of the WEDDING SUPPER, and these PEOPLE cannot ASCEND above the SIXTH LEVEL in HEAVEN, that which allows them to reach the EQUIVALENCY of the ANGEL. ***GOD*** being RIGHTEOUS in ALL that ***HE*** does, only allows MAN to reach the EQUIVALENCY of the ANGEL while being in CHRIST, and only a SELECT FEW ever attain this.

At the TIME of the FALL of Lucifer, there were TWENTY-ONE BILLION ANGELS in HEAVEN, and LUCIFER took SEVEN BILLION of those Angels with him when he fell from the GRACE of ***GOD.*** Since then, with every lifecycle of the EARTH (7000-YEAR PERIOD), ***GOD*** brings ONE BILLION NEW ANGELS into HEAVEN, along with FOUR BILLION NEW SOULS. Of the FOUR BILLION NEW SOULS (MAN), only ONE HUNDRED and FOUR MILLION are of the BRIDE of CHRIST, and the balance of the FOUR BILLION (3,896,000,000) of the NEW SOULS (MAN), are "CALLED", the WEDDING GUESTS. This is why JESUS CHRIST said, ***"MANY WILL BE CALLED, BUT FEW CHOSEN"(Matthew 20:16).*** The ONE'S who are "CHOSEN" are the BRIDE of CHRIST, and the ONE'S who are "CALLED" are them who are CALLED to attend the WEDDING SUPPER.

Only on SABBATHS (HOLY DAYS), are the WEDDING GUESTS allowed to ASCEND to the SEVENTH LEVEL, for it is at the SEVENTH LEVEL where the TEMPLE of ***GOD*** resides. However the WEDDING GUESTS can NEVER ASCEND to the LEVEL of CHRIST (the EIGHTH LEVEL), albeit they NEVER feel DEPRIVED, for the GUESTS in HEAVEN cannot be DEPRIVED.

Even though the ANGELS are SUPERIOR to MAN in HEAVEN, all GUESTS are treated as WELCOME GUESTS, for the ANGELS are a

HUMBLE SORT, and see MAN as their BROTHERS and SISTERS, and not as strangers. The ANGELS have appearances similar to both men and women in HEAVEN, however except for the FIVE, (the FOUR COVENANTS and RAPHAEL) ANGELS do not have a GENDER. The Angel Uriel is not included in this NUMBER even though she has a gender, for she resides at the Gates of HELL, and only periodically RECEIVES ACCESS to HEAVEN. And, even when allowed ACCESS to HEAVEN, she cannot ASCEND above the FIRST LEVEL.

Although the men and women making up the GUESTS of the WEDDING SUPPER are allowed to have mates and marry in HEAVEN, they are never GRANTED CHILDREN, for all of the NEW SOULS come forth from CHRIST, the KEEPER of SOULS. Except for the COVENANT ANGELS, the ANGELS of HEAVEN do not mate nor are they given in marriage. The ANGELS are in a COMPLETE FORM without GENDER, and neither need nor desire a mate.

When the ANGEL is sent to the EARTH they are split into genders and only one-half of them DESCENDS at a time, and while on the Earth they are allowed to both marry and have children. Their children are always of the GENTILE, and when their children's life terminates on the Earth each one returns back to the DUST of the Earth from whence they were taken. Each half of the New Angel must experience carnal life. So the Angel comes once as a female and once as a male, and when either half experiences death of the flesh, they at that time ASCEND to PARADISE rather than to HEAVEN and maintain their GENDER. The Angel returns to HEAVEN in the same way as does the MAN, at the END of the LAST DAY!

The NEW ANGELS are RECEIVED back into HEAVEN by "DIVINE RIGHT", and needn't be BAPTIZED, whereas the MAN bearing a SOUL does require BAPTISM. When ONE-HALF of the ANGEL comes to the EARTH, in GENDER, they are COUNTED as being ONE PERSON rather than ONE-HALF of an ANGEL, and only after their LAST HALF has come to EARTH and lived in a carnal form are they considered COMPLETE. The ONE BILLION ANGELS are really FIVE HUNDRED MILLION, even though they consist of one billion people on the EARTH. They are FIVE HUNDRED MILLION female and FIVE HUNDRED MILLION male on EARTH, and are COUNTED in regard to world population as being ONE BILLION ANGELS. This method of counting the EARTH Angels continues on throughout the MILLENNIUM PERIOD. However, when the EARTH Angel ASCENDS to HEAVEN, they ASCEND as FIVE HUNDRED MILLION COMPLETE ANGELS rather than ONE BILLION PEOPLE.

Chapter 6
Lucifer and his Fallen Regime

As explained in "The ROD of IRON", the EARTH replicates HEAVEN before the fall of Lucifer, having in it both GOOD and EVIL. After Lucifer's falling from the GRACE of ***GOD,*** all EVIL along with him was cast out of HEAVEN, and he was given the EARTH for his domain and allowed to rule over it in increments of SIX THOUSAND-YEAR periods. This fixed time period began after Lucifer's first reign of 8224 years in the OLD WORLD, the world NOAH lived in prior to the GREAT FLOOD.

After his falling, Lucifer was given SEVEN additional names (TITLES), and his names are, "The Prince of the WORLD", "Satan", "That OLD SERPENT", "The Great Red Dragon", "LEVIATHAN", "The King over the children of PRIDE" and "The DEVIL". He is also referred to as "The Tempter" and "The Adulterer" and through the years men have given him other names as well, but the seven names that have been listed are the ones that represent the SEVEN HEADS of Lucifer. The TEN HORNS on the SEVEN HEADS spoken of in Revelation 12:3, represent the TEN CHIEF FALLEN ANGELS, who under his rule carry out his orders and lead the others within his regime.

> ***Revelation 12:3*** *And there appeared another wonder in HEAVEN; and behold a GREAT RED DRAGON, having SEVEN HEADS and TEN HORNS, and seven crowns upon his HEADS.*

The following is a list of the TEN FALLEN ANGELS (the TEN HORNS) who hold high positions in Lucifer's regime and are CHIEFTAINS in HELL.

1. Abigor, Grand Duke of HELL
2. Amducias, Grand Duke of HELL
3. Azazel, Standard-Bearer of HELL
4. Baalberith, Secretary of HELL
5. Balan, 2nd King of HELL

6. Beelzebub, Prince of HELL
7. Furfur, Count of HELL
8. Malphas, Grand President of HELL
9. Nebiros, Field Marshal of HELL
10. Zaebos, Grand Count of HELL

All TEN of these FALLEN ANGELS before the FALL of Lucifer were Angels of the SIXTH CHOIR in HEAVEN, and they as well were cast out of HEAVEN for joining Lucifer in his rebellion against THE ***HOLY SPIRIT (IXOTE).*** In total, seven billion Angels followed the lead of Lucifer, representing at that time one-third of the Angels in HEAVEN.

> ***Revelation 12:4*** *And his tail drew the THIRD PART of the STARS of HEAVEN, and did cast them to the EARTH: and the DRAGON stood before the WOMAN which was ready to be DELIVERED, for to DEVOUR her CHILD as soon as it was BORN.*

Lucifer's Plan

It is Lucifer's plan to DESTROY and CORRUPT all of ***GOD'S*** CHILDREN, prior to and at the very onset of their SPIRITUAL REBIRTH (***HOLY SPIRIT*** BAPTISM). He does this to deprive ***GOD'S*** CHILDREN of HEAVEN and ETERNITY. For those of the BLESSED SEED who ***GOD*** has determined to be the BRIDE of CHRIST, the CORRUPTION of them becomes very difficult. This is because he faces time constraints and must conquer and corrupt the group called the BRIDE prior to their BAPTISM; for PROTECTION against him comes immediately after they are BAPTIZED leaving him no further ACCESS to them.

However, for the WEDDING GUESTS, who can be either of the BLESSED SEED or of the GENTILE, there is a FORTY-DAY period between the time of BAPTISM and it being CONFIRMED in HEAVEN. This delays the WEDDING GUESTS from RECEIVING the PROTECTION provided by the BAPTISM. During this FORTY-DAY period the WEDDING GUESTS are most VULNERABLE to Lucifer's attack, and it is the most likely time that he will attack. During the GREAT TRIBULATION, the FORTY-DAY period for SPIRITUAL CONFIRMATION is shortened to TEN DAYS. The time is shortened to give those remaining on the EARTH a chance to survive his attack, for if it remained at FORTY DAYS, nearly all would fall to Lucifer and very few SOULS could be SAVED.

Even though Lucifer can read MINDS, he cannot IDENTIFY SPIRITS. When he attacks someone, it is unknown to him at that time which Spiritual type of person he's attacking. He can't even identify the CANAANITE spiritually, who is his own offspring, prior to his attacking them. However, once the SPIRIT REACTS to his attack, Lucifer knows by its reaction what SPIRITUAL TYPE it is. If he finds by their reaction that it is the CANAANITE or the GENTILE who hasn't been SAVED, he will withdraw from his attack, for they haven't any value. However, if it is the BLESSED SEED or a GENTILE that has been SAVED but not yet protected by FAITH, he will step up his attack most vigorously, until he either corrupts or conquers that spirit.

For the WEDDING GUESTS who can either be of the BLESSED SEED or of the GENTILE, once the CHILD is BORN (has RECEIVED SPIRITUAL BAPTISM), it is as though a RED FLAG is raised IDENTIFYING that SPIRIT as being REBORN in CHRIST. Therefore at BAPTISM, Lucifer knows SPIRITUALLY who these PEOPLE are and makes them his PRIME TARGETS. He also knows that his time is now limited in conquering and taking POSSESSION of those SPIRITS, so he immediately starts attacking them. This is why the aforementioned Scripture taken from the Book of Revelation says, "and the DRAGON stood before the WOMAN which was ready to be DELIVERED, for to DEVOUR her CHILD as soon as it was BORN".

The NEWBORN CHILD referred to in the Scripture, refers to the REBORN CHILD in CHRIST, the NEWLY BAPTIZED, prior to them RECEIVING PROTECTION from ***GOD.*** If the NEWLY BAPTIZED PERSON then yields to Lucifer's attack, and capitulates to his CONTROL, they then will lose their SOUL and become forever DAMNED, for they have committed the unforgivable SIN, a SIN against THE ***HOLY SPIRIT.***

The UNFORGIVABLE SIN

In "The ROD of IRON", in the 14th Chapter, titled "Carnal Life, the GLIMPSE", it is WRITTEN; at the time of the fall of Lucifer from HEAVEN, ***GOD*** DECREED from that time forward, that any SIN being committed against ***IXOTE*** (THE ***HOLY SPIRIT***) would thereafter be an UNFORGIVABLE SIN! With BAPTISM being an ACT of THE ***HOLY SPIRIT***, any SIN placed upon ONE'S SOUL after BAPTISM is considered to be a BLASPHEMY AGAINST THE ***HOLY SPIRIT.***

BAPTISM is given on the BASIS of COMMITTING ONE'S SOUL to ***GOD,*** and the SOUL must be CLEAN when OFFERED to ***HIM.*** When that

COMMITMENT is VIOLATED and the SOUL OFFERED is TARNISHED by SIN, a BLASPHEMY against THE ***HOLY SPIRIT*** has been made, for it is ***HE*** WHO OFFERS the SOUL to ***GOD.*** BAPTISM is the CLEANSING of the SOUL and the WORK of THE ***HOLY SPIRIT.*** Therefore, once the SOUL has been made CLEAN by THE ***HOLY SPIRIT,*** it is a requirement of the ONE bearing the SOUL to keep it CLEAN!

After the BAPTISM has been CONFIRMED SINNING no longer becomes an issue. This is because by the FAITH RECEIVED from THE ***HOLY SPIRIT*** as a GIFT after the CONFIRMATION, the SAVED can no longer SIN, for the SOUL NOW BELONGS to ***GOD,*** and ***GOD*** CANNOT SIN! However, prior to CONFIRMATION, if the SOUL becomes tarnished by SIN for any reason, THE ***HOLY SPIRIT*** still keeps ***HIS*** COMMITMENT to ***GOD*** by RE-CLEANSING IT, and RETURNING the SOUL to CHRIST. However this SOUL is now without a Spirit and the Spirit formerly having the SOUL is now SOULLESS and forever DAMNED, ***SAITH THE LORD.***

As previously said, the BLESSED SEED can be either the BRIDE of CHRIST or a GUEST of the WEDDING SUPPER. The BRIDE, unlike the WEDDING GUEST, cannot be wittingly fooled by the DEVIL once their BAPTISM has been PERFORMED, for it is INSTANTANEOUS. However the WEDDING GUESTS are most VULNERABLE immediately after their BAPTISM and during the time prior to CONFIRMATION, and can fall from ***GOD,*** for they are the "CALLED" and not the "CHOSEN".

The DEVIL uses several methods to TRICK the NEWLY BAPTIZED SOULS prior to their CONFIRMATION and receipt of PROTECTION. Due to ONE having to rely on their own faith during this time, rather than the FAITH of ***GOD*** coming as a GIFT from THE ***HOLY SPIRIT*** after CONFIRMATION, the DEVIL will immediately instill DOUBT in the MIND of the NEWBORN.

He will use that DOUBT to try to CONVINCE those whom he attacks that ***HOLY SPIRIT*** BAPTISM had not taken place, and explain the EXPERIENCE of the BAPTISM as being a figment of imagination. He will then use your own MIND against you by saying through it, you can still SIN and be forgiven by ***GOD***. However at this point, SIN cannot be forgiven as it could be before the BAPTISM, for the SIN now is against THE ***HOLY SPIRIT*** who PERFORMED the BAPTISM on your behalf.

This PERIOD of TIME prior to CONFIRMATION, whether it be FORTY DAYS or TEN DAYS is called the TIME of TRIAL and TRIBULATION. This is a very crucial TIME, for if you FAIL after BAPTISM your fate is certain. Once FAILED, there will be no redemption for you, for you are DAMNED!

Any SIN being committed during the TIME of TRIAL and TRIBULATION is an UNFORGIVABLE SIN, and a BLASPHEMY against ***THE LORD of HOSTS.***

READ the parable given by JESUS CHRIST about this very SUBJECT, written in the Gospel of Matthew, Chapter 12, verses 43-45. JESUS says in the Scriptures, once a man's soul has been cleansed through ***HOLY SPIRIT*** BAPTISM, and he once more returns to a SINFUL STATE, his latter state is worse than his former state. In his former state, the man could be forgiven for the SIN, but in his latter state he cannot!

The Threat of Death, Lucifer's Ace in the hole!

Lucifer's PRIME THREAT is the threat of physical death. Prior to BAPTISM, all people fear death, and this is because they have not yet RECEIVED the GIFT of FAITH allowing them to BELIEVE that through JESUS CHRIST death can be DEFEATED! This is why in the Scriptures of the GOSPEL of John (John 11:20 through 11:27) it was Martha who ***GOD*** sent to JESUS, rather than Mary Magdalene her sister, who was closer to JESUS than she, to request HIS HELP regarding the death of their brother Lazarus.

Mary Magdalene at the time of her brother Lazarus' death was disappointed that JESUS had not come as they had so requested HIM to do, and HEAL Lazarus to keep him from dying. So when JESUS showed up at Bethany after Lazarus' death, Mary's faith had faltered in JESUS, for HE had not saved the life of her brother. So ***THE LORD*** sent Martha to JESUS rather than Mary, because Martha had the NECESSARY FAITH for JESUS to PERFORM the miracle of RAISING Lazarus from the dead. The MESSAGE in the story of Lazarus is, that FAITH was the KEY ingredient needed for Lazarus' life to be restored, and it was Martha who had the NEEDED FAITH.

The NEW COVENANT is a COVENANT of FAITH, and only by FAITH can DEATH be DEFEATED. The DEVIL is death, DEATH of the SPIRIT, and because he hasn't any control over the ***GOD*** GIVEN SPIRIT, he uses physical death as his PRIME THREAT. By Lucifer being the Prince of the WORLD he has control over most earthly things, and can certainly bring about one's death. JESUS' crucifixion was a PRIME example of what Lucifer can do in regard to one's life in this world. However, Lucifer must have ***GOD'S*** permission before he can take any life and it is MAN'S fear of death that causes HIM to stumble and fall from the GRACE of ***GOD***. This is why JESUS says in the Scriptures that the SPIRIT is WILLING, but the FLESH is WEAK!

Matthew 26:41 WATCH AND PRAY, THAT YE ENTER NOT INTO TEMPTATION: THE SPIRIT INDEED IS WILLING, BUT THE FLESH IS WEAK.

This was a WARNING given by JESUS to HIS Disciples prior to their BAPTISM. JESUS knew that the DEVIL would soon start ATTACKING the Disciples and instill the fear of DEATH in them. Then by their FEARING physical death the DEVIL could manipulate them into SINNING against ***GOD***.

However, after BAPTISM and CONFIRMATION, the physical spirit given from the earth separates from the ***GOD*** GIVEN SPIRIT who becomes the DOMINANT SPIRIT of the NEWBORN CHILD in CHRIST. At this point in time, ALL FEAR of death is CONQUERED, and DEATH ITSELF is DEFEATED by FAITH, leaving the DEVIL nothing left to THREATEN the NEWBORN CHILD with.

The TEMPTER invades YOUR MIND

Unlike the SPIRIT of a CHILD of ***GOD***, the MIND of man is EARTH given. It is the MIND of the biological person that analyzes brainwaves and causes thoughts to occur. Whereas the SPIRIT RECEIVES its information by inspirations from the SOUL by way of EMOTION, the MIND receives thoughts from the brain by way of electrical impulses. The brain puts out electrical signals as impulses to the central nervous system and when the impulses are detected, the MIND analyzes them and this is called THOUGHT.

Prior to BAPTISM and CONFIRMATION, thoughts caused by the MIND cannot be segregated from emotional FEELINGS sent forth by the SOUL, and the SPIRIT sees thoughts and FEELINGS as being the SAME. This causes the SPIRIT to yield to either a thought or an INSPIRED FEELING in very much the same way, reacting to either of them in a POSITIVE or NEGATIVE way depending on how the MIND perceives them.

When the DEVIL attempts to CONTROL ONE'S thoughts, he does so by tampering with the MIND. He will continually reverse the POLARITY of the brain impulses, so it appears to the MIND that GOOD is BAD and BAD is GOOD. This reversal of THOUGHT POLARITY causes the SPIRIT to become CONFUSED because it can no longer DIFFERENTIATE between GOOD and EVIL. While in this state of confusion caused by the MIND, the SPIRIT surrenders to the MIND allowing it to override the SOUL and any EMOTION coming from it. Then due to the ABSENCE of FEELING (EMOTION), the person's actions are no longer judged, thus allowing the person to unknowingly commit EVIL ACTS without remorse!

When this phenomenon occurs it is called DEVIL or DEMON POSSESSION, and it happens daily throughout the world. However, it is generally on a small-scale basis, affecting very few people at any particular time. Most doctors see this phenomenon as a breakdown in one's mental faculties and a state of mental illness, and try to treat the symptoms with chemicals. But all the treatment does is to temporarily disconnect the body from the thought process, and as soon as the drugs dissipate, the prior state of MIND returns.

Lucifer uses both DEMONS and FALLEN ANGELS in the MIND DISRUPTING PROCESS, and can implant up to a LEGION (6,000) of them in a single person at one time. An Angel is made up of what is called "SUBTLE MATTER" and can EXPAND or CONDENSE in size at will. When in a CONDENSED FORM, 10,000 Angels can stand on the head of a pin. So when DEMONS or FALLEN ANGELS are being hosted by a physical being they CONDENSE, and scatter themselves throughout the central nervous system allowing them to control as many of the body functions they so desire.

This type of POSSESSION by a multitude of DEMONS and FALLEN ANGELS is spoken about in three of the FOUR GOSPELS. In the GOSPEL of Mark, Chapter 5, verses 1 through 13, JESUS so encounters a man hosting a multitude of EVIL SPIRITS. In that Chapter when JESUS asked the evil spirit his name, the spirit said his name was called "LEGION" for there was a legion of evil spirits within the man.

Demons are the offspring of the Fallen Angels, however the Demon declines in angelic power down through the generations. Each succeeding generation of Demons loses some of its parental angelic power, and this decline continues on as the hosts of hell are increased. Angels cannot reproduce like man because they do not have a gender, so Lucifer uses a "Spiritual Splitting Process" to increase the numbers of the hosts of Hell. This "Splitting Process" can only produce one offspring from each generation, and because the offspring is a split from the prior generation, it inherits only one half of the power its parent has.

When a Demon or Fallen Angel POSSESSES a person, they can produce an electrical impulse within the central nervous system that is identical in every aspect to that which the brain produces, therefore giving them absolute physical and mental control over the person hosting them. It is usually the GENTILE whom provides the vehicle of flesh for the fallen ones, however, they prefer to invade the BLESSED SEED prior to their BAPTISM and control a CHILD of ***GOD.***

Seemingly odd, the Demon or the fallen Angel rarely POSSESS the

CANAANITE, for they do not like to be hosted by one of their own. Furthermore, the CANAANITE need not be POSSESSED for they will willingly follow the instructions given to them by the DEVIL. The GENTILE and the BLESSED SEED however require MIND manipulation to be controlled, and can only be PHYSICALLY POSSESSED and not SPIRITUALLY POSSESSED, prior to any DAMNATION of them by ***GOD.***

When one is Spiritually POSSESSED by the DEVIL they are in constant communication with HELL, and will capitulate to whatever Lucifer or his Delegates orders them to do without the need of PHYSICAL POSSESSION. Their information comes to them spiritually and is transferred to their MIND from their Spirit without the need of invading forces to manipulate the MIND to accept the information given to it. The Spiritually Possessed can be likened to a machine receiving its information from a central computer, that can only function while linked to the computer, for it hasn't its own resources for independent operation.

Lucifer's SEVEN HEADS

Lucifer has OMNI-PRESENCE in a limited form, and because of his OMNI-PRESENCE he can be in all places on the earth at the same time. However, he does not have OMNIPOTENCE, that which would allow him to use his POWER while being in ALL PLACES. Therefore, Lucifer can personally attack only one person at a time, even though he can be in ALL places at the same time.

This is what necessitates his need for the Demons and the Fallen Angels; for they must carry out his mischief while he identifies the targets for them to attack. Lucifer with his OMNI-PRESENCE can DIRECT the forces under his command simultaneously at the multitudes, identifying the targets with his OMNI-PRESENCE. Unlike the OMNI-PRESENCE of JESUS CHRIST or the ***DELIVERER,*** or even RAPHAEL who is the ANGEL of THE ***HOLY SPIRIT,*** Lucifer's OMNI-PRESENCE only operates within the EARTH PLANE, or while in HELL. It may also be noted that if he were to personally take POSSESSION of a physical body, while in that body his OMNI-PRESENCE would cease to function.

When in all places at the same time (in the OMNI-PRESENT STATE), Lucifer is referred to as the DEVIL, for it is the Spirit of the DEVIL that FILLS the world with EVIL. However when Lucifer personally attacks, he is referred to as "The Great Red Dragon", and when he POSSESS a body of flesh he is referred to as "The King over the children of PRIDE". You should be able to SEE from the aforementioned, that each one of the SEVEN HEADS of Lucifer represents his being in SEVEN DIFFERENT Spiritual States. When Lucifer personally tries to TEMPT a CHILD of ***GOD,*** he is referred to, as being "That OLD SERPENT", for he appeared as a SERPENT while in the GARDEN of EDEN and TEMPTING ADAM and EVE to SIN.

When allowed by ***GOD*** to TORMENT someone, Lucifer is referred to as the "LEVIATHAN" as he was referred to in the Book of Job, when he was allowed to TORMENT Job. When Lucifer takes POSSESSION of the Antichrist, and RULES over the WORLD, he will be referred to as "The Prince of the World", and while RULING in HELL he is called "Satan".

SIN Specialists

Even though the Demons and Fallen Angels can implant a whole host of EVIL THOUGHTS within the MIND, there are some of them who specialize in specific tasks. For instance, it is the Fallen Angel "Asmodeus" who oversees the Demons specializing in "LUST and ANGER", and when he is summoned by Lucifer to CORRUPT, he instills LUST and ANGER in its most potent form. A rapist is generally POSSESSED by a Demon being under the control of the Fallen Angel "Incubus", for it is Incubus who is the "Seducer of Women". However, it is the Fallen Angel "Succubus" who oversees homosexuality, for he is the "Seducer of Men and the Corrupter of Gender", and both he and his Demons are them who entice either men or women to share in "SAME GENDER" sexual activities. When Succubus is summoned by Lucifer to personally CORRUPT, the homosexual or heterosexual act will be most brutal, displaying acts of sodomy, bondage, sadism and masochism, which will generally result in the death of one or more of the participants.

The closer a PERSON is to ***GOD,*** the more likely that PERSON will be targeted by a "SIN Specialist" prior to their BAPTISM, and only the STRONGEST will SURVIVE the attack! Prior to BAPTISM and CONFIRMATION, ***GOD*** will only INTERVENE when the PERSON who is being attacked by the DEVIL has been PREDESTINED for HEAVEN. ***GOD'S*** INTERVENTION only APPLIES to the Angel, when in the form of a MAN or a WOMAN, or to ***HIS*** CHOSEN, them who are called, "THE BRIDE of CHRIST"; for neither of them can FALL. However, ***GOD*** will not INTERVENE on behalf of the "WEDDING GUESTS", who can either be of the BLESSED SEED or of the GENTILE.

HELL OPENED

Once the Fallen Angel Balan (called in the Scriptures A-bad'-don, Revelation 9:11), is released from HELL, more than fifty-three billion Demons and seven billion Fallen Angels will follow him out. This EVENT occurs at the very onset of the GREAT TRIBULATION, shortly after the Angels, the "BRIDE", and THE ***HOLY SPIRIT*** have left the EARTH.

The EARTH'S population at that time will be just under SIX BILLION people, leaving a ratio of greater than 10:1 of Fallen Angels and Demons over the population of people on the earth. Other than the 144,000 Tribulation Saints and the TWO WITNESSES that are PROTECTED by the ***SEAL of the LIVING GOD,*** ALL who will be SAVED at this time are called the "WEDDING GUESTS". These "WEDDING GUESTS" will all be under attack by the "Hosts of Hell" during the entire GREAT TRIBULATION (Forty-two months), and unless those being attacked are willing to GIVE UP their LIVES in the NAME of ***GOD,*** and for the TESTIMONY of JESUS CHRIST, they cannot be SAVED. However, those who are willing to die for the CAUSE will NOT LOSE THEIR LIFE as a result of it, and only the "BEHEADED SOULS" will die and be resurrected at the DAWNING of the LAST DAY!

> ***Luke 21:35 FOR AS A SNARE SHALL IT COME ON ALL THEM THAT DWELL ON THE FACE OF THE WHOLE EARTH.***
>
> ***Luke 21:36 WATCH YE THEREFORE, AND PRAY ALWAYS, THAT YE MAY BE ACCOUNTED WORTHY TO ESCAPE ALL THESE THINGS THAT SHALL COME TO PASS, AND TO STAND BEFORE THE SON OF MAN.***

During the GREAT TRIBULATION the Demons and Fallen Angels will be in both the Spiritual form and in the Fleshly form of them they POSSESS. Those in the Spiritual form will be visible to the human eye and will appear to their onlookers as HORRIFIC CREATURES from HELL! However, the evil ones that are in the Fleshly Form will look like normal people, and only the Tribulation Saints and the TWO WITNESSES will be able to IDENTIFY the POSSESSED. During this time every SIN Specialist from HELL will be out in force to assist Lucifer's Regime in the DESTRUCTION of the EARTH and all of its OCCUPANTS!

War of the ANGELS

After Lucifer seizes control over the EARTH, the ANGELS from HEAVEN will come down to fight against him and his regime, and anyone on the EARTH at that time who has not RECEIVED the ***SEAL of the LIVING GOD,*** will be considered by the ANGELS as the ENEMY. During this time it will be very difficult for the UNSAVED to RECEIVE the ***SEAL of the LIVING GOD.*** This is because ***GOD*** will no longer hear any individual's prayer other than those of the TRIBULATION SAINTS. And, as the people approach the TRIBULATION SAINTS seeking sanctities from them, the ANGELS from HEAVEN will see those people as being a threat to the SAINTS and will attack them. The unsaved will then run the risk of being attacked by either side, and many will be killed while trying to reach the TRIBULATION SAINTS, for the unsaved will know that only the TRIBULATION SAINTS can help them.

> ***Daniel 9:27*** *And* ***HE*** *shall CONFIRM the COVENANT with many for ONE WEEK: and in the midst of the WEEK* ***HE*** *shall cause the SACRIFICE and the OBLATION to CEASE, and for the overspreading of ABOMINATIONS* ***HE*** *shall make it DESOLATE, even until the CONSUMMATION, and that determined shall be POURED upon the DESOLATE.*

NOTE: This Scripture says that ***GOD*** will CONFIRM the COVENANT (BAPTIZE and SEAL) MANY during the SEVEN YEARS of TRIBULATION, for the WEEK in the Scripture represents one week of years (seven years). Then in the midst of the WEEK (three and one-half years into the TRIBULATION), the GREAT TRIBULATION will begin, and at that time ***GOD*** will no longer listen to one's prayers (the SACRIFICE and the OBLATION will CEASE). The Scripture then says that this will continue on until the entire world has been made DESOLATE, and the WRATH of ***GOD*** has been POURED OUT upon the EARTH.

THE METATRON are RELEASED

The FOUR ANGELS spoken of in the Book of Revelation (Revelation 9:14) that are released from the great river Euphrates are the FOUR METATRON of HEAVEN. Their names are, ANAFI-EL, SAN-DAL'-PHON, ME'-SO-LOT, and OR'-THA-BEL. Except for the FOUR SERAPHIM, the FOUR

METATRON are the MOST POWERFUL beings in all of HEAVEN, and once they are released upon the EARTH, even Lucifer will fear their PRESENCE, for the POWER they wield is at least ONE THOUSAND TIMES greater than Lucifer's.

It is the METATRON who will reverse the magnetic poles on the EARTH and move it out of its orbit around the Sun. These EVENTS are explained in the 24th Chapter of the Book of the Prophet Isaiah. The METATRON will FIRST reverse the MAGNETIC POLARITY of the EARTH (referred to in the Scriptures as turning the earth upside down), and this will disrupt all magnetically sensitive instrumentation rendering the equipment useless. The MAGNETIC REVERSAL of the POLES will also cause all the fault lines within the EARTH to dislodge. Then there will be great earthquakes caused by the dislodging of the faults that will shake the EARTH so VIOLENTLY the earth's occupants will be tossed about like gravel in a tumbler.

> ***Isaiah 24:1*** *BEHOLD,* ***THE LORD*** *maketh the EARTH empty, and maketh it waste, and turneth it UPSIDE DOWN, and SCATTERETH abroad the INHABITANTS thereof.*

This EVENT happens as a result of the POURING OUT of the SEVENTH VIAL of the WRATH of ***GOD*** (Revelation 16:17 through 16:21), and it is the METATRON who orchestrate the catastrophe. They will also MOVE the EARTH out of its place (its orbit around the Sun), and hurl it through space like a ball. The EARTH will then come to rest in an orbit around another star, however its axis will be perpendicular to its poles; and there it will remain until it is DESTROYED at the END of the LAST DAY.

> ***Isaiah 24:19*** *The EARTH is utterly broken down, the EARTH is clean dissolved, the EARTH is MOVED EXCEEDINGLY.*

> ***Isaiah 24:20*** *The EARTH shall reel to and fro like a drunkard, and shall be REMOVED like a cottage; and the transgression thereof shall be heavy upon it; and it shall FALL, and NOT RISE AGAIN.*

At the END of the LAST DAY Lucifer is once again cast into HELL to rejoin his regime, and HELL is shut up until the next generation of the earth begins. The cycle of the earth then repeats itself starting with NOAH landing in the NEW WORLD, and Lucifer being released from the Ark (referred to in the Scriptures as the RAVEN) to once more rule for another SIX THOUSAND

YEARS! The CYCLE of the EARTH continues on throughout ETERNITY with Lucifer ruling over it for SIX out of its SEVEN THOUSAND-YEAR LIFE CYCLE!

> ***Revelation 20:10*** *And the DEVIL that deceived them was cast into the LAKE of FIRE and BRIMSTONE, where the BEAST and the FALSE PROPHET are, and shall be TORMENTED day and night for ever and ever.*

> ***Revelation 20:15*** *And whosoever was NOT FOUND written in the BOOK of LIFE was cast into the LAKE of FIRE.*

Chapter 7
SPEAKING to the SPIRIT

Certainly by now you have noticed that this BOOK is composed in a rather odd way, as were the other TWO BOOKS, "Revealing The Bible's Truth" and "The ROD of IRON" composed in the same manner. Throughout the text in ALL THREE BOOKS TYPE STYLE changes routinely from lower to UPPER case letters, from standard to **BOLD TYPE,** and from regular to ITALIC font. Although some people might see these changes in TYPE STYLE as an annoyance, there is a SPECIFIC REASON as to why the BOOKS have been COMPOSED in this way.

When FIRST WRITING for ***THE LORD,*** it was unbeknown to ME at the time of the WRITING that the changes in TYPE STYLE were occurring throughout the text, and it wasn't until after I had went back and REVIEWED what had been WRITTEN that I became AWARE of it. Initially, I went back and changed the various TYPE STYLES back to normal. However after doing so, I found that the MESSAGE GIVEN in the TEXT had lost its PUNCH. I then asked ***THE LORD*** what was the REASONING behind the various changes in TYPE STYLE, and I was TOLD that the BOOK I was WRITING was being WRITTEN by the ***SPIRIT of GOD*** and not by the MIND of MAN. ***GOD*** told ME that the changes in TYPE STYLE were acting as KEY INDICATORS placed within the text to ENLIGHTEN the SPIRIT and GIVE it MESSAGES from the SOUL.

It was further EXPLAINED to ME that the SPIRIT sees certain individual WORDS as complete STATEMENTS, and when the human eye detects the CHANGES in TYPE STYLE, this ALERTS the SPIRIT of the STATEMENT; somewhat like a ringing phone. The TYPE STYLE CHANGES then inform the SPIRIT that it is about to RECEIVE an EMOTIONAL MESSAGE, and that the MESSAGE RECEIVED will be coming from its SOUL. Then once the SPIRIT RECEIVES the MESSAGE from the SOUL, a DIALOGUE between the SPIRIT and SOUL takes place, allowing the TWO to openly COMMUNICATE.

The SOUL is the CONNECTION to CHRIST, and once the SPIRIT LEARNS to COMMUNICATE and LOOK to the SOUL rather than to the

MIND for its DIRECTION and JUDGMENT, ERRORS in its ACTIONS can no longer be made. This is because the SOUL makes its JUDGMENT based solely on TRUTH, whereas the MIND prefers to look towards LOGIC for its truth, and its LOGIC is knowledge based. This is to say that the MIND is limited in its DECISION MAKING to what it knows, whereas the SOUL makes its DECISIONS based on FEELINGS resulting from TRUTH. The SOUL KNOWS only TWO very SIMPLE WORDS, "GOOD" or "EVIL" and this results in either a "YES" or a "NO" answer when asked any QUESTION.

The MIND operates by playing out "what if" SCENARIOS for its decision making process, because it is a knowledge based system. This is not only a very slow process, but is also a very inaccurate one, for MAN'S KNOWLEDGE is very LIMITED! However the SOUL uses a "TRUTH BASED SYSTEM" for its DECISION MAKING PROCESS, not needing to play out any scenarios whatsoever, but rather LOOKING towards EMOTION for its simple YES or NO answer when called on by the SPIRIT for DIRECTION.

When the MIND speaks, it has a tendency to speak in many words, and this at times is consistent with its inability to answer a particular question, or many words may also be used to buy itself time while it continues to search for the answer. Its answer will always be an explanation rather than an AFFIRMATION and use an array of played out "what if" scenarios to justify the answer. LOGIC relies on DATA for its accuracy, and when the DATA is limited the analysis is FLAWED.

It was told to you in the previous chapter, how Lucifer uses the MIND to manipulate and CONFUSE the Spirit. So when one looks to their MIND for direction, they are playing right into Lucifer's hand; for the MIND can be CORRUPTED, and even if not corrupted, the MIND is a very LIMITED RESOURCE to use for FEEDBACK and DIRECTION. If a person were to write a book on a particular subject and relied totally on his or her own knowledge for its content, the book would be quite limited in its information. On the other hand, if the writer used every available resource for informational support, along with his or her own knowledge, the book would then be significantly more informative.

When the SPIRIT starts to listen to its SOUL rather than to the physical MIND, it shortly thereafter realizes that it has now become linked to an INFINITE SOURCE of INFORMATION. The SPIRIT also REALIZES that the INFORMATION now being RECEIVED is TRUTH BASED and not knowledge based as was the information coming from the MIND. This allows the SPIRIT to TRUST in the ANSWER given to it by the SOUL, because the INFORMATION and DIRECTION is BASED on TRUTH, precluding any possibility of ERROR.

EMOTION from WORDS

Most people never consciously realize the EMOTION emitted by WORDS. If I were to say to you, "I think that you are a **WONDERFUL** person" and you knew in your SPIRIT that I TRULY meant what I said, the SOUL would send out a MESSAGE of ACCEPTANCE to the SPIRIT, and the SPIRIT would FEEL ACCEPTED! However, if I were to say, "I think that you are a **HORRIBLE** person, the SOUL would send out a MESSAGE of REJECTION to the SPIRIT, and the SPIRIT would feel REJECTED. As you can SEE, both sentences contain all the same WORDS being used in the same sequence, EXCEPT for a single WORD being DIFFERENT in each sentence.

It should be obvious from the aforementioned example; a single WORD TRIGGERED the SPIRIT in both sentences. The WORD **WONDERFUL** TRIGGERED a POSITIVE FEELING, whereas the WORD **HORRIBLE** TRIGGERED a NEGATIVE one. You should also SEE from the example, the SOUL'S MESSAGE to the SPIRIT was a simple "POSITIVE" in the case of using the WORD "WONDERFUL" and a "NEGATIVE" when using the WORD "HORRIBLE". This is because the SOUL simply replies to the SPIRIT in "YES" or "NO" terms, and even though the SOUL realizes that the STATEMENT made in either of the sentences is merely an opinion, and not necessarily a TRUTH, it still LOOKS towards the TRUTH for its answer. In regard to the statement saying that the person is found to be HORRIBLE, the SOUL FINDS that any SPIRIT bearing a ***GOD*** GIVEN SOUL can NEVER be HORRIBLE. It therefore sends a NEGATIVE MESSAGE to the SPIRIT saying to it, the statement made in the WORD "HORRIBLE" is UNTRUE and UNACCEPTABLE. Therefore once the SPIRIT sees that the SOUL has rejected the WORD, the SPIRIT FEELS itself REJECTED, because the WORD was DIRECTED at the SPIRIT.

When an answer of either "YES" or "NO" is given to a question by the SOUL, no further interpretation of the answer is required, for the WORDS "YES" and "NO" stand alone because they are COMPLETE STATEMENTS. Although the MIND at times prefers to EXPLAIN the reasoning behind its "YES" or "NO" answers to justify its truth, the same answer GIVEN by the SOUL needn't be explained for it is the TRUTH, and the TRUTH is self-explanatory without the need for justification.

JESUS told HIS Disciples that whenever the authorities should QUESTION them, the answers they were to give were to be SIMPLE "YES" and "NO" answers. HE said that they should not think about what they were to say before hand, for they would RECEIVE the answer needed about an hour before it was to be given.

JESUS was WARNING them against the use of their MINDS and how more than a SIMPLE "YES" or "NO" answer would be coming from their MINDS and not from their SOUL. JESUS knew that THE ***HOLY SPIRIT*** would SPEAK to their SPIRITS through the SOUL, and was TEACHING them that the SOUL knows only TWO WORDS, "GOOD" and "EVIL", which translate into either a YES or a NO.

> ***Matthew 5:37 BUT LET YOUR COMMUNICATION BE, YEA, YEA; NAY, NAY; FOR WHATSOEVER IS MORE THAN THESE COMETH OF EVIL.***

Listening to the SOUL

The SOUL responds to WORDS without the need of CONSCIOUS THOUGHT, and is instantaneous in giving its answer to the SPIRIT. However, many times it SPEAKS in a subtle voice, and one must learn how to listen to it, not allowing the MIND to drown it out.

Although the SOUL only gives simple "YES" and "NO" answers, with each of its answers comes an EMOTIONAL FEELING. These FEELINGS can either be POSITIVE or NEGATIVE ones depending on how the SOUL receives and interprets the WORDS. Any WORDS being directed to the SPIRIT is immediately received by the SOUL, and the SOUL searches out the TRUTH in the WORDS and does its evaluation based on the TRUTH or the lack of TRUTH in the WORDS.

An EGO cannot disrupt the TRUTH, and when NEGATIVE WORDS are directed at the SPIRITUAL CHARACTER of the person (ONE'S OWN SELF WORTHINESS), if the WORDS bear the TRUTH they are given MERIT by the SOUL as being ACCEPTABLE. This is TRUE even though the WORDS received by the SOUL might be demeaning to the CHARACTER of the SPIRIT and although the EMOTION produced by the SOUL may sadden the SPIRIT, the SPIRIT ACCEPTS the WORDS as TRUTHFUL CRITICISM. The SOUL also evaluates the character of the person or persons who are directing the WORDS at the SPIRIT, and responds to their INTENTIONS accordingly.

If the CRITICISM is directed at the SPIRIT intentionally to discredit it, then the SOUL sends out the MESSAGE to the SPIRIT, saying that the WORDS are TRUE, however the ONE'S directing the WORDS are doing so for an EVIL purpose. On the other hand, if the SOUL sees the person or persons that are DI-

RECTING the WORDS at the SPIRIT doing so with CONSTRUCTIVE rather than DESTRUCTIVE intentions, it says, the WORDS are TRUE and them who are DIRECTING the WORDS at the SPIRIT do so for RIGHTEOUS REASONS; not meaning to discredit the SPIRIT but rather to IMPROVE its CHARACTER.

In either of the two scenarios, the SPIRIT RECEIVES the TRUTH from the SOUL, and also receives from the SOUL the TRUTHFUL INTENTIONS behind the WORDS of them that are saying them. The SOUL bases all of its JUDGMENT on TRUTH, and the ***GOD*** GIVEN SPIRIT can always ACCEPT the TRUTH, even when the TRUTH may cause PAIN to the SPIRIT.

EGO blocks TRUTH

Whereas the SOUL acts as a GUIDE to the SPIRIT, the EGO acts as a SHIELD to the MIND. When the MIND refuses to ACCEPT the TRUTH, it is the EGO that shields it from the TRUTH and will create reasons to justify its denial of the TRUTH.

The ***GOD*** GIVEN SPIRIT has the ability to continually learn, because its KNOWLEDGE is TRUTH BASED, relying on its SOUL for its UNDERSTANDING and DIRECTION. As was explained earlier in this BOOK, the SOUL carries with it ONE'S PURPOSE, and it is the SPIRIT that IDENTIFIES the ONE bearing that PURPOSE. Although each CHILD of ***GOD*** serves a specific PURPOSE for ***GOD*** with each one being DIFFERENT, ALL CHILDREN of ***GOD*** commonly SHARE in ***GODLIKE*** QUALITIES. ***GOD*** is ALL KNOWING and expects ***HIS*** CHILDREN to strive to be as ***HE*** is, also, ALL KNOWING.

It is the CHILD of ***GOD'S*** ability to ACCEPT the TRUTH for their KNOWLEDGE BASIS that enables them to continually learn, and as they learn ASCEND beyond this world and its physical limitations. However, the EGO, which is a creation of the MIND, hinders that learning process and limits the person of the EGO in their learning ability; for the EGO tells the SPIRIT that it is already ALL KNOWING based on the MINDS knowledge. Furthermore, because the EGO refuses to believe that the MIND could ever be wrong, it limits the person in even the understanding of physical things, much less their being able to UNDERSTAND SPIRITUAL things.

It is your EGO that will tell you that the Changes in TYPE STYLE within this BOOK are annoying and serve no purpose, so you should set the BOOK aside. It does this because the MIND directs the EGO to SHIELD the SPIRIT from any SPIRITUAL UNDERSTANDING. The MIND is a product of the

EARTH, acting like a spirit without a SOUL and wanting to dominate the body of flesh. Therefore the MIND views the SPIRIT as a threat to its existence, and will do whatever may be necessary to maintain its control over the body of flesh, even to the point of it causing the SPIRIT within it to die! And, the MIND will do this without REMORSE, so be cautious of it!

Spiritual death is referred to in the Scriptures as being "the SECOND DEATH", and the SECOND DEATH applies to any spirit not having a ***GOD*** GIVEN SOUL. A spirit without a SOUL serves no PURPOSE in ***GOD*** outside of the "EARTH PLANE" and therefore needn't exist after physical death. There are two types of spiritual death, with one type occurring at the time of physical death, and the other type occurring when the SOUL is taken from the spirit after JUDGMENT and given back to CHRIST. For the CANAANITE (the offspring of the DEVIL) the SECOND DEATH always occurs at the time of their physical death, whereas for the BLESSED SEED who has failed and for the GENTILE who has not been SAVED, the SECOND DEATH occurs after JUDGMENT.

This BOOK and its COMPOSITION is intended to WAKE UP the SPIRIT within YOU. However this only applies to those of you with ***GOD*** GIVEN SPIRITS bearing a SOUL, and not to the CANAANITE nor to the UNSAVED GENTILE, for they will find the BOOK OFFENSIVE. Once the SPIRIT is AWAKENED and a DIALOGUE between the SPIRIT and the SOUL has been ESTABLISHED, the MESSAGE within this BOOK will be RECEIVED by the SOUL and given to the SPIRIT, and the SPIRIT will be ENLIGHTENED by it!

Lost in TRANSLATION

This BOOK and its THREE COMPANIONS, The HOLY BIBLE, Revealing The Bible's Truth, and The ROD of IRON are all IDENTICALLY composed. If the HOLY BIBLE were originally WRITTEN in the ENGLISH language rather than in Hebrew, Latin and Greek, the changes in TYPE STYLE would appear throughout its text just as they do in this BOOK. However, only in the Hebrew text and in the Book of Revelation, that which was WRITTEN in LATIN, were the more obvious SPIRITUAL DECLARATIONS detected by the Translators and included in the TRANSLATION.

In 1611, when King James TRANSLATED the HOLY MANUSCRIPTS, (which were IDENTICAL in all respects to the "Dead Sea Scrolls" found in 1948) into the ENGLISH LANGUAGE, many of the changes in SCRIPT CHARACTER within the MANUSCRIPTS were missed and therefore not included in the TRANSLATION. Only some of the gross changes in the MANU-

SCRIPTS TEXT were caught and characterized during the TRANSLATION by the Interpreters, leaving many of the SUBTLE changes in the SCRIPT CHARACTER out.

However, the Book of Revelation that which was ORIGINALLY WRITTEN in Latin made the CHANGES in SCRIPT CHARACTER more obvious to the Interpreters, and throughout its TEXT various changes from lower to upper case LETTERS can be readily detected. If you have a 1611 King James "AUTHORIZED VERSION" of the HOLY BIBLE, WE will point out where some of these changes in TYPE STYLE appear. However, even in the Book of Revelation there are still MANY such changes in SCRIPT CHARACTER that were missed by the Interpreters and left out of the HOLY BIBLE.

In the King James 1611 AUTHORIZED VERSION of the HOLY BIBLE, the FIRST appearance of the changes in TYPE STYLE in the Book of Revelation occur in Revelation 2:27.

> ***Revelation 2:27*** **And HE SHALL RULE THEM WITH A ROD OF IRON; AS THE VESSELS OF A POTTER SHALL THEY BE BROKEN TO SHIVERS; even as I received of my Father.**

Although WE typically NOTE *SCRIPTURE* in *ITALIC CHARACTERS*, WE purposely entered the SCRIPTURE in standard type, for this is how it should appear in your BIBLE. The **BOLD CHARACTERS** represent the WORDS of JESUS CHRIST, and in most Bibles they will appear in **RED INK,** rather than in **BOLD TYPE.** You should also readily SEE from the SCRIPTURE that a COMBINATION of lower and upper case letters are used, just as WE have done in this BOOK.

There are some that will say, the only reason for the change from lower to upper case TYPE STYLE, is because the Scripture cites that which was said in previous Biblical Scripture, Psalms 2:8 and 2:9. However, in the very NEXT CHAPTER, Revelation 3:7, TYPE STYLE changes again, and this time the Scripture does not refer to other BIBLE SCRIPTURE and STANDS ENTIRELY on its own.

> ***Revelation 3:7*** **And to the angel of the church in Philadelphia write; These things saith he that is holy, he that is true, HE THAT HATH THE KEY OF DAVID, HE THAT OPENETH, AND NO MAN SHUTTETH; AND SHUTTETH, AND NO MAN OPENETH;**

Although part of this Scripture relates to other Scripture, the OPENING STATEMENT, **"HE THAT HATH THE KEY OF DAVID"** is only so STATED in the Book of Revelation, and does not appear elsewhere in the Scriptures.

Changes in TYPE STYLE occur again in Chapter 7 verse 10 and as well in the 15th verse of the 11th Chapter, and this FORMAT continues on throughout the Book of Revelation, sometimes referring to previous Biblical Scripture, and sometimes not! The one Scripture in particular that is highlighted in a gross change in TYPE STYLE is the TITLE given to the GREAT WHORE in Revelation 17:5. Some people, as did the Publisher of my particular Bible make reference to the Epistle of Paul, 2 Thessalonians 2:7; implying that he too was referring to the GREAT WHORE by TITLE. However, they do ERR in their thinking!

Even though Paul in his Epistle was WARNING the CHURCH about how the Devil would eventually take control of it, he makes no reference to the TITLE given to the GREAT WHORE, for the "GREAT WHORE" spoken of in the Scriptures is the CHURCH!

It is also NOTEWORTHY to point out that the USE of upper case lettering for TYPE STYLE indicates the STRENGTH in WORDS and does NOT necessarily mean that the AUTHOR is SHOUTING. The upper case letters rather indicate the AUTHORITY given to the AUTHOR'S WORDS, and them that have rather LARGE EGOS will find this OFFENSIVE, as will the DAMNED find the changes in TYPE STYLE offensive.

If you find that the changes in TYPE STYLE offend you, you are either DAMNED by ***GOD***, or are dealing with an EGO that is so overwhelming it controls your Spirit. Pray to ***GOD*** that it be the LATTER and not the FORMER, and that ***HE*** will help you to overcome your EGO. For if the EGO controls the Spirit, the Spirit cannot hear the SOUL, for THE ***HOLY SPIRIT*** SPEAKS through the SOUL to the SPIRIT.

WE will close this Chapter by citing TWO Scriptures taken from the Book of the Prophet Zechariah, thus showing the CHANGES in TYPE STYLE that WE have been pointing out to you. THIS HAS ALWAYS been the WRITING STYLE of THE ***HOLY SPIRIT of GOD.***

> ***Zechariah 3:8*** Hear now, O Joshua the high priest, thou and thy fellows that sit before thee: for they are men wondered at: for, behold, I will bring forth my servant the **BRANCH.**

Zechariah 6:12 And speak unto him, saying, Thus speaketh the Lord of Hosts, saying, Behold the man whose name is The **BRANCH**; and he shall grow up out of his place, and he shall build the temple of the Lord:

Chapter 8
The FOUR SONS of GOD

In Chapter 6 of the Book of Genesis, and in Chapters 1 and 2 of the Book of Job, the Scriptures make reference (in plural) to the SONS of ***GOD***. Many people over the course of years when READING these Scriptures have become somewhat confused and troubled by them, because they seem to differ from what JESUS had said in the GOSPELS. Most clergy teach when questioned about these particular Scriptures, that the Scriptures refer to the Fallen Angels, and justify this misunderstanding by saying ***GOD*** has only one son, JESUS.

However, the Scriptures mean EXACTLY what they SAY, for there are FOUR SONS of ***GOD*,** and when JESUS refers to HIMSELF in the GOSPELS as being the ONLY BEGOTTEN of the ***FATHER***, this is also TRUE. ***THE LORD*** wants ME to clear up any CONFUSION resulting from the MISINTERPRETATION of these Scriptures, for ***GOD*** says the Scriptures have become a STUMBLING BLOCK to them who READ them.

JESUS was sent to the EARTH to be MAN'S PERFECT EXAMPLE, and ALL of MANKIND bearing a SOUL from ***GOD*** has come through the LINEAGE of JESUS CHRIST. When a person RECEIVES ***HOLY SPIRIT*** BAPTISM and is REBORN in CHRIST, that PERSON in the EYES of ***GOD*** becomes ***GOD'S*** ONLY BEGOTTEN SON, and this is what JESUS was saying in the GOSPELS.

GOD SEES ALL them BEARING a SOUL, after BAPTISM, as ***HIS*** ONE and ONLY SON, whether they are MALE or FEMALE in GENDER. ***GOD*** does not want YOU to see your RELATIONSHIP with ***HIM*** as being one of many, but rather wants YOU to SEE YOUR RELATIONSHIP with ***HIM*** in the same way an ONLY CHILD would SEE their RELATIONSHIP with their FATHER. This relates to the INTIMACY ***GOD*** has regarding YOUR RELATIONSHIP with ***HIM***; and how ***GOD*** wants YOU to FEEL about ***HIS LOVE*** towards YOU; for it is a ONE of a KIND LOVE that cannot be shared or compared to another. It is because of this UNIQUE LOVE ***GOD*** has for YOU, that YOU should not only BELIEVE, but also come to EXPECT; that in the EYES of ***GOD*** YOU are ***HIS*** ONLY BEGOTTEN SON!

GOD does not SEE YOU as ONE of MANY sons, but rather SEES YOU in a SINGULAR FORM, and this is why the Scriptures refer to YOU in the SINGULAR FORM.

> ***Revelation 21:7*** *He that overcometh shall INHERIT ALL THINGS; and **I** will be his **GOD,** and HE shall be **MY** SON.*

There are FOUR SON'S of ***GOD***, and not just one, because the FOUR are the DIRECT DESCENDANTS of ***GOD*** outside of the ***TRINITY (THE GODHEAD).*** Whereas the ANGEL is a CREATION of ***GOD,*** the FOUR SONS of ***GOD,*** called the SERAPHIM, (or the FOUR LIVING BEASTS), DESCENDED from ***GOD*** and are called ***HIS*** SONS**.** This is why JESUS says in the Scriptures that HE had COME OUT from ***GOD;*** for HE indeed had meant it LITERALLY; HE DESCENDED from THE ***GODHEAD.*** In the other TWO BOOKS, "Revealing The Bible's Truth" and "The ROD of IRON", the FOUR SERAPHIM were explicitly covered. However, for those of you who haven't READ the other BOOKS, WE will review some of what was covered in them.

There is FOUR SERAPHIM RULING in HEAVEN as FOUR KINGS, and they are CALLED the SONS of ***GOD;*** and no one OUTSIDE of ***GOD*** is more POWERFUL than they. ALL FOUR SERAPHIM have NAMES and have been given NUMBERS also in regard to the timing of their APPEARANCES on EARTH, and their NUMBERING starts from the time of NOAH. The reason why their NUMBERS start from the time of NOAH rather than from the time of ADAM, is because ADAM'S WORLD was DESTROYED prior to the SERAPHIM coming to the EARTH as MEN, thus making ADAM'S era irrelevant to that TIMING. Every single person in this WORLD and in the many WORLDS yet to come, will have come through the LINEAGE of NOAH, a DELIVERER. This is TRUE whether they are of the BLESSED SEED, of the DAMNED SEED, or of the GENTILE, for NOAH carries forward the SEED from the FIRST WORLD.

Prior to the DESTRUCTION of the FIRST WORLD, the SERAPHIM came to the EARTH in the FORM of SERAPHIM and not in the form of men. The Scriptures make note of their coming into the FIRST WORLD, and how they took women for wives and had children with them. The SERAPHIM on EARTH were nine cubits (15 feet) tall, and had the appearances of GIANT MEN, and when the women gave birth to the children of the SERAPHIM, the children grew to be over six cubits in height (9 feet tall). ***GOD*** disapproved of this activity by the SERAPHIM, and ALL of the SERAPHIM offspring were

DESTROYED during the GREAT FLOOD.

> ***Genesis 6:4*** *There were GIANTS in the EARTH in those days; and also after that, when the SONS of* ***GOD*** *came in unto the daughters of men, and they bare children to them, the same became mighty men which were of old, men of renown.*

The DELIVERERS

ALL DELIVERERS come through the LINEAGE of the FOURTH SERAPHIM. NOAH, being a SPIRITUAL DESCENDANT of THE ***DELIVERER*** (The FOURTH SERAPHIM), walked on the EARTH "with ***GOD***" as the Scriptures say, but not "as ***GOD***", and NOAH was ONE of THREE DELIVERERS spoken of in the OLD TESTAMENT. Whereas when THE ***DELIVERER*** comes to the EARTH, ***HE*** on EARTH will be AS ***GOD.***

The other TWO DELIVERERS of the OLD TESTAMENT were JOSEPH and MOSES, with JOSEPH coming TWICE, once as the Son of Jacob, and ONCE as the FATHER of JESUS CHRIST. You will not see the NAMES of NOAH, JOSEPH or MOSES in HEAVEN, for each of their THREE NAMES represent ONE-THIRD of the ***DELIVERER*** and COMBINE in HEAVEN to make ***ONE SINGLE NAME.***

NOTE: By each one of the THREE DELIVERERS being ONE-THIRD that of THE ***DELIVERER*** (the FOURTH SERAPHIM) it cannot be said that THE ***DELIVERER*** has already COME to the EARTH. For only ONE-THIRD of ***HIM*** was here in each of HIS appearances. It would have taken ALL THREE of these men (NOAH, JOSEPH, and MOSES) coming at the same time as ONE SINGLE PERSON, before it could be said, THE ***DELIVERER*** had COME. Furthermore, because the THREE had come as THREE separate PERSONS and not as a SINGLE PERSON, none of the THREE could REPRESENT THE ***HOLY SPIRIT*** in FLESH; for only THE ***DELIVERER*** called the ***182 PERSON*** can REPRESENT THE ***HOLY SPIRIT of GOD*** in the FORM of a MAN.

To further complicate matters, the SERAPHIM come to the earth in the reverse order to that of their EXISTENCE in HEAVEN, with the LAST SERAPHIM coming FIRST, and the FIRST SERAPHIM coming LAST. To further clarify what is being said (for WE know that it is somewhat difficult to UNDERSTAND), WE will start OUR EXPLANATION by giving you the NAMES of the FOUR SERAPHIM.

The 1st SERAPHIM is called "DAVID", for DAVID was the FIRST SERAPHIM after the time of NOAH to COME to the EARTH, and while on the

EARTH, DAVID was the father of SOLOMON. In HEAVEN, SOLOMON is the 2nd SERAPHIM, and because the order of the SERAPHIM'S appearances in HEAVEN is REVERSED from that of the EARTH, in HEAVEN SOLOMON is the FATHER of DAVID, for SOLOMON came out from the ***GODHEAD*** prior to DAVID.

The 3rd SERAPHIM'S NAME is JESUS, and although JESUS came to the EARTH after SOLOMON and DAVID, HE was before SOLOMON in HEAVEN, making JESUS SOLOMON'S FATHER and DAVID'S GRANDFATHER in HEAVEN. The 4th SERAPHIM is THE ***DELIVERER,*** and ***HE*** has THREE NAMES that when the LETTERS making up those NAMES are converted to NUMBERS and sum totaled, they EQUAL the NUMBER ***182;*** just as the THREE NAMES (NOAH, JOSEPH, and MOSES) when converted to NUMBERS sum total to the NUMBER ***182.***

THE ***DELIVERER*** (the FOURTH SERAPHIM) is the FIRST DESCENDANT of ***GOD*** and while OUTSIDE of the ***TRINITY, HE*** is THE ***HOLY SPIRIT of GOD (GOD'S IDENTITY)*** in FLESH. THE DELIVERER is also the FATHER of JESUS CHRIST, and this is TRUE both outside of the ***TRINITY*** and WITHIN it as well. This is because WITHIN the ***TRINITY (THE GODHEAD)*** THE ***DELIVERER IS THE HOLY SPIRIT of GOD, IXOTE, and THE FATHER of YESHUA,*** and ***YESHUA*** OUTSIDE of the ***TRINITY*** is JESUS CHRIST.

Inside the ***TRINITY (THE GODHEAD),*** neither ***YESHUA*** nor ***IXOTE*** have a GENDER, whereas outside of the ***TRINITY*** both ***YESHUA*** and ***IXOTE*** are MALES; both having FEMALE counterparts, the COVENANT ANGELS, ASAPH and ***JAEL*** for THEIR MATES. Also, while outside of the ***TRINITY,*** both ***YESHUA*** and ***IXOTE*** have ENGLISH NAMES, ***YESHUA*** is JESUS CHRIST and ***IXOTE*** is THE ***DELIVERER 182.*** THE ***DELIVERER'S*** ENGLISH ***NAME*** consists of THREE NAMES, and when those THREE NAMES are CONVERTED to NUMBERS and sum totaled they equal the NUMBER ***182,*** and this is why ***HIS NAME*** is expressed by the NUMBER ***182,*** for ***HE IS THE SEVEN SPIRITS of GOD (7x26=182).*** This is also why the SCRIPTURES IDENTIFY the LAMB of ***GOD*** as having SEVEN HORNS and SEVEN EYES, and being the ***SEVEN SPIRITS of GOD.***

The SEVEN HORNS and SEVEN EYES represent the NUMBER 77, for that is the NUMBER given to the NAME "CHRIST". The letter "C" is the 3rd letter of the English alphabet; the letter "H" is the 8th letter, the letter "R" the 18th letter, the letter "I" the 9th letter, the letter "S" the 19th letter and the letter "T" the 20th letter. When each of the letters making up the NAME "CHRIST" are added together, they EQUAL the NUMBER "77" (3+8+18+9+19+20 = 77).

The WORD ***"GOD"*** EQUALS the NUMBER "*26*", for when its letters are converted to NUMBERS and added together they equal the NUMBER ***26***. This makes the ***SEVEN SPIRITS of GOD*** the same as the multiplied NUMBER of ***7 x 26*** or the NUMBER ***182 (7 x 26 = 182).***

Also, when taking the letters making up the WORDS, ***"SEVEN SPIRITS of GOD",*** and CONVERTING them to NUMBERS and then sum totaling them, you will SEE that the NUMBER they sum total to is the NUMBER "*222*". This is the NUMBER of the ***THREE NAMES*** within the ***TRINITY (THE GODHEAD),*** for the NAME ***YAHWEH*** equals the NUMBER "*70*", the NAME ***IXOTE*** equals the NUMBER "*73*", and the NAME ***YESHUA*** equals the NUMBER "*79*". When the ***THREE NAMES of THE GODHEAD*** are added together they total the NUMBER ***222,*** as does the WORDS ***"SEVEN SPIRITS of GOD"*** sum total to ***222.***

> ***Revelation 5:6*** *And I beheld, and, lo, in the midst of THE THRONE and of THE FOUR BEASTS, and in the midst of the ELDERS, stood a LAMB as it had been SLAIN, having SEVEN HORNS and SEVEN EYES, which are the* ***SEVEN SPIRITS of GOD*** *sent forth into all the EARTH.*

CHRIST *(THE LAMB)* represents ***GOD*** in a DESCENDED FORM, and the FOUR SERAPHIM are CHRIST. However, outside of the ***GODHEAD,*** only THE ***DELIVERER*** represents ***GOD,*** and JESUS CHRIST the SON of ***GOD,*** both being in FLESH as MEN; thus making THE ***DELIVERER, GOD,*** in the form of "MAN", and JESUS CHRIST, "THE SON of MAN".

When ***GOD*** DESCENDS within the ***TRINITY*** it is called the DESCENDING FORM of ***GOD,*** and when DESCENDING OUTSIDE of the ***TRINITY*** it is CALLED the DESCENDING NATURE of ***GOD*** or CHRIST; for OUTSIDE of the ***TRINITY,*** THE ***HOLY SPIRIT* of *GOD*** is in the NATURE (LIKENESS) of MAN (in FLESH).

> ***Genesis 6:3*** *And* ***THE LORD*** *said,* ***MY SPIRIT*** *shall not always strive with MAN, for that* ***HE*** *also is FLESH: yet* ***HIS*** *days shall be an hundred and twenty years.*

Bridging the GAP

The ANGEL was before the SERAPHIM and also before ***YESHUA,*** the ***THIRD PERSON of the GODHEAD.*** Therefore ***GOD*** would not DESCEND to CHRIST without INCLUDING the ANGEL, who had been ***HIS*** LOYAL SERVANTS prior to both TIME and CREATION. In HONOR of the ANGELS, THE ***HOLY SPIRIT*** SPLIT the SERAPHIM into GENDER, and the FEMININE portion of the SERAPHIM was taken from them. THE ***HOLY SPIRIT*** then took those FEMININE QUALITIES of the SERAPHIM and made from them a FEMALE ANGEL. The FEMALE ANGEL was then called the COVENANT ANGEL, and was the FIRST OUTSIDE of the ***GODHEAD*** to partake in the COVENANT of MARRIAGE, and also the FIRST of the ANGELS to be given GENDER. The FOUR COVENANT ANGELS then became the FOUR BRIDES of CHRIST; thus continuing to allow the ANGEL ACCESS to ***GOD*** as it had been before the SERAPHIM, only now their ACCESS to ***GOD*** would be through CHRIST.

The FOUR COVENANT ANGELS were also given NAMES: The BRIDE of DAVID is called ZARALL, the BRIDE of SOLOMON is called CHAMUEL, the BRIDE of JESUS was called URIEL, and the BRIDE of THE ***DELIVERER*** is CALLED ***JAEL.*** However, after the woman called EVE (who was the SPIRIT of URIEL) caused the MAN ADAM to SIN in the GARDEN of EDEN, THE ***HOLY SPIRIT*** removed Uriel from her POST of being a COVENANT ANGEL. The ANGEL ASAPH was then given a FEMALE GENDER, and it is SHE who replaced Uriel as the 3rd COVENANT ANGEL of CHRIST and the BRIDE to JESUS.

It is the COVENANT ANGEL that BRIDGES the GAP between the ANGEL and CHRIST, for it is the COVENANT ANGEL who allows the ANGEL to ASCEND into CHRIST. ALL BEINGS in HEAVEN are composed of LIGHT, however the LIGHT COMPOSITION of the ANGEL is different than that of the SERAPHIM. Therefore the TWO different forms of LIGHT cannot be unified (COMBINED) without a CONDUIT to CONNECT the TWO. It is the COVENANT ANGEL who acts as that CONDUIT and PROVIDES the CHANNEL to CHRIST by MARRIAGE of the ANGEL to MAN.

CHRIST

Although the WORD "CHRIST" means ***GOD'S ANOINTED,*** the WORD "CHRIST" ALSO represents a FAMILY NAME. CHRIST is the SONS of ***GOD,*** the FOUR SERAPHIM, or ***GOD*** in the FORM of MAN. This can be best UNDERSTOOD by visualizing a FAMILY TREE, starting with the FIRST PERSON of the FAMILY who is ***THE FATHER*** (in this case ***GOD*** or the ***GODHEAD***), and then DESCENDING DOWN through ALL the GENERATIONS of MANKIND having SOULS. This PROCESS started with the FIRST out of the ***GODHEAD,*** THE ***DELIVERER,*** and this is why ***HE*** is referred to in the Scriptures as being the ***SEVEN SPIRITS of GOD.***

This is also why the NUMBERING of the SERAPHIM starts with NOAH rather than ADAM, because THE ***DELIVERER*** started the sequence of MAN in HEAVEN. Each TIME the EARTH is REGENERATED it starts with NOAH entering into the ARK, as stated in the 7th Chapter of the Book of Genesis. NOAH, being a ONE-THIRD SPIRITUAL DESCENDANT of THE ***DELIVERER*** starts the PROCESS of the REGENERATION of Man on EARTH. This is because only a DELIVERER can PRODUCE the OFFSPRING of EACH of the THREE SEEDS of MAN and it is always the DELIVERER, NOAH that sows the THREE SEEDS of MAN on EARTH.

ADAM was the DESCENDANT of JESUS CHRIST, the FIRST MAN with a SOUL, and from him came forth only the BLESSED SEED, whereas ALL THREE SEEDS (the BLESSED, the DAMNED, and the GENTILE) come through the LINEAGE of NOAH and HIS THREE SONS, for NOAH is a DELIVERER.

Getting back to the FAMILY TREE: Within the ***GODHEAD*** the FIRST of the FAMILY TREE is ***YAHWEH,*** for ***HE*** is ***THE FATHER*** to ALL. The next is ***IXOTE*** who is ***YAHWEH'S SON*** and as with ***YAHWEH, IXOTE*** has ALWAYS BEEN with ***GOD*** throughout ETERNITY. Then through ***IXOTE*** came forth ***YESHUA*** and ***YESHUA*** is ***IXOTE'S SON and YAHWEH'S GRANDSON.***

Within the ***GODHEAD***, ***GOD*** DESCENDS in a ***SPIRITUAL FORM,*** having no NEED for a GENDER, and ONLY THE ***DELIVERER*** OUTSIDE of the ***GODHEAD*** was BORN of THE ***SPIRIT of GOD*** while being in the NATURE of MAN. ALL of MANKIND after THE ***DELIVERER*** is of the OFFSPRING of THE ***DELIVERER*** and ***JAEL HIS*** MATE.

OUTSIDE of the ***GODHEAD*** the FIRST DESCENDANT of ***GOD*** is the OFFSPRING of BOTH ***IXOTE*** and ***YESHUA*** and ***HE*** is called THE ***DELIVERER*** (the ***182 PERSON***)***.*** After ***HE*** was SPLIT into GENDER, ***HE*** and ***HIS*** MATE ***JAEL*** GAVE BIRTH to the SON of MAN and ***HE*** is ***GOD*** in the NATURE of MAN. The FIRST DESCENDANT from the MAN (THE ***DELIVERER*** and ***JAEL***) was called JESUS CHRIST, thus making JESUS the FIRST OFFSPRING from ***GOD*** OUTSIDE of the ***GODHEAD.*** The next DESCENDANT of ***GOD*** is SOLOMON, and SOLOMON came forth from JESUS and ASAPH, and then DAVID was born in HEAVEN, and HIS PARENTS are SOLOMON and CHAMUEL.

NOTE: THE LORD wants ME to point out to YOU that OUTSIDE of the ***GODHEAD*** only THE ***DELIVERER*** DESCENDED IMMACULATELY from

THE ***GODHEAD,*** therefore ONLY ***HE*** can REPRESENT ***GOD*** on EARTH. This is why THE ***DELIVERER*** COMES LAST to the EARTH, allowing ***HIM*** to fulfill the Scripture WRITTEN about ***HIS*** COMING.

> ***Isaiah 41:4*** *Who hath wrought and done it, calling the GENERATIONS from the BEGINNING?* ***I THE LORD, THE FIRST, AND WITH THE LAST; I AM HE.***

This is also why JESUS CHRIST was BORN IMMACULATELY on EARTH, for HIS ***FATHER,*** THE ***DELIVERER,*** was BORN IMMACULATELY in HEAVEN. THE ***DELIVERER,*** will PASS DOWN to ***HIS*** SON, JESUS CHRIST, the ***AUTHORITY of GOD*** during the MILLENNIUM, and JESUS WILL BE GOD on EARTH during the MILLENNIUM. However, in HEAVEN, THE ***DELIVERER*** WILL BE ***GOD*** in the FORM of MAN, for THIS IS HIS INHERITANCE FROM ***GOD***!

The FOUR LIVING BEASTS (CHRIST)

In Chapter 4 of the Book of Revelation, the Apostle John was taken up to HEAVEN in a VISION, and while there was shown the FOUR LIVING BEASTS. ALL things shown to John regarding HEAVEN was shown to him SYMBOLICALLY; for if John BEHELD the GLORY of these things through his human eyes, he would have been forever changed and no longer allowed by ***GOD*** to return to EARTH.

This is because ALL things in HEAVEN are HOLY, and the unholy (earthly) cannot be commingled with the HOLY. This is also why MOSES was told to remove his shoes while he was in the PRESENCE of ***GOD*** and standing upon HOLY GROUND. MOSES' shoes were manmade objects, whereas the body of MOSES and the EARTH upon which he stood were a CREATION of ***GOD.***

When the Apostle John saw the FOUR LIVING BEASTS, he saw the 1st BEAST having an image of a LION, and the LION represented DAVID, for KING DAVID was called the LION of the TRIBE of JUDAH. John saw the 2nd BEAST having the appearance of a CALF (an OX), and this represented KING SOLOMON. When KING SOLOMON fashioned the THRONE of DAVID, it was encompassed with LIONS in honor of KING DAVID, and when the MOLTEN SEA was made and placed in the courtyard of the TEMPLE of ***GOD*** in JERUSALEM, it rested on the backs of TWELVE OXEN. The TWELVE OXEN supporting the MOLTEN SEA represented KING SOLOMON being BURDENED with the building of the TEMPLE of ***GOD*** in JERUSALEM for the TWELVE TRIBES of ISRAEL.

When the Apostle John saw the 3rd BEAST, it had the FACE of a MAN. This represents JESUS CHRIST, for HE is the FATHER of the SOUL BEARING MAN, and also the HEAD of CHRIST, who enables MAN to enter into the HEAVENLY DOMAIN through HIM. This is also a STATEMENT; proclaiming that ALL of CHRIST must at least once live on earth as a MAN, and MAN can only ACCESS CHRIST and HEAVEN through the 3rd BEAST, JESUS.

When John in his REVELATION VISION saw the 4th LIVING BEAST, he saw ***HIM*** as a FLYING EAGLE, for the FLYING EAGLE symbolically represents DELIVERANCE. The EAGLE is the SYMBOL of THE ***DELIVERER,*** the ***182 PERSON,*** and the ***SEVEN SPIRITS of GOD,*** for ONLY ***GOD*** can DELIVER. When MOSES PRAISED ***GOD*** for the DELIVERANCE of the CHILDREN of ISRAEL out of BONDAGE in Egypt, he referred to ***GOD*** as being the FLYING EAGLE who had carried ISRAEL out of Egypt on its WINGS.

The WRATH of the LAMB (The FOUR SERAPHIM)

Starting in Chapter 6 of the Book of Revelation, the FIRST of SEVEN SEALS are BROKEN on a BOOK that THE ***HOLY SPIRIT*** has HANDED down to CHRIST (the FOUR LIVING BEASTS). The BOOK represents the *WORD of* ***GOD*** that of which was HANDED DOWN to CHRIST and ALSO to the EARTH by THE ***HOLY SPIRIT***.

Each SEAL of the BOOK that is BROKEN represents an incremental PUNISHMENT for the EARTH that is handed down by the LAMB of ***GOD*** (CHRIST) to those who have disregarded or ABUSED the *WORD of* ***GOD.*** Each of the SEVEN INCREMENTAL PUNISHMENTS represents ***GOD'S*** AUTHORIZATION for the DESTRUCTION of the EARTH. John is told by each of the FOUR LIVING BEASTS as to what each PUNISHMENT ENTAILS for the first FOUR SEALS that are BROKEN.

The first FOUR SEALS that are BROKEN are referred to in the Scriptures as being the FOUR HORSEMEN of the APOCALYPSE, who are released upon the EARTH to begin its DESTRUCTION. DAVID, the FIRST LIVING BEAST, announces the FIRST of the HORSEMEN to be released, and the FIRST HORSEMAN rides upon a WHITE HORSE. The WHITE HORSEMAN REPRESENTS THE ***HOLY SPIRIT*** going through the EARTH with ***HIS*** ANGELS, to take back control of it from the DEVIL.

When the SECOND SEAL is BROKEN, it is SOLOMON (the SECOND SERAPHIM) who tells John of the EVENT, and John sees another HORSE-

MAN being sent out, this time riding on a RED HORSE. This PUNISHMENT entails the instilling of CHAOS and CONFUSION into the MINDS of them on the EARTH who have NOT HONORED ***GOD***, and PEACE is taken from the EARTH. People will no longer be able to trust in each other, neither in family or friends, and they will turn against one another, and kill one another; believing they must do so to preserve their own lives.

JESUS, the 3rd LIVING BEAST, announces the BREAKING of the THIRD SEAL, and the THIRD HORSEMAN is sent out riding upon a BLACK HORSE and having in his hand a BALANCE SCALE. The BALANCE SCALE represents the imbalance at this time on EARTH between the forces of GOOD and EVIL, with EVIL overwhelming the EARTH, and of the JUDGMENT the EARTH is about to RECEIVE. It also represents the rationing of food due to food shortages throughout the world. But JESUS tells John in the Scriptures that neither the ANOINTED nor ***GOD'S*** CHILDREN will be affected by the calamities or shortages; referring to the ANOINTED as the OIL and to the BLESSED (***GOD'S*** CHILDREN) as being the WINE.

NOTE: In between the BREAKING of the THIRD and FOURTH SEALS of the BOOK handed down to CHRIST, the FIRST TRUMPET will SOUND, marking the BEGINNING of the GREAT TRIBULATION, and those of the BRIDE of CHRIST will RECEIVE RAPTURE. At the time of the SOUNDING of the FIRST TRUMPET, 10,400,000 people will be taken from the EARTH and put into a PLACE of PROTECTION. This group is called the BRIDE of CHRIST and will consist of only 800,000 adults ages twenty and older, and 9,600,000 children, ages from infant to nineteen years old. The balance of the BRIDE of CHRIST are them residing in PARADISE, who will remain there until the SOUNDING of the SEVENTH TRUMPET; and at that time join those of the FIRST RAPTURE. Anyone else being alive that may be DESTINED for HEAVEN will do so as a WEDDING GUEST; for only the WEDDING GUESTS are left on EARTH. Those of the WEDDING GUESTS will remain living on the EARTH for an additional TWENTY-ONE MONTHS, after the SOUNDING of the FIRST TRUMPET. These people will unfortunately have to endure the first TWENTY-ONE MONTHS of the GREAT TRIBULATION; for at the SOUNDING of the FIRST TRUMPET, Lucifer is released upon the earth and the GREAT TRIBULATION begins.

WE will not at this time further critique the EVENTS of the END TIME, and have only included them in this Chapter to IDENTIFY the ROLE that the FOUR SERAPHIM play in the Scriptures of the Book of Revelation. However it MUST be understood that ALL of the ANGELS in HEAVEN report to the SERAPHIM, and it is the SERAPHIM who will DIRECT the ANGELS in ALL that they do during the END TIME!

Summary

In summary, the FOUR SONS of ***GOD*** consists of the FOUR SERAPHIM and their MATES, the FOUR COVENANT ANGELS. It is the FOUR SONS of ***GOD*** who provide the LINK for both the ANGEL and MAN to ***GOD,*** through CHRIST. Those who are RECEIVED into HEAVEN by SAVING GRACE are CALLED the WEDDING GUESTS, and them who are CHOSEN to be "THE BRIDE" are RECEIVED back into HEAVEN by DIVINE RIGHT; for they are the DESCENDANTS of CHRIST. MANY ARE "CALLED" but FEW ARE "CHOSEN".

Of the FOUR, only JESUS allows MAN'S ACCESS to CHRIST through HIS DEATH and RESURRECTION. For "THE BRIDE", who is the DESCENDANT of CHRIST, this is AUTOMATIC, for they RETURN to HEAVEN by the DIVINE RIGHT as does the Angel, and through CHRIST they have ACCESS to ***GOD.*** However, for the "WEDDING GUESTS", ***HOLY SPIRIT*** BAPTISM is not automatic, and even though they may ENTER HEAVEN and have ACCESS to CHRIST, they CANNOT ACCESS ***GOD*** for they are not in CHRIST!

The Churches improperly teach many things; however the most deceptive thing they teach is in the BELIEF that anyone can be RECEIVED into HEAVEN and has ACCESS to ***GOD.*** This is simply UNTRUE; for only the DESCENDANT of ***GOD,*** CHRIST, has ACCESS to ***HIM.*** At the Time of the END there will have been TWENTY-ONE BILLION people who had lived upon the face of the EARTH. Of the TWENTY-ONE BILLION, only FIVE BILLION will be RECEIVED into HEAVEN, and ONE BILLION of them will have been of the Angel. Of the remaining FOUR BILLION, only ONE HUNDRED and FOUR MILLION are the DESCENDANTS of CHRIST (THE BRIDE), and the balance of THREE BILLION, EIGHT HUNDRED and NINETY-SIX MILLION people, are all "WEDDING GUESTS". Whereas the "WEDDING GUESTS" represent 18.6% of the World's historical population, "THE BRIDE" represents only one-half of one per cent of it. This means that only one in five thousand are those of "THE BRIDE"!

It was TOLD to you in both "Revealing The Bible's Truth" and "The ROD of IRON" that the NUMBER 444 represents the SONS of ***GOD***. WE would like to close this Chapter by CONFIRMING this to you by using the NUMBERS of the NAMES of the FOUR SONS of ***GOD***.

One of the things the CHURCH neglects to teach is the subject of REIN-

CARNATION. The BIBLE speaks most frequently about REINCARNATION and three of the FOUR GOSPELS speak directly to the subject. JESUS told HIS Disciples in the GOSPELS that John the Baptist was the REINCARNATED Elijah, who had come back to the EARTH to ANNOUNCE the COMING of CHRIST (Malachi 4:5). However, what isn't made clear in the Scriptures is that Elijah is the REINCARNATED KING SOLOMON, for this is buried DEEP within them.

It was also said in "Revealing The Bible's Truth" that KING DAVID was the REINCARNATED Enoch, the son of Jared, from the FIRST WORLD, thus making him NOAH'S Great Grandfather. However, because Enoch was of the FIRST WORLD, the NAME Enoch is forever gone, although his SPIRIT NOW RESIDES in HEAVEN renamed as KING DAVID. Only NOAH and HIS family survived the GREAT FLOOD and all NAMES before NOAH are forever gone!

It may also be noted that only the NAMES of SOLOMON and Elijah are recognized in HEAVEN as being one PERSON, with the name of John the Baptist being omitted. This is because John the Baptist's being in the SPIRIT of ELIJAH was disclosed in the GOSPEL of Luke, therefore making the name, John, irrelevant as an IDENTITY for SOLOMON. If it were announced by the ANGEL GABRIEL that John the Baptist was in the SPIRIT of SOLOMON rather than in the Spirit of Elijah, then the NAME John would stand!

> ***Luke 1:17*** *And he shall go before him in the SPIRIT and power of E-LI'-JAH, TO TURN THE HEARTS OF THE FATHERS TO THE CHILDREN, and the disobedient to the wisdom of the just; to make ready the people prepared for THE LORD.*

NOTE: As with most of the NAMES in the OLD TESTAMENT, the NAME ELIJAH is spelled incorrectly in the NEW TESTAMENT, it is spelled Elias. This is also true with the NAMES NOAH being spelled "NOE", Isaiah being spelled Esaias, and the name Jonah being spelled Jonas. The differences in spelling between the OLD and New TESTAMENTS is a result of dialect changes in the HEBREW language due to the many years of CAPTIVITY the Children of Israel endured in foreign nations. The OLD TESTAMENT has the CORRECT SPELLING of the NAMES whereas the NEW TESTAMENT does not.

When the letters making up the NAMES of the FOUR SONS of ***GOD*** are converted to NUMBERS based on where each of the letters fall within the English Alphabet and are then sum totaled, the following NUMBERS are achieved; thus proving how the NUMBER 444 represents the FOUR SONS of ***GOD.***

- The NAME DAVID = the NUMBER 40
- The NAME SOLOMON (Elijah) = the NUMBER 103 + (45) or 148
- The NAME JESUS = the NUMBER 74
- The NAME of THE **DELIVERER 182** = the NUMBER **182** or, 40+148+74+**182** = THE NUMBER 444

It may also be noted that the NUMBER (4) in the 444 represents the FOURS SONS of ***GOD,*** and the TRIPLICATE (4s) indicate that the 4 SONS of ***GOD*** had come out from THE ***TRINITY.*** This further clarifies what JESUS had meant when HE said HE had come out from ***GOD*****!**

LETTER and NUMBER Reference Guide

Each letter of the Alphabet has a corresponding NUMBER running from the NUMBER 1 through the NUMBER 26 depending on where the letter falls within the English Alphabet. The following is a list of letters and their corresponding NUMBERS.

The letter "A"=1, "B"=2, "C'=3, "D"=4, "E"=5, "F"=6, "G"=7, "H"=8, "I"=9, "J"=10, "K"=11, "L"=12, "M"=13, "N"=14, "O"=15, "P"=16, "Q"=17, "R"=18, "S"=19, "T"=20, "U"=21, "V"=22, "W"=23, "X"=24, "Y"=25, and "Z"=26.

Chapter 9
EARTH Angels

WE have told you in this BOOK and as well in the TWO PREVIOUS BOOKS, that of the FIVE BILLION PEOPLE that RECEIVE RAPTURE, ONE BILLION of them are Angels. Although the ONE BILLION represent one billion people, they only represent FIVE HUNDRED MILLION ANGELS in HEAVEN.

This is because in order for the ANGEL to be BORN out of CHRIST and come to the EARTH, they must first be given a GENDER. ***THE LORD*** divides the ANGEL of CHRIST into TWO Half-Angels, giving one-half the MALE qualities of the Angel, and the other half the FEMALE qualities. Each half of the Angel then becomes a person on EARTH, but not at the same time! If the MALE part of the Angel comes first, then the FEMALE part comes with them only in SPIRIT and becomes the other's GUARDIAN Angel while on EARTH; and the opposite would be TRUE if the FEMALE GENDER were to come rather than the MALE.

If BORN out of CHRIST the ANGEL is DESTINED to be an Angel on EARTH, and it is a prerequisite that both the MALE and FEMALE GENDERS of the Angel, live on the EARTH as both a MAN and a WOMAN. However, both GENDERS cannot come to be a person at the same time.

The first half of the Angel may come several thousand years before the other, or the second half may come shortly after the first Carnal Angel is deceased. The timing of either GENDER coming to the EARTH varies amongst the ANGELS, with only ***GOD*** KNOWING when or who will be SENT first.

While in HEAVEN, the ANGEL remains GENDERLESS, and it isn't until the TIMING of the FIRST to leave HEAVEN, that GENDER is given to the ANGEL. Then shortly thereafter, either the MALE or the FEMALE counterpart is sent to the EARTH, and the SPIRIT of both halves of the ANGEL DESCEND to the EARTH. However, one of the two will remain in SPIRIT, while other takes on a CARNAL FORM.

The Beginning of EARTH Angels

Prior to the Fall of Lucifer, ANGELS could only access the EARTH in a SPIRITUAL FORM; although at times, the Angels had appeared to them who were experiencing VISIONS of Angels, as being MEN rather than ANGELIC SPIRIT. In the OLD TESTAMENT, only a select few of the SEVENTH LEVEL ANGELS were allowed to come to the EARTH and be in a CARNAL FORM. However, since the RESURRECTION of JESUS CHRIST, ***GOD*** has sent many Angels to the EARTH to live, once as a MAN and once as a WOMAN.

While in the CARNAL FORM, the Angel is stripped of all of its angelic powers, and is as vulnerable to evil as any other carnal person on EARTH. The Angel's memory is also taken from them, as it is with anyone DESCENDING from HEAVEN to EARTH, and no recollection of HEAVEN is retained once they have entered into their carnal life. While on the EARTH, the Angel hasn't any idea whatsoever of them being different from any of the other people, and they are not told of their Angelic Status until after they have drawn their final breath in carnal life.

Increasing the NUMBER of ANGELS

While Lucifer was yet in HEAVEN, the population of the ANGELS was held constant at TWENTY-ONE BILLION. When Lucifer fell from the GRACE of ***GOD***, he took with him seven billion of the angels. This is why there are SEVEN BILLION PEOPLE who enter the MILLENNIUM, a period of HEAVEN on EARTH; FIVE BILLION of which who are DESTINED for HEAVEN, with ONE BILLION of those FIVE BILLION being Angels, and TWO BILLION of the BEHEADED SOULS (all being GENTILES) DESTINED to return to the DUST of the EARTH.

With each CYCLE of the EARTH, the population of ANGELS in HEAVEN increases by FIVE HUNDRED MILLION, all of which COME OUT FROM CHRIST, unlike the ANGELS of OLD. The Angels coming out from CHRIST can be ANGELS from the FIRST through the SIXTH CHOIR in ANOINTING, however the lower level numbers are significantly greater than those of the SIXTH LEVEL.

Unlike the CHILDREN of ***GOD***, the Angel never RECEIVES less than THREE GIFTS from THE ***HOLY SPIRIT***. And in HEAVEN, the ANGEL is SUPERIOR to MAN up to the SIXTH LEVEL, the LEVEL of the SAINT, and at the SIXTH LEVEL the ANGEL and SAINT become EQUIVALENT in ANOINTING. However, THE ***HOLY SPIRIT*** who is ***THE LORD of HOSTS,*** never SEES MAN EQUIVALENT to the ANGEL, except for those in CHRIST, who can ASCEND in CHRIST to the EIGHTH LEVEL.

After the CREATION of CHRIST (the DESCENDING of ***GOD*** into MAN) and the fall of Lucifer, all ANGELS have since come out through CHRIST; therefore fulfilling THE ***HOLY SPIRIT'S*** PROMISE of never placing MAN above the ANGEL, neither in HEAVEN nor on the EARTH! The ANGEL was before MAN in HEAVEN and ***GOD*** HONORS their SENIORITY!

Due to the ANGEL living twice on EARTH and being recombined with their MATE upon arrival in HEAVEN, it can be said that the ANGEL is twice that of MAN when in HEAVEN. However, MAN is not treated as such in HEAVEN by ***GOD*** or the ANGEL, and is TREATED as a WELCOME GUEST by ALL of the HEAVENLY HOSTS.

Angelic OFFSPRING and EARTHLY Marriage

ANGELS are not ALLOWED to MATE and produce Angelic Offspring neither in HEAVEN nor while on EARTH and in a CARNAL FORM. Therefore when the EARTH Angel selects a MATE on EARTH, the one SELECTED will always be of the GENTILE, and all of their OFFSPRING will be of the GENTILE, who returns to the DUST of the EARTH at death. This is also TRUE for the SPOUSE to the Angel; they also will return to the DUST of the EARTH; for Marriage of an ANGEL, other than on EARTH is FORBIDDEN, and can only be TEMPORARY.

While on the EARTH, the Angel is allowed to participate in the same lifestyles as does the MAN, and this includes marriage and the bringing forth of children. And, although the Spouse to the Angel and their children are of the GENTILE who can never be SAVED or RECEIVE a SOUL, this particular group will NEVER suffer the SECOND DEATH and be cast into HELL. This is their BLESSING for their SERVICE to ***GOD,*** by being either a SPOUSE or CHILDREN to the EARTH Angel.

All Angelic families will endure a GOOD LIFE on EARTH, even though short lived. ***GOD*** SEES to all of the families NEEDS and BLESSES them in all of their endeavors. The Angelic family rarely goes through DIVORCE, for the married partner to the Angel fulfills all marital vows. ***GOD*** normally will not allow an Angel's marriage on EARTH to fail, unless the spouse interferes with the Angel's PURPOSE.

DIVINE PURPOSE

ALL CHILDREN of ***GOD*** serve a PURPOSE in ***GOD*** both on EARTH and in HEAVEN, because the SOUL carries with it the PURPOSE that ***GOD*** has intended for the SPIRIT to SERVE. For each CHILD of ***GOD*** the PURPOSE of the SPIRIT will be different, and in varying degrees the CHILD will fulfill his or her PURPOSE during their life on EARTH, with no two PURPOSES being the same.

In many cases, the PURPOSE the SPIRIT serves while on EARTH will be quite subtle, and neither obvious to the SOUL bearing PERSON or to anyone else who may be close to that PERSON. This is because what they do during their carnal life makes up only a very small portion of a much GREATER PURPOSE that is yet to be SERVED for ***THE LORD.*** Each one of the PURPOSES being served by the CHILDREN of ***GOD*** can be viewed like one single piece to a very large PUZZLE, that if any one single piece might be lost, the PUZZLE could never be completed. This is why a CHILD of ***GOD*** can NEVER be LOST; for ***GOD*** will not allow any one PIECE to the PUZZLE to either be lost or misplaced!

Just like the pieces to a PUZZLE, although there are many that look alike, only the proper piece fits perfectly into its intended place; allowing for no substitutions of that PIECE in its PLACE. Each PIECE, when added to the PUZZLE, REVEALS a tiny bit more of the PUZZLE'S IMAGE, and the IMAGE of this PUZZLE WE SPEAK about, is the PICTURE ***GOD*** PAINTED of ***HIS*** SON, CHRIST, before CREATION.

As with each piece of the PUZZLE being unique, so are each of ONE of ***GOD'S*** CHILDREN UNIQUE, with each and every SPIRIT and SOUL being a "ONE of a KIND". ***THE LORD*** has explained this phenomenon to ME in this way:

Imagine a MASTER ARTIST painting ***HIS*** MASTERPIECE on a GLAZED EARTHEN VESSEL (POTTERY), and then BREAKING the VESSEL into BILLIONS of tiny little pieces; making sure while gathering up the PIECES of the BROKEN VESSEL, that not a SINGLE PIECE be lost. Now further IMAGINE the EARTHEN VESSEL be made of LIGHT, rather than CLAY, and SEE each one of its tiny pieces as being a SINGLE POINT of LIGHT.

Each SINGLE POINT of LIGHT can then be VIEWED as ONE SINGLE SPIRIT, and the PURPOSE of that SINGLE POINT of LIGHT can be VIEWED as ITS PLACE within the MASTERPIECE where it had once RESIDED. As EACH PIECE is then put back into its RIGHTFUL PLACE within the VESSEL, more of the MASTERPIECE painted on the VESSEL is REVEALED.

By only the MASTER ARTIST knowing what the PAINTED IMAGE entails, only ***HE*** can put EACH and EVERY PIECE back into its PROPER PLACE within the VESSEL, and do so without FLAW. For ***HE CREATED BOTH THE VESSEL*** and ***THE IMAGE ON THE VESSEL*** and KNOWS its every DETAIL.

Let US now SEE the VESSEL in its ORIGINAL and COMPLETED FORM, and IMAGINE at the TIME of the BEGINNING when ***GOD*** said, ***"LET THERE BE LIGHT",*** let that be the TIME when the VESSEL made of LIGHT be BROKEN to SHIVERS. This can be likened to what the scientists call "THE BIG BANG THEORY", the TIME when the UNIVERSE was created from a SINGLE POINT of LIGHT.

Now, if WE call the VESSEL made of LIGHT, ***GOD,*** and the IMAGE on the VESSEL, CHRIST, and EACH of the PIECES of the BROKEN VESSEL, ***GOD'S*** CHILDREN, WE THINK YOU WILL START TO SEE THE PICTURE, of who you are, and where you came from!

> ***Revelation 2:26 AND HE THAT OVERCOMETH, AND KEEPETH MY WORKS UNTO THE END, TO HIM WILL I GIVE POWER OVER THE NATIONS;***
>
> ***Revelation 2:27 AND HE SHALL RULE THEM WITH A ROD OF IRON; AS THE VESSELS OF A POTTER SHALL THEY BE BROKEN TO SHIVERS; EVEN AS I RECEIVED OF MY FATHER.***

EACH ANGEL that comes to the EARTH to live in a CARNAL FORM also serves a PURPOSE in ***GOD.*** The Earth Angel SERVES a DIVINE PURPOSE in ***GOD*** whereas ***GOD'S*** CHILDREN serve an INTERMEDIATE PURPOSE. It is the Angel who initiates KEY EVENTS, and those EVENTS form the foundation that the CHILDREN of ***GOD*** build on, who otherwise could not find their PLACE in ***GOD*** and fulfill their PURPOSE.

The Earth Angels can also be VIEWED like PIECES to the PUZZLE, the same as the CHILDREN of ***GOD***. However, the PIECES the Angels form of the PUZZLE can be likened to the BORDER of the PUZZLE that is needed for the center PIECES to FIND their rightful place. When the BORDER PIECES are not in PLACE, the CENTER PIECES have nothing to attach to, and ***GOD*** uses the Earth Angel as a GUIDE for ***HIS*** CHILDREN, thus helping them find their

PLACE in the PUZZLE.

The FIRST CORNER of the PUZZLE that is needed to start the assembly is CALLED JESUS CHRIST, and none of the PIECES of the PUZZLE can be installed until after that CORNER has been put into its RIGHTFUL PLACE. The FIRST CORNER was put into its PLACE at the TIME of JESUS' RESURRECTION, and for the past TWO THOUSAND YEARS the BORDER and most of the CENTER PIECES have been put into their PROPER PLACES, leaving only a few of the CENTER PIECES and the FINAL CORNER left to be INSTALLED.

The FINAL CORNER PIECE is CALLED THE ***DELIVERER 182,*** and this is the LAST PIECE of the PUZZLE. Once it is INSTALLED, the MASTERPIECE is COMPLETE, and ALL of ***GOD'S PURPOSES*** on EARTH will have been SERVED!

UNEXPECTED HELP

The Earth Angel during his or her course of carnal life will perform many acts on behalf of ***GOD,*** with some of the acts seemingly trivial while others can be quite miraculous. This is the young man who just happened to drive by a nearly frozen pond and sees a car with a woman and her children in it, and the car submerging into the pond, and dives into the freezing water to rescue them. Or, this is the woman who noticed an odd bundle lying next to the road in a rural area, and something inside of her tells her to stop and see what's in the bundle; and when she does she finds a tiny infant wrapped up in a blanket who had been discarded by the mother. She then drives 20 miles in the opposite direction from where she was going to the nearest hospital, and gets the child to safety.

These people are Earth Angels, and they themselves are not aware of it. Generally when asked why they had performed their acts of heroism, these heroic people cannot give a definite answer; and simply say that they were compelled by something to do what they had done. Most frequently, when asked why they had risked their life to save another, the answer will be; "I don't know". "It all happened so fast that I didn't have time to think about what I was doing, I just did it!" ***GOD*** put these Angels in the RIGHT PLACE at the RIGHT TIME, for ***HE KNEW*** when and where the HELPLESS would need HELP!

When these types of stories are heard, most people honor those who performed the heroic acts. However, the ones who had been rescued, they know that it was ***GOD*** who was looking after their well being, albeit they as well are thankful for those whom ***GOD*** had chosen to perform the acts.

Acts of the Earth Angel

Earth Angels do much more than come to the aid of the helpless; they also send MESSAGES from ***GOD*** to the people; for the Angels are ***GOD'S*** MESSENGERS! Earth Angels can be Writers of screenplays, Athletes, Marketers, Authors of books, Celebrities, an Artist, or any of which who can deliver a MESSAGE accurately to a rather large audience when required.

GOD will INSPIRE the Earth Angel in all of their works in such a way as to put forward the MESSAGE ***HE*** intends to give to either a SINGLE PERSON, or to a multitude of PEOPLE. Whenever you might see one's work as being INSPIRED WORK, the craftsman of the WORK will more than likely be an Earth Angel.

The GREATEST ARTISTS, and MUSICIANS, and INVENTORS are ALL Earth Angels. For instance; Michael Angelo, Leonardo De Vinci, Thomas Edison, Mozart, Rembrandt, Benjamin Franklin, and even Orville and Wilbur Wright were ALL Earth Angels, to name but a few. Any of the GREAT MEN and WOMEN throughout the world's history, after the RESURRECTION of JESUS CHRIST, that had impacted the future of the world in a POSITIVE way by their WORKS, was ALL Earth Angels.

The only COMMON TRAIT these GREAT PEOPLE had was in their UNIQUENESS of WORK, for other than that they were all DIFFERENT with not a two of them being alike in any way. However, not all Earth Angels are the Michael Angelo types. Many of them go unnoticed through their entire lives, for the SEEDS they plant may not sprout for many years, and they receive no earthly notoriety for their WORKS. But although their WORK goes unnoticed on EARTH, they are surely REVERED in HEAVEN, and the ANGELS rejoice at their HOMECOMING!

Chapter 10
Gender and Sexual Behavior

Gender began in HEAVEN, FIRST with THE ***DELIVERER 182,*** and then with the remaining three SONS of ***GOD***. The SONS of ***GOD*** SPIRITUALLY were SPLIT into a MALE and a FEMALE, and BOTH shared in the SAME SOUL. The MALE gender was called the SERAPHIM, and the FEMALE was called the COVENANT ANGEL. This was the FIRST COVENANT of MARRIAGE, and ***GOD*** saw that the MARRIAGE was GOOD, so ***GOD*** used Gender again in the CREATION of the SIXTH DAY MAN, the GENTILE. However in the case of the GENTILE, the man and the woman were made independent of one another unlike the SONS of ***GOD***, because the GENTILE had not a Soul. Lacking a Soul, the GENTILE man and woman hadn't the spiritual connection needed to draw them together, and initially neither of the two had the desire to copulate.

Whereas the animal mated instinctively during mating seasons, the man and the woman of the SIXTH DAY were made different and were not drawn together instinctively as was the animal. They were made to be like the SERAPHIM and the COVENANT ANGEL in HEAVEN; however without a soul for the two to share in, the GENTILE male and female hadn't any interest sexually in one another. So ***GOD*** gave the GENTILE a PHYSICAL SEXUAL DESIRE by making the two physically attracted to each other, and substituted a PHYSICAL connection (hormones) to compensate for the lack of the SPIRITUAL CONNECTION provided by the SOUL. This physical attraction drew the GENTILE male and female together in the physical act of sex, and they then started to mate and multiplied.

Prior to ***GOD'S*** making ADAM and as time went on, the GENTILE male and female's sexual desires intensified, and the males started killing other males so they could take the other's mates. The GENTILE females also learned very quickly how to manipulate the males by making themselves sexually desirable, and started changing their appearances to promote their feminine qualities and intensify the males sexual attraction to them.

The more popular females would accentuate everything they had that was different from that of the male. They would tie leather straps under and around their breasts to make them look fuller and larger, because they knew that the larger breasted females were always taken first when a male was looking for a mate. They also tied leather straps around their buttocks, for the females with the full well rounded buttocks appeared more attractive to the males.

GOD did not approve of the GENTILES sexual behavior, but allowed it to continue for a prolonged period of time, and as the time went on the GENTILES sexual conduct worsened. ***GOD*** decided then to make for ***HIMSELF*** another MAN, and this MAN was to be given a SOUL. So ***GOD, HIMSELF,*** made the MAN from the DUST of the EARTH and gave HIM a SOUL and the name of ADAM. ***GOD*** did not want the MAN with the SOUL to live among the GENTILES because this MAN was different from the GENTILE. So prior to the CREATION of ADAM, ***THE LORD*** made a BEAUTIFUL GARDEN for the MAN, ADAM to live, and ***GOD*** called the GARDEN, EDEN.

ADAM, being made like the ANGEL without GENDER had both MALE and FEMALE qualities, and like the ANGEL, ADAM should not have desired a MATE. However, after the passing of time ADAM became lonely; because ADAM was made from the DUST of the EARTH whereas the ANGEL was borne out of HEAVEN, and ***GOD*** saw that ADAM'S needs were different from that of the ANGEL. So ***GOD*** did on EARTH PHYSICALLY as ***HE*** had done with the SONS of ***GOD*** in HEAVEN SPIRITUALLY, and REMOVED the FEMININE QUALITIES from ADAM, and made from them a WOMAN. ADAM then NAMED the woman EVE, and ***GOD*** sanctified the TWO in MARRIAGE, as it was with the SERAPHIM and COVENANT ANGEL in HEAVEN.

Unlike ***GOD'S*** SIXTH DAY CREATION the GENTILE whom ***GOD*** told to go forth and multiply, ADAM and EVE were WARNED against it. Both ADAM and EVE were placed under the same conditions, as was the ANGEL who had been given GENDER; for ADAM and EVE were made like the Angel.

NOTE: Before an ANGEL can receive GENDER, they must first swear themselves to CELIBACY before ***GOD*** and can NEVER take a MATE or have OFFSPRING; and at the time of ADAM and EVE, only the ARK ANGEL LUCIFER had been given GENDER. The FOUR COVENANT ANGELS are different from all the other ANGELS in HEAVEN. Albeit having a FEMALE GENDER, they are allowed by ***GOD*** to MATE, for they are DESCENDANTS of ***GOD*** rather than CREATIONS of ***GOD*** as are the other ANGELS. ***GOD'S*** SIXTH DAY CREATION, the GENTILE, hadn't any such bond to HEAVEN as did ADAM and EVE, and were not of the HEAVENLY or angelic realm; so they were allowed to both mate and have offspring. Whereas ADAM and EVE were a cross between the ANGEL and the SERAPHIM and were forbidden to physically mate.

After disobeying ***GOD*** and mating, SIN had been placed upon the SOUL that ADAM and EVE shared and the SPIRITUAL CONNECTION between the TWO ceased, for the ***SPIRIT of GOD*** had left them. They then took on the carnal characteristic of the GENTILE, so ***GOD*** put the TWO out of the GARDEN, making ADAM and EVE live out the remainder of their days amongst the GENTILES and CANAANITES. Once removed from the GARDEN, it was only the physical attraction and a sexual desire that kept ADAM and EVE together, for once they had SINNED their SPIRITUAL CONNECTION was BROKEN. At the time of ADAM and EVE'S sinning, there was no forgiveness of SIN, for at that time ***GOD*** would not forgive sin!

NOTE: It wasn't until ***GOD*** made ***HIS*** FIRST COVENANT with ABRAHAM that animal sacrifice became an ACCEPTABLE means to RECEIVE FORGIVENESS. Although animal sacrifices were made to ***GOD*** prior to ABRAHAM, the sacrifices provided only a method of WORSHIP, and FORGIVENESS was not given in exchange for the sacrifice until ABRAHAM.

Sexual Desire versus SPIRITUAL LOVE

Although there are some similarities between a sexual act and SPIRITUAL LOVE MAKING, the two cannot be compared. The sexual act is a physical act that allows only the man's penis to enter the woman's vagina, and any further physical contact can only be an external contact. However, when TWO SPIRITS come together in an ACT of LOVE, the FEMALE SPIRIT RECEIVES the MALE SPIRIT in its ENTIRETY, and the TWO SPIRITS become as ONE during the ACT. Whereas the physical act of fornication is based on reaching a climax that lasts for only a few moments, the SPIRITUAL ACT of LOVE starts with a feeling equivalent to that of the sexual climax. It then INTENSIFIES to the point of RAPTURE, and then SPIRITUAL ECSTASY is experienced for as long as the TWO PARTNERS so desire. By the Spirit being eternal, SPIRITUAL ECSTASY can be experienced for prolong periods of time, one hour, one day, one week, or one month, for time is irrelevant in ETERNITY.

It is generally the male whom initiates the event of carnal sexual intercourse by arousing the female to the point of her sexual acceptance of the act, and this is called sexual foreplay. However, this is not so with SPIRITUAL LOVE MAKING, for it is the FEMALE SPIRIT who entices the MALE SPIRIT to MAKE LOVE with HER. The FEMALE SPIRIT (SOUL MATE) knows exactly what the MALE SPIRIT enjoys, and SHE can excite the MALE in the most SENSUAL and INTIMATE manner for SHE desires exactly what HER MALE desires. What ONE PARTNER experiences during the ACT of LOVE, the other experiences the SAME, with both SHARING in the SAME thoughts and ECSTATIC FEELING, for the TWO become ONE in the ACT of LOVE.

This can be somewhat related to the sexual fantasies that one experiences during physical copulation, which intensifies the feeling of orgasm during climax. However, in the physical form of sex, these feelings are not shared with the partner, and while one may be enjoying the act, the other may not. This is also why one might need imaginary sexual fantasies to reach a climax, for their partner cannot fulfill their sexual desires. And in many cases, the sexual fantasies are not inclusive of the partner, thus making the physical act of two, an intimate act by one; similar to masturbation.

Physical Attraction

Physical attraction is not a lasting attraction, and if there isn't a SPIRITUAL CONNECTION between partners, the relationship will fail. This is because the two partners are drawn together physically rather than SPIRITUALLY, and once the physical act of sex has been performed, neither person has further interest in the other.

Many people select their mate based on physical appearances, and when either of the two people tires of the other's appearance, they no longer have an attraction to them. Most often the two haven't any spiritual bond keeping them together, and in time find that their mate's exterior appearance is no longer sexually appealing. Then once the exterior of either person changes to the others dislike, the relationship fails, generally ending up in separation. Due to the aging process, appearances change, and if the two partners are bound only by a physical attraction, as the appearance of aging sets in, the physical attraction diminishes.

GOD gave the GENTILE their sexual desire by way of a physical attraction of one gender to the other, and did so only to enable them to multiply. The GENTILES did not marry nor were they capable of loving one another; for without a SOUL, LOVE cannot be experienced. The GENTILE males took several females for mates, and when the male tired of his females, he replaced them. This is not what ***GOD*** intended for ***HIS*** CHILDREN; for ADAM was given only EVE to be his mate, and she wasn't chosen by ADAM, but rather given to him by ***GOD.***

While in a carnal form the EARTH has a tendency to dominate one's thoughts and desires, and this includes one's sexual desires. However you need not be like the GENTILE, even though you live among them. ***GOD*** has made ***HIS*** CHILDREN in SPIRIT like ***HIM***, for ***GOD*** is ***SPIRIT.*** If you look to the EARTH to fulfill your desires, you will take on the characteristic of the GENTILE who is a product of the EARTH, just like ADAM and EVE had done, causing their demise. However, if you look to fulfill your SPIRITUAL DESTINY rather than your EARTHLY desires, ***GOD*** will PROVIDE you with the SPIRITUAL GUIDANCE needed to fulfill your DESTINY, by way of THE ***HOLY SPIRIT.***

The coming together of MAN and WOMAN is intended to be a SPIRITUAL MARRIAGE, bound and sanctified in THE ***SPIRIT of GOD.*** And, although on EARTH ONE'S TRUE SPIRITUAL PARTNER cannot be found, another SPIRIT similar in nature to it can be, so look to the SPIRIT of the PERSON, and not to their physical appearance. Let the SPIRIT rather than your hormones, be your GUIDE!

Chapter 11
NUMBERS

Revelation 13:18 *Here is WISDOM. Let him that hath UNDERSTANDING count the NUMBER of the BEAST: for it is the NUMBER of a MAN; and his NUMBER is SIX HUNDRED THREESCORE and SIX.*

After reading this Scripture for the first time, I asked ***THE LORD*** how a man's name could be associated with a NUMBER? ***THE LORD*** then showed ME how each letter in the English Alphabet had a NUMBER assigned to it, based on where the letter falls within the twenty-six letters making up the Alphabet. I was also told at that time that the HOLY BIBLE and its NUMBERS could only be discerned after it had been TRANSLATED into the English language, as King James had done in 1611; however the most recent spelling of the English WORDS needed to be used, rather than the older form used by King James when converting the WORD to a NUMBER.

THE LORD then started to show ME various WORD and NUMBER associations within the BIBLE, and started with the WORD ***"GOD".*** I was shown how the WORD ***"GOD"*** adds up to the NUMBER ***TWENTY-SIX***, because the Letter "G" is the 7th Letter of the Alphabet, the Letter "O" is the 15th Letter, and the Letter "D" is the 4th Letter; and when added together (7+15+4) its sum total equals ***TWENTY-SIX.*** I was told that the English Language is what is spoken in HEAVEN, other than at the THRONE where the HEBREWAH LANGUAGE is SPOKEN; and this is why the English Language has ***TWENTY-SIX*** letters in it, because it is REPRESENTATIVE of ***GOD'S LANGUAGE.***

THE LORD showed ME that the ***SEVEN SPIRITS of GOD*** proceeding from the THRONE of ***GOD*** is REPRESENTED by the NUMBER ***182,*** because the WORD ***"GOD"*** is REPRESENTED by the NUMBER ***"26",*** therefore making the ***SEVEN SPIRITS of GOD*** the SAME as the NUMBER of ***7 x 26*** or the NUMBER ***"182".*** To CONFIRM this personally to ME, I was told by ***THE LORD*** to look at the page in MY BIBLE where MOSES' 4th Book, the Book of

NUMBERS started; and when I did, I found that the Book of NUMBERS in MY BIBLE started on page ***182*** (reference the Nelson 883C "Giant Print" printing of the King James 1611 Version).

Further CONFIRMATIONS were given to ME; I was shown when the WORD "HOLY" is converted to a NUMBER it totals "60", and when the WORD "BIBLE' is converted to a NUMBER it totals "30", and when the WORD "NUMBERS" is converted to a NUMBER it totals "92". And, because the HOLY BIBLE consists of both ***GOD'S*** WORD and ***GOD'S*** NUMBERS, when the WORDS "HOLY BIBLE NUMBERS "are added together they equal the NUMBER ***182,*** thus REPRESENTING the ***SEVEN SPIRITS of GOD*** (The HOLY BIBLE), that which proceeds from the THRONE of ***GOD.***

The following CONVERSION of letters of WORDS to NUMBERS will illustrate what is being said:

H = 8	B = 2	N = 14
O = 15	I = 9	U = 21
L = 12	B = 2	M = 13
Y = 25	L = 12	B = 2
	E = 5	E = 5
		R = 18
		S = 19

or

8 + 15 + 12 + 25 + 2 + 9 + 2 + 12 + 5 + 14 + 21 + 13 + 2 + 5 + 18 + 19 = **182**

After several months of being taught about HOLY WORD and NUMBER association, many of which are covered in "Revealing The Bible's Truth" and "The ROD of IRON", ***THE LORD*** started to show ME how certain NUMBERS applied to ME personally. I was told to add up all of my resident street addresses I had had during the course of my life, and when I did I found that when sum totaled, they equaled the NUMBER ***70,*** just as the NAME ***YAHWEH*** equals the NUMBER ***70*** when converted to a NUMBER.

My first street address number was "1785", and the second was "728", the third was "1168" and my current address number is "7072". Then when I put the addresses into a string of numbers and added them together, I got: 1+7+8+5+7+2+8+1+1+6+8+7+0+7+2 = ***70.***

THE LORD also told ME to ADD up the NUMBERS making up my two major forms of IDENTIFICATION, my Driver's License and Social Security Numbers. My Drivers License has the letter "M" preceding the number, so ***THE LORD*** told ME to replace the "M" with the NUMBER 13, for the letter

"M" is the 13th Letter in the Alphabet. After doing so and adding the NUMBERS making up my Driver's License, they added to the NUMBER "36". I then added the numbers making up MY Social Security Number, and they added to the NUMBER "41". ***THE LORD*** then had ME add the two numbers (36+41) together, and when I did they added to the NUMBER "77", which is the SAME NUMBER as the WORD "CHRIST", for its letters also add to "77".

I was further told to multiply the NUMBERS making up my Social Security Number and divide that NUMBER by the sum total of my Driver's License NUMBER, and when I multiplied the numbers of my Social Security Number it equaled the NUMBER 252,000. I then divided the number 252,000 by the number "36" which is that of my Driver's License, and found it equaled ***7000***, just as the NUMBER of YEARS making up the LIFE CYCLE of the EARTH.

THE LORD told ME that there was a DIRECT SPIRITUAL RELATIONSHIP between JESUS CHRIST and I, and if I were to take the NUMBER of the NAME JESUS (74) and multiply it by the NAME ROBERT (78), it would equal the NUMBER "5772". It was then told to ME that the NUMBER of the WORD "EARTH" is the NUMBER "52", and this is why there are 52 WEEKS in one year. ***GOD*** said the NUMBER "5772" that was the product of the NAMES JESUS and ROBERT had the meaning of "CHRIST amidst the EARTH"; for the NUMBER "77" in "5772" fell between the NUMBERS "5" and "2" in the NUMBER "5772".

THE LORD then had ME divide the NUMBER "5772" by the NUMBER of ***GOD (26)***, and when I did, it equaled the NUMBER ***222***, which REPRESENTS the ***THREE NAMES*** of the ***TRINITY***, ***YAHWEH***, ***IXOTE***, and ***YESHUA***. The following is the exercise in NUMBERS that ***THE LORD*** had ME follow: (The NUMBERS next to the NAMES are the sum totals of the letters making up the NAMES.)

ROBERT = 78	***YAHWEH*** = 70
JESUS = 74	***IXOTE*** = 73
EARTH = 52	***YESHUA*** = 79
78 x 74 = 5772	or
5772 / **26** = **222**	**70 + 73 + 79 = 222**

The Antichrist

After being shown these things, ***THE LORD*** had made it clear to ME how a man's name could be expressed by a NUMBER, and in the case of the Antichrist the NUMBER would be the NUMBER 666. However, when running several sets of test names and CONVERTING them to NUMBERS, none of the NAMES I had tried had sum totaled to a NUMBER greater than 400, and some of the names tested were quite long names having many letters in them. I then confronted ***GOD*** on the matter.

It was then explained to ME that the NUMBER 666 has several meanings. ***THE LORD*** said one of its meanings is that the FIRST 6, in the "666" makes reference to ***GOD'S*** SIXTH DAY CREATION, the GENTILE man, and the SECOND TWO following 6's, make reference to the WORD "WOMAN", for the sum total of the letters making up the WORD "WOMAN", adds to the NUMBER "66". It was explained that the WOMAN referred to in the SECOND set of 6's, referred to both the EARTH (who ***GOD*** calls the WOMAN) and the CHURCH, (who ***GOD*** calls the GREAT WHORE).

Another EXPLANATION of the THREE 6's was also given to ME by ***THE LORD***. ***HE*** said that the THREE 6's also means that the Antichrist will be THREE PERSONS and not only ONE; the DEVIL, the BEAST, and the FALSE PROPHET; and these THREE will all be of the GENTILE, ***GOD'S*** SIXTH DAY CREATION.

NOTE: It was explained earlier in this BOOK that DEMON spirits rarely possesses the CANAANITE, for they don't like to be hosts to one of their own. Therefore the fact that the ANTICHRIST comes through the GENTILE rather than the CANAANITE should come as no surprise; for this only supports that which you have been PREVIOUSLY TOLD!

The FALSE PROPHET

THE LORD then had ME go into the Book of Revelation, specifically Chapter 17, verse 5.

> ***Revelation 17:5*** *And upon her forehead was a name written,* ***MYSTERY, BABYLON THE GREAT, THE MOTHER OF HARLOTS AND ABOMINATIONS OF THE EARTH.***

After reading the Scripture, ***THE LORD*** showed ME how the NAME of the

GREAT WHORE was expressed as a TITLE, rather than only a NAME, and explained how the NUMBER 666 could IDENTIFY ALL THREE of the ANTICHRISTS, the DEVIL, the BEAST, and the FALSE PROPHET. ***GOD*** said that the THREE would have official titles they would go by on the EARTH, and the Beast and the DEVIL would share in the SAME NAME & TITLE, whereas the FALSE PROPHET would go by a TITLE having the same NUMBER as the WORDS "THE EARTH".

I was also told that when the NUMBER of the TITLE of the FALSE PROPHET was added to the NUMBER of the TITLE given in the Scripture of Revelation 17:5, and the NUMBER of the ***SEVEN SPIRITS of GOD (182)*** was taken from it, for it is VOID of THE ***SEVEN SPIRITS of GOD***, the NUMBER 666 would be revealed.

So the first thing I did was to convert the TITLE given in the Scripture of Revelation 17:5 to a NUMBER, and it coverts as follows:

MYSTERY = 125
BABYLON = 71
THE = 33
GREAT = 51
THE = 33
MOTHER = 79
OF = 21
HARLOTS = 93
AND = 19
ABOMINATIONS = 132
OF = 21
THE = 33
EARTH = 52

or

125+71+33+51+33+79+21+93+19+132+21+33+52 = 763

And, although I didn't KNOW the NAME of the TITLE that was to be added to the NUMBER "763", I did know after CONVERTING the Scripture's TITLE to a NUMBER, that the NUMBER of the WORDS "THE EARTH" added to the NUMBER "85". I then added the NUMBER "85" to the NUMBER "763" and arrived at the NUMBER "848" (763 + 85 = 848). After MY doing this ***THE LORD*** reminded ME that the NUMBER of the ***SEVEN SPIR-***

ITS of GOD (7 x 26 =182) was to be taken from the NUMBER 848 for the GREAT WHORE (FALSE PROPHET) is VOID of THE ***HOLY SPIRIT of GOD;*** and when I subtracted ***182*** from the NUMBER 848, I arrived at the NUMBER 666.

All that was needed now for ME to IDENTIFY the FALSE PROPHET, was for ME to find the PERSON whose official title had the same NUMBERS as the WORDS "THE EARTH". So I then asked ***GOD*** for some GUIDANCE, and ***THE LORD*** told ME that the FALSE PROPHET was associated with the CHURCH, and that he considered himself to be ***GOD*** on EARTH.

Not being very familiar with the various religions, I temporarily drew a blank, and was puzzled as to what religious leader of the CHURCH would consider himself to be ***GOD*** on EARTH. But MY answer came shortly thereafter: While listening to a news broadcast, the Commentator of the News Network was interviewing a Priest of the Catholic Church, and in response to one of the questions being asked the Priest, the Priest said that The Pope, whom he called "The Holy Father", was ***GOD*** on "THE EARTH".

I then immediately took the title, "THE POPE", and CONVERTED it to NUMBERS. After CONVERTING the WORDS, "THE POPE", to NUMBERS, it was REVEALED to ME that they were IDENTICAL to the NUMBERS of the WORDS "THE EARTH"! (The NUMBERS in parenthesis after each WORD is the sum of the letters making up the WORD).

THE (33) EARTH (52) = 85
THE (33) POPE (52) = 85

Regardless of what any CHURCH says, no man can consider himself to be GOD, or be called GOD. This is clearly stated throughout the HOLY BIBLE, and any such person or organization that follows after this order is DESTINED for HELL, ***SAITH THE LORD.*** Even THE ***DELIVERER 182,*** whom is THE ***HOLY SPIRIT*** in the FORM of a MAN, does not refer to ***HIMSELF*** as ***GOD,*** albeit ***HE*** could, should ***HE*** so DESIRE. The reference in the Scripture, Revelation 17:5, to "**BABYLON THE GREAT**", refers to King Neb-u-chad-nez'-zar of Babylon, for he also considered himself to be ***GOD***, as does the FALSE PROPHET.

The DEVIL and the BEAST

As previously stated, the DEVIL and the BEAST share in the same EARTHLY NAME & TITLE, but ***THE LORD*** will not allow ME at this time to disclose both the TITLE and NAMES of them in their entirety. However, I can in partiality disclose parts of the NAME & TITLE they both will share. This sharing in NAME & TITLE will continue up until the time that the DEVIL, Lucifer, is proclaimed by the 2nd BEAST to be "THE GOD OF FORCES". Then after the 2nd BEAST proclaims the 1st BEAST to be "THE GOD OF FORCES", only the 2nd BEAST will continue with the TITLE bearing the NUMBER 666.

The NAME & TITLE:

_ _ _ _ G _   _ E _ _ _ _ T   _ _ _ K _ _   _ _ S _ ,
the 4 _ _ _ President of the United States of America.

Once the proper letters are put into the blank spaces in the NAME & TITLE, the NUMBER 743 will be the sum of the LETTERS and NUMBERS. Then when the NUMBER of the WORD, CHRIST (77), is removed from the NUMBER 743 (for they are the Antichrist (-77)), the NUMBER 666 will be REVEALED.

At this point in time neither the PERSON whom will play HOST to the DEVIL, nor the PERSON who will play HOST to the BEAST are aware of their TRUE IDENTITIES. It will not be made known to them until after the FIRST TRUMPET has SOUNDED and the DEVIL, Lucifer, has been cast down to the EARTH. Then shortly thereafter they will KNOW who they are; for they will be empowered by the DEVIL to commit atrocities of evil that will be beyond imagination.

After Empowerment

The empowerment given to the 1st and 2nd BEASTS occurs at the same instance as does the RAPTURE; for at that time, THE ***HOLY SPIRIT*** leaves the EARTH as the ***DELIVERER 182 PERSON,*** taking with ***HIM*** "THE BRIDE of CHRIST". This is why the NUMBER ***182*** is taken from the NUMBER of the FALSE PROPHET, for the FALSE PROPHET will not be empowered and take control of the CHURCH until after THE ***HOLY SPIRIT*** has left the EARTH.

Religion of all sorts will then run amuck throughout the world, and the FALSE PROPHET will cleverly invent an explanation as to what happened to the 10,400,000 PEOPLE who had suddenly VANISHED from the EARTH without a trace, but he will not call it RAPTURE. Those who had been LEFT BEHIND by their loved ones will find his explanation difficult to believe, but they will force themselves to believe it, because they will be in denial and refuse to believe that they had been left behind.

Many of them that had been LEFT BEHIND will curse ***GOD,*** for they will say they had dedicated their lives to serving ***HIM,*** and were not appreciated for their service. Then those who do curse ***GOD*** will have sealed their own fate for they are DESTINED for HELL!

NUMBERS of IMPORTANCE

There are certain NUMBERS that identify KEY WORDS making up the *WORD of* ***GOD***, and WE will list some of those WORDS. However FIRST, to enlighten your UNDERSTANDING prior to giving you those WORD/NUMBER associations, WE will take you into the Scriptures of the Book of Revelation to show you how the NUMBERS complement the *WORD of* ***GOD*** and aid in the PROPER INTERPRETATION of the Scripture.

> ***Revelation 12:1*** *And there appeared a GREAT WONDER in HEAVEN; a WOMAN clothed with the sun, and the moon under HER feet, and upon HER head a CROWN of TWELVE stars:*

> ***Revelation 12:2*** *And SHE being with CHILD cried, travailing in BIRTH, and pained to be DELIVERED.*

As previous told to you in this Chapter, ***GOD*** refers to the EARTH as a WOMAN. In the first Scripture, the WOMAN is said to be clothed with the sun, and the moon under HER FEET. This refers to the EARTH at high noon, for when the sun is above and shining upon the earth, the moon is not visible, similar to if the EARTH was standing over it and shadowing the moon. The WOMAN is also said to be wearing a CROWN of TWELVE STARS. The NUMBER TWELVE represents the EARTH'S twelve months, ***GOD'S*** CHILDREN (the TWELVE TRIBES of ISRAEL), and the TWELVE Disciples who carried forward to *WORD of* ***GOD*** given to them by JESUS CHRIST. The TWELVE STARS represent TWELVE LIGHTS, and the WORD "LIGHT" represents the "TRUTH" given in the GOSPELS, both that which was WRITTEN, and also that which all TWELVE of the Disciples had PREACHED on the EARTH, by WORD of MOUTH.

The WOMAN, in the second verse, is also said to be PREGNANT and bearing a CHILD, and having labor pains, thus indicating that the TIME of BIRTH is near. The "CHILD" represents the NEWBORN CHILD in CHRIST, ***GOD'S***

CHILDREN, who are waiting to be BORN in CHRIST through ***HOLY SPIRIT*** BAPTISM, and COME out of the EARTH, much like a baby is DELIVERED out of the mother's WOMB. However, the next two Scriptures WARN of how the DEVIL wants to DESTROY the CHILD, as soon as it is BORN.

> ***Revelation 12:3*** *And there appeared another wonder in HEAVEN; and behold a GREAT RED DRAGON, having seven heads and ten horns, and seven crowns upon his heads.*

> ***Revelation 12:4*** *And his tail drew the third part of the stars of HEAVEN, and did cast them to the EARTH: and the DRAGON stood before the WOMAN which was ready to be DELIVERED, for to DEVOUR HER CHILD as soon as it was BORN.*

As explained in Chapter 6 of this BOOK, the seven heads on the GREAT RED DRAGON represent the seven names given to Lucifer after his falling from the GRACE of ***GOD***. The ten horns represent the ten Chief fallen angels whom Lucifer has empowered over HELL, and they serve in his regime and administer the evil he so delights in. The seven crowns upon the seven heads represents the power that ***THE LORD*** has given Lucifer over the EARTH; and the Scripture says, regardless of which of the seven names may be used to IDENTIFY him, his power is not restrained.

The one-third of the stars in HEAVEN that he did cast to the EARTH represent the ONE-THIRD of the Angels in HEAVEN that followed Lucifer in his revolt against ***GOD,*** and were cast out with him. The Scripture then explains how Lucifer waits until the time of SPIRITUAL BAPTISM, and then prior to CONFIRMATION of the BAPTISM, tempts the NEWBORN CHILD in CHRIST to sin, thus causing their demise. This failure in BAPTISM only applies to the WEDDING GUESTS during their time of TRIAL and TRIBULATION, for CONFIRMATION of BAPTISM is instantaneous for the BRIDE of CHRIST. However the vast MAJORITY of them to be SAVED are of the WEDDING GUESTS.

You should by now be able to SEE how NUMBERS assist in the PROPER INTERPRETATION of the Scriptures and unveil the TRUTH within them. UNDERSTANDING NUMBERS and applying them properly to a Scripture, PRESENT the Scripture to the SPIRIT in a COMPLETE FORM, allowing the SPIRIT to REALIZE the ENTIRE MESSAGE and not just a portion of it. The following is a list of IMPORTANT NUMBERS for you to remember and apply when READING Scripture.

TRINITY NUMBERS:

The NUMBER ***111*** is the FIRST NUMBER of the ***TRINITY.*** It represents UNITY within the ***TRINITY*** between ***THE FATHER, THE SON,*** and THE ***HOLY SPIRIT.*** The NUMBER ***111*** also REPRESENTS a PLACE where ***GOD*** has put ***HIS NAME,*** and can be arrived at when the NAMES ***SHILOH (71)*** and ***BANDS (40)*** are CONVERTED to NUMBERS and ***COMBINED.***

The NUMBER ***222*** is the SECOND NUMBER of the ***TRINITY***, and it REPRESENTS the ***THREE NAMES of GOD*** within the ***TRINITY, YAHWEH (70), IXOTE (73)*** and ***YESHUA (79).*** When the NUMBER of the ***THREE*** is ***COMBINED*** it equals the NUMBER ***222.***

The NUMBER ***333*** is the THIRD and FINAL NUMBER of the ***TRINITY.*** It REPRESENTS the ***SEVEN SPIRITS of GOD (222)*** COMBINED with the NAMES ***SHILOH (71)*** and ***BANDS (40).*** It also REPRESENTS the ***SEVEN SPIRITS of GOD*** expressed in a NUMERIC FORM ***(7 x 26 = 182)*** and when ***COMBINED*** with the NUMBER of THE ***HOLY SPIRIT (151)*** or the NAME JESUS (74) CHRIST (77) (74 + 77 = 151) it yields the NUMBER ***333 (182 + 151 = 333).***

Other TRIPLICATE NUMBERS:

The NUMBER 444 represents the SONS of ***GOD,*** the FOUR SERAPHIM, the FOUR COVENANT ANGELS, and the BRIDE of CHRIST.

The NUMBER 555 represents the CHURCH and the WEDDING GUESTS.

The NUMBER 666 represents the "Mark of the Beast" and ETERNAL DAMNATION.

The NUMBER ***777*** REPRESENTS the ***WRATH of GOD,*** and the END!

TWIN NUMBERS:

The NUMBER 11 represents the TWO COMINGS of CHRIST to the EARTH.

The NUMBER ***44*** REPRESENTS the WORDS, ***GODHEAD (44),*** ABRAHAM (44), JUDAH (44) and ***FAITH (44).***

The NUMBER 66 represents the WORD, "WOMAN (66)" or the female GENTILE. The NUMBER 69 can also represent "WOMAN" as being pregnant with child.

The NUMBER ***77*** REPRESENTS the NAME, CHRIST (77) and the WORDS, "POWER (77)" and "GLORY (77)".

The NUMBER 88 REPRESENTS the NAME ***IMMANUEL (88),*** which means as ONE with ***GOD,*** or UNITY in ***GOD,*** ONENESS.

The NUMBER 99 refers to RAPTURE (99).

Other IMPORTANT NUMBERS:

The NUMBER 6 refers to ***GOD'S*** SIXTH DAY CREATION, specifically the GENTILE male.

The NUMBER *7* REPRESENTS ***GOD'S COMPLETENESS,*** or ***FINALITY.*** The NUMBER *7* has been HALLOWED unto ***GOD,*** and anything bearing the NUMBER *7* BELONGS to ***GOD.***

The NUMBER 8 refers to UNITY and also to INFINITY when the 8 is turned on its side.

The ***NUMBER 9*** is the NUMBER of THE ***HOLY SPIRIT,*** for ***HE*** brings with ***HIM 9 GIFTS,*** and both ***HIS*** CREATION of HEAVEN and HELL have 9 LEVELS. The NAME ***IXOTE*** is preceded with the Roman Numeral NINE (IX) and its HEBREWAH TRANSLATION into English means the NUMBER ***98, DELIVERANCE (98)*** and THE ***DELIVERER (98).***

The NUMBER 10 is the NUMBER of DECEPTION and refers to individuals or organizations that are DECEPTIVE in NATURE. Lucifer was the TENTH ANGEL created in HEAVEN and Judas Iscariot was the TENTH Disciple picked by JESUS CHRIST.

The NUMBER 12 REPRESENTS ***GOD'S*** CHILDREN, the 12 Disciples of JESUS CHRIST, and the 12 MONTHS of the year. The NUMBER 12 also REPRESENTS ***GOD'S*** DIVISION, outside of the ***TRINITY (GODHEAD).***

The NUMBER 13 REPRESENTS the SONS of ***GOD.***

The ***NUMBER 26*** refers to ***GOD*** and ***GOD'S LANGUAGE*** (English).

The NUMBER 28 represents both the WORD "MAN (28)" and the WORD "LAMB (28)".

The NUMBER 30 represents the WORD, "EAGLE (30)", and it also refers to ***DELIVERANCE.***

The NUMBER 36 represents both the WORDS "LAW (36)" and "FEET (36)" and it refers to the DELIVERANCE of the LAW.

The NUMBER 41 makes reference to the WORD "KING (41)".

The NUMBER 49 refers to the WORD "LORD (49)", for it is ***SEVEN SQUARED.***

The NUMBER 52 refers to the WORD "EARTH (52)" and represents something of the EARTH relating to TIME; for there are 52 weeks in the yearly cycle of the EARTH.

Significant NUMBERS:

The ***NUMBER 182*** REPRESENTS the NUMERICAL EXPRESSION of the ***SEVEN SPIRITS of GOD*** PROCEEDING from the THRONE of ***GOD.***

The NUMBER ***151*** REPRESENTS the NAMES, ***LORD of HOSTS (151),***

HOLY SPIRIT (151) and JESUS CHRIST (151).

The NUMBER ***152*** REPRESENTS the ***COMBINED NUMBERS of the NAMES*** of ***IXOTE (73)*** and ***YESHUA (79)*** and the NAMES of ROBERT (78) and JESUS (74). It may also be NOTED that when the WORD "EAGLE (30)" is added to either of the TWO NAME COMBINATIONS, the ***NUMBER*** is ***182,*** that of THE ***DELIVERER.***

The NUMBER 153 REPRESENTS MIRACULOUS EVENTS, and also DEPICTS the FIRST and LAST MIRACLE of JESUS CHRIST while on EARTH. JESUS' FIRST MIRACLE was the CONVERSION of 15 firkins of water into 153 gallons of WINE and HIS LAST MIRACLE was the catching of 153 fish in the Disciples net.

NOTE: When converting firkins to gallons, there are 10.2 gallons per firkin.

As you become more familiar with the Scriptures and CONVERT KEY WORDS to NUMBERS, you will SEE that the NUMBERS WE have given YOU repeatedly appear throughout THE HOLY BIBLE. And, only the King James 1611 TRANSLATION of the HOLY Scriptures into the English Language will yield the CORRECT NUMBERS.

Chapter 12
MIRACLES

What construes a MIRACLE? The Dictionary explains a miracle to be an EVENT that takes place that cannot be explained by the use of the "Laws of Nature". However, the more correct explanation of a MIRACLE, is, ***GOD'S*** intervention into a set of circumstances, changing the expected, into the unexpected.

JESUS' MIRACLES

While on EARTH, JESUS performed many MIRACLES. The Disciple John said:

> ***John 21:24*** *This is the Disciple that testifieth of these things, and wrote these things: and we know that his testimony is true.*
>
> ***John 21:25*** *And there are also many other things which JESUS did, the which, if they should be written every one, I suppose that even the world itself could not contain the books that should be written. A-men'.*

These last two Scriptures are the closing statements made by the Disciple John in the "GOSPEL According to John". John was very cautious as to what he wrote about JESUS, and only recorded the EVENTS he had personally experienced with JESUS. Even though John believed many of the things he had been told by Mary, the Mother of JESUS, and by the other Disciples, he only wrote about that which he himself had seen and experienced. This is one of the reasons why John was given the Revelation of JESUS CHRIST to write, rather than it being given to one of the other Disciples.

John says in the final Scriptures of his GOSPEL, in his closing statement, that JESUS performed so many MIRACLES that if they were to be written into BOOKS, there would be so many BOOKS the world itself could not contain them. Was John exaggerating in his statement, or did he really mean what he had written? John meant every WORD he had wrote, in his GOSPEL, and also in the Book of Revelation, for they are both error free!

Shortly after JESUS' ***HOLY SPIRIT*** BAPTISM, HE began to perform MIRACLES, starting with the making of water into wine, and ending with HIS filling the Disciples net with 153 fish. In between those two MIRACLES, JESUS performed MIRACLE after MIRACLE over a three-year span, many of which went unnoticed by HIS Disciples until after HE had left the EARTH and they came to REALIZE what HE had done.

JESUS made the blind to SEE, the deaf to HEAR, HE healed the SICK, and calmed the seas; HE even gave LIFE after DEATH. All the MIRACLES that JESUS once performed, continue on, albeit, HE does so now in the SPIRIT, that which HE had done previously in the FLESH. These MIRACLES continue on even this day, and they shall never cease ***SAITH THE LORD,*** for they are ongoing.

Over the past two thousand years, since JESUS' DEPARTURE, if every person touched by JESUS CHRIST were to write a BOOK on the events and MIRACLES taking place in their lives after their BAPTISM, the world itself could not contain those BOOKS. JESUS continues to perform MIRACLES and has not ceased in doing so since HIS ***HOLY SPIRIT*** BAPTISM. JESUS LIVES ON, AND SO DO HIS MIRACLES!

GOD PERFORMS MIRACLES

I have seen with my own EYES what ***THE LORD*** can do, and it is LIMITLESS! ***GOD*** can do whatsoever ***HE*** chooses to do, as often as ***HE*** so desires, and ***GOD*** LOVES to PERFORM MIRACLES. One of the most WONDERFUL things about ***THE LORD*** is ***HIS*** COMPASSION towards them who LOVE and WORSHIP ***HIM. GOD*** WILL PERFORM MIRACLE after MIRACLE for them whom ***HE*** LOVES.

I have asked ***THE LORD*** to do MANY things for ME, and only a few of the things I have asked for thus far, has ***HE*** yet to GIVE ME. ALL the other things I have asked for ***HE*** has done, with ***HIM*** telling ME to be patient and wait for the things that ***HE*** has not yet done, for they will SURELY come to pass. Furthermore, what ***THE LORD*** has done for ME thus far, is even better than that which I had EXPECTED! In each and every circumstance I have RECEIVED MORE than I had asked for. However, when ***GOD*** ANSWERS MY PRAYERS, they are always ANSWERED in a DIFFERENT WAY than how I had expected.

When I ask ***GOD*** for something, I usually get an immediate ANSWER from

HIM, whether it is a YES, or a NO to MY SUPPLICATION, and in the past year and a half it has always been a YES ANSWER! Once ***THE LORD*** has told ME ***HE*** will grant ME my request, I most often try to figure out how ***HE*** will do it. However, I can tell you to date, MY assessment of how I think ***GOD*** will GRANT MY request has thus far been WRONG every time.

I am very close to ***THE LORD,*** however ***HE*** never tells ME how ***HE*** intends to do something, even though ***HE*** tells ME what ***HE*** is going to do before ***HE*** does it. I BELIEVE ***GOD*** does this, not to keep ME in the dark, but rather does so to add excitement to the EVENT when it comes to pass, for then the EVENT is unexpected. It is the unexpected that makes the MIRACLE a MIRACLE, for if it is expected it can then be explained, and if it can be explained, it is not a MIRACLE.

Things Don't Just Happen!

Most of ***GOD'S*** MIRACLES appear to be things that just happen, however, I can assure you that NOTHING, just happens. ***GOD*** enjoys being COVERT in ***HIS*** actions, and DELIGHTS in MAN'S curious nature, by him always trying to figure out ***THE LORD***. MAN always feels the need to explain away what ***THE LORD*** has done, and when he hasn't any answers, it tickles ***THE LORD*** to see him in his frustration. This is especially TRUE when MAN is forced to explain the EVENT as being a RANDOM act or a COINCIDENCE; because there aren't such things as RANDOM ACTS, and nothing is COINCIDENTAL, ***SAITH THE LORD.***

Things don't just happen, for if that were so, then there would be certain things outside of ***GOD'S*** CONTROL, and NOTHING is outside of ***GOD'S CONTROL!*** Everything that happens has a REASON for it happening, therefore leaving NOTHING to CHANCE, for ALL THINGS that HAPPEN are PREDETERMINED by ***GOD.***

GOD is not like a MAN, ***HE*** has no boundaries of TIME nor is ***HE*** limited in what ***HE*** can do. This is why ***GOD*** cannot LIE, for by ***HIS VOICE*** alone can ***HE*** INVERT the UNIVERSE and fold it within itself. FURTHERMORE, what ***GOD*** says, IS, and ***HE*** can make whatsoever ***HE*** chooses into ANYTHING at any time, and no person or spiritual entity can keep ***GOD*** from doing what ***HE*** wants to do.

GOD HIMSELF is a MIRACLE that goes on throughout ETERNITY, who has no explanation as to ***HIS*** COMPLEXITY or MAKEUP. ***HE*** does not need to think, for ***HE*** is ALL KNOWING, and by ***HIS*** WISDOM ***GOD*** can do as ***HE*** so pleases without restraint or limitation.

Simply look around you and SEE ***GOD'S MIRACLES.*** A world that is self-supportive, continually producing life, and the necessities needed to support that life. A world with seasons needed for the various trees and plant life to exist, having its own water supply that continually recycles itself from sea to land. A world that produces an air supply suitable to sustain human and animal life, and trees and plants that use man's spent air and make new air from it. These MIRACLES happen routinely, yet the people who need them for their very own existence, take the MIRACLES for granted, and fail to THANK ***GOD*** for them.

Life in itself is a MIRACLE of ***GOD***; Mankind, animals, fish, trees, and plants that reproduce from their own seed maintaining their existence throughout the generations, as long as the world in which they live continues to cycle and support them. When one of the world's species dies out, ***GOD,*** to replace them CREATES another; and the regeneration of life continues on as long as the world supportive of life continues on.

These things did not just happen. The world in which you live did not just happen!

MIRACLES turned to WRATH

Soon you will all SEE the POWER and the MIGHT of the ***ALMIGHTY GOD,*** for the days of ***HIM*** being COVERT are SOON to come to an end, and ***HE*** will then let ***HIS PRESENCE*** be known to the WORLD.

> ***Revelation 6:14*** *And the heaven departed as a scroll when it is rolled together; and every mountain and island were moved out of their places.*
>
> ***Revelation 6:15*** *And the kings of the EARTH, and the great men, and the rich men, and the chief captains, and the mighty men, and every bondman, and every free man, hid themselves in the dens and in the rocks of the mountains;*
>
> ***Revelation 6:16*** *And said to the mountains and rocks, FALL ON US, and HIDE US from the* ***FACE of HIM*** *that sitteth on THE THRONE, and from the WRATH of THE LAMB:*
>
> ***Revelation 6:17*** *For the GREAT DAY of* ***HIS WRATH*** *is come; and who shall be able to stand?*

The many MIRACLES happening daily that the world has come to take for granted will ABRUPTLY END over the course of the GREAT TRIBULATION. The seasons will deteriorate and the rain will be scarce ***SAITH THE LORD of HOSTS.*** This will be a TIME when ***GOD'S MIRACLES*** are turned into ***HIS WRATH.***

The WIND and the SEAS will be disrupted, the CROPS will CEASE, and the TREES will shed their leaves in the SPRING and will no longer bring forth FRUIT. There will be DRAUGHT and FAMINE throughout the world, the likes of which have never been seen since its very existence. The MAGNETIC POLARITY of the EARTH will be REVERSED, thus making the NORTH POLE the SOUTH POLE, for ***GOD*** will magnetically TURN the EARTH UPSIDE DOWN.

GOD PERFORMED many MIRACLES through JESUS CHRIST, so MANKIND through JESUS might RECEIVE FAITH in ***GOD,*** and many have. However many, many, more have not ***SAITH THE LORD of HOSTS,*** and them who have not WILL SEE and FEEL ***MY WRATH.*** THE ***TIME FOR MIRACLES TO TURN TO WRATH COMES VERY SOON, IT IS EVEN AT THE DOOR; AND WHEN IT KNOCKS, THE DOOR SHALL BE OPENED, AND A TIME FOR REPENTANCE WILL HAVE PASSED, SAITH THE LORD of HOSTS!***

Once the FIRST TRUMPET SOUNDS and the GREAT TRIBULATION begins, only those who have been MARKED and SEALED by the ***LIVING GOD*** will continue to RECEIVE MIRACLES. ALL the others left upon the face of the EARTH will SEE ***GOD'S MIRACLES*** turn to WRATH

Chapter 13
Welcome HOLY SPIRIT; THE DELIVERER 182

THE LORD has told ME that THE ***DELIVERER 182 PERSON*** is on the EARTH at this TIME, and has already been made aware of both ***HIS IDENTITY*** and ***HIS PURPOSE*** for being here! I have been told to detail ***HIS DESCRIPTION*** in this Chapter through the Biblical Scripture given about ***HIM,*** and to note certain KEY EVENTS that ***HE*** will TRIGGER by ***HIS PRESENCE*** on the EARTH.

THE ***DELIVERER*** at this time has with ***HIM*** FIVE ANGELS of the SEVENTH LEVEL. However the ANGELS are currently in SPIRIT ONLY and have not yet taken on a carnal form to accompany ***HIM*** during ***HIS*** mission; but that will SOON CHANGE. The people who have known this MAN haven't any idea as to ***HIS*** TRUE ***IDENTITY,*** and those who know ***HIM*** see ***HIM*** now only on occasion, whereas before ***HIS*** PRESENCE was routine.

THE LORD has PURPOSELY ISOLATED this MAN from family and friends for their own PROTECTION, because SINNING against ***HIM*** in ***HIS*** current SPIRITUAL STATE will not be FORGIVEN ***SAITH THE LORD. THE LORD*** says, there are some that have already SINNED AGAINST ***HIM,*** but they are unaware of what they have done and what price they must pay for their actions; even though they had unknowingly BLASPHEMED THE ***HOLY SPIRIT.*** This a CRITICAL TIME for the world, and although those who SINNED against ***HIM*** were not aware of what they had done, it has cost them their ETERNITY, ***SAITH THE LORD of HOSTS! FOR SINCE THE FALL OF LUCIFER, ANY BLASPHEMY AGAINST THE HOLY SPIRIT SEALS ONE'S FATE IN HELL!***

Reference:

> ***Isaiah 41:4*** *Who hath wrought and done it, calling the generations from the BEGINNING?* ***I THE LORD, THE FIRST, AND <u>WITH</u> THE LAST; I AM HE.***

Genesis 6:3 *And* ***THE LORD*** *said,* ***MY SPIRIT SHALL NOT ALWAYS STRIVE WITH MAN, FOR THAT HE ALSO IS FLESH:*** *yet* ***HIS*** *days shall be an hundred and twenty years.*

Matthew 12:31 WHEREFORE I SAY UNTO YOU, ALL MANNER OF SIN AND BLASPHEMY SHALL BE FORGIVEN UNTO MEN: BUT THE BLASPHEMY AGAINST THE HOLY GHOST SHALL NOT BE FORGIVEN UNTO MEN.

Matthew 12:32 AND WHOSOEVER SPEAKETH A WORD AGAINST THE SON OF MAN, IT SHALL BE FORGIVEN HIM: BUT WHOSOEVER SPEAKETH AGAINST THE HOLY GHOST, IT SHALL NOT BE FORGIVEN HIM, NEITHER IN THIS WORLD, NEITHER IN THE WORLD TO COME.

I have been told that there are FIVE people thus far that have SINNED against THE ***DELIVERER 182.*** And, while ALL but one of the FIVE believed they would go to HEAVEN, they will not, and are now DESTINED for HELL. At the TIME of JUDGMENT, these people will be cast into the LAKE of FIRE whose FLAME cannot be QUENCHED, and there they shall remain FOREVER ***SAITH THE LORD!***

There is also in addition to the FIVE, ONE, who is of the Angel that has also SINNED against ***MY DELIVERER SAITH THE LORD.*** And even though she has a DIVINE RIGHT to HEAVEN, she shall spend her days outside of it and guard the Gates of HELL.

JESUS said that you should LOVE one another, and not JUDGE each other, and HE also WARNED about SINNING against THE ***HOLY SPIRIT.*** If any of the FIVE had FOLLOWED the DIRECTION given by JESUS rather than their own minds and had taken heed to HIS WARNINGS, their SOULS could have been SAVED. But now it is too late ***SAITH THE LORD, WHAT IS DONE IS DONE!***

THE DELIVERER'S DESCRIPTION According to Habakkuk

The Prophet Habakkuk was given a VISION in regard to THE ***DELIVERER'S JUDGMENT*** of the world. The VISION told Habakkuk of THE ***DELIVERER'S COMING*** and also gave a DESCRIPTION of ***HIM*** and how the CHURCH would criticize ***HIM*** once ***HIS PRESENCE*** was known.

The Scriptures say that ***HE*** will be called a DRUNKARD, a SINNER, and a PERSON PROCLAIMING ***HIMSELF*** to be someone ***HE*** is not.

I found the Scriptures of Habakkuk to be somewhat ironic, for the CHURCH will SEE THE ***DELIVERER*** in much the same manner as the JEWS saw JESUS CHRIST; for they also called JESUS a DRUNKARD, a SINNER, and said HE was PROCLAIMING HIMSELF to be someone HE was not!

Reference:

> ***Matthew 11:18 FOR JOHN CAME NEITHER EATING NOR DRINKING, AND THEY SAY, HE HATH A DEVIL.***
>
> ***Matthew 11:19 THE SON OF MAN CAME EATING AND DRINKING, AND THEY SAY, BEHOLD A MAN GLUTTONOUS, AND A WINEBIBBER, A FRIEND OF PUBLICANS AND SINNERS. BUT WISDOM IS JUSTIFIED OF HER CHILDREN.***
>
> ***John 8:13*** *The Pharisees therefore said unto HIM, Thou bearest record of thyself; thy record is not true.*
>
> ***John 8:14*** *JESUS answered and said unto them,* ***THOUGH I BEAR RECORD OF MYSELF, YET MY RECORD IS TRUE: FOR I KNOW WHENCE I CAME, AND WHITHER I GO; BUT YE CANNOT TELL WHENCE I COME, AND WHITHER I GO.***

There are a great deal of similarities between the PERSONALITIES of THE ***DELIVERER*** and JESUS CHRIST. However, JESUS came to SAVE the world, whereas THE ***DELIVERER*** will JUDGE it, REMOVE the WORTHY from it, and then DESTROY IT! The MAJOR differences between the TWO, is that JESUS FORGIVES one of their SINS, whereas THE ***DELIVERER*** CONDEMNS them that SIN AGAINST ***HIM; SO BEWARE!***

THE LORD has told ME that whosoever SINS against THE ***DELIVERER 182*** commits the UNFORGIVABLE SIN, and if that person's NAME is entered into the ***LAMBS BOOK of LIFE*** at the TIME of their SIN, their name SHALL be REMOVED. This is TRUE regardless of what that person may or may not have done prior to their SINNING against THE ***HOLY SPIRIT.*** This would apply to even a person who had spent their entire life in the service of ***GOD;*** for there are NO EXCEPTIONS ***SAITH THE LORD of HOSTS!***

As WE proceed into the Scriptures of the Book of Habakkuk, you shall SEE that the ***PERSON*** of THE ***HOLY SPIRIT*** (THE ***182*** PERSON) is QUITE DIFFERENT than any of the others that have COME before ***HIM.*** Scripture describes ***HIM*** as being a heavy drinker and also a very PROUD PERSON, whose ACTIONS and WORDS appear to be quite controversial to them that believe they themselves are serving ***GOD.*** They will find both ***HIS WORDS*** and ***HIS ACTIONS*** to be OFFENSIVE and will be public in their denunciations of ***HIM,*** thus causing their own DEMISE.

There will be MANY of the CHURCH and CLERGY that will be made to endure the GREAT TRIBULATION by their denouncing of ***HIM,*** who would have otherwise RECEIVED RAPTURE. Only them called "THE BRIDE of CHRIST" will BELIEVE ***HIM*** to be who ***HE*** proclaims ***HIMSELF*** to be, and this is why ONLY the "BRIDE of CHRIST" is taken in the FIRST RAPTURE.

Shortly after the RAPTURE of the "BRIDE", those left behind will KNOW that their failure in RECOGNIZING THE ***DELIVERER 182*** has caused them to endure much PAIN and SUFFERING. However, at that time it will be too late for them to do anything about it. They must now SURVIVE the GREAT TRIBULATION and the "Mark of the Beast", for this will be the PUNISHMENT that ***GOD*** has levied upon them.

The WARNING:

> ***Habakkuk 2:2*** *And* ***THE LORD*** *answered me, and said,* ***WRITE THE VISION, AND MAKE IT PLAIN UPON THE TABLES, THAT HE MAY RUN THAT READETH IT.***
>
> ***Habakkuk 2:3 FOR THE VISION IS FOR AN <u>APPOINTED TIME</u>, BUT AT THE <u>END</u> IT SHALL SPEAK, AND NOT LIE: THOUGH IT TARRY, WAIT FOR IT; BECAUSE IT WILL SURELY COME, IT WILL NOT TARRY.***

NOTE: In these last two Scriptures, ***THE LORD*** is telling Habakkuk about the coming of THE ***DELIVERER 182 PERSON,*** and how them who may READ and UNDERSTAND the Scriptures about ***HIM***, should be FEARFUL of ***HIM***. ***THE LORD*** says that the VISION is SET for an APPOINTED TIME, at the "END TIME". ***GOD*** tells Habakkuk, the ***182 PERSON*** shall SPEAK only the TRUTH, because ***HE*** cannot LIE. The Scripture further says that THE ***HOLY SPIRIT'S PRESENCE*** on the EARTH in ***SPIRIT,*** will linger for a LONG period of TIME (***THOUGH IT TARRY***) and that one should patiently wait for BAPTISM in the ***SPIRIT,*** while THE ***SPIRIT*** is still in a SPIRITUAL FORM. The THIRD LAYER of the Scripture says, once THE ***HOLY SPIRIT*** takes on the FORM of a MAN, as THE ***DELIVERER 182, HE*** will no longer

TARRY; meaning, ***HE*** will leave the EARTH shortly thereafter. This is a WARNING to anyone who hasn't yet been BAPTIZED; for once THE ***HOLY SPIRIT*** takes on the FORM of THE ***DELIVERER 182 PERSON***, BAPTISM in the SPIRIT can no longer take place.

> ***Habakkuk 2:4 BEHOLD HIS SOUL WHICH IS LIFTED UP IS NOT UPRIGHT IN HIM: BUT THE JUST SHALL LIVE BY HIS FAITH.***

NOTE: The Scripture states that which WE have previously TOLD you: The ***PERSON*** of THE ***HOLY SPIRIT*** is REVERSED from ALL of the others in the SPIRIT of ***GOD. HE*** comes FIRST in the ***SPIRIT*** and then in the FLESH, rather than first in the flesh and then in the SPIRIT, as does everyone else on EARTH bearing THE SPIRIT ***of GOD***. The Scripture also CONFIRMS that a PERSON can only be SAVED and RECEIVE "AFTERLIFE", by their RECEIVING the GIFT of FAITH through ***HOLY SPIRIT*** BAPTISM ("*But the JUST shall LIVE by* ***HIS*** *FAITH*"). FAITH is the 1st GIFT GIVEN by THE ***HOLY SPIRIT*** and ONE cannot be SAVED and RECEIVE an AFTERLIFE without it!

> ***Habakkuk 2:5 YEA ALSO, BECAUSE HE TRANSGRESSETH BY WINE, HE IS A PROUD MAN, NEITHER KEEPETH AT HOME, WHO ENLARGETH HIS DESIRE AS HELL, AND IS AS DEATH, AND CANNOT BE SATISFIED, BUT GATHERETH UNTO HIM ALL NATIONS, AND HEAPETH UNTO HIM ALL PEOPLE.***

NOTE: The last Scripture IDENTIFIES THE ***DELIVERER 182*** as being a drinker of alcohol and a PROUD person. It also says that this ***PERSON*** is quite cautious as to what ***HE*** may bring into ***HIS*** home, and allows nothing pertaining to EVIL (death or HELL) to come into it. It further states that THE ***DELIVERER 182*** will take the control of the EARTH and its PEOPLE back from the DEVIL, so ***HE*** may give them to ***HIS SON***, JESUS CHRIST to RULE OVER, as it has been so NOTED in the Scriptures.

Reference:

> ***Daniel 7:13*** *I saw in the night VISIONS, and, BEHOLD, ONE like the SON of MAN came with the CLOUDS of HEAVEN, and came to the* ***ANCIENT of DAYS****, and they brought HIM near before* ***HIM.***

Daniel 7:14 *And there was given HIM DOMINION, and GLORY, and a KINGDOM, that ALL PEOPLE, NATIONS, and LANGUAGES, should serve HIM: HIS dominion is an EVERLASTING DOMINION, which shall not pass away, and HIS KINGDOM that which shall not be destroyed.*

The Rebuking by the CHURCH:

Habakkuk 2:6 SHALL NOT ALL THESE TAKE UP A PARABLE AGAINST HIM, AND A TAUNTING PROVERB AGAINST HIM, AND SAY, WOE TO HIM THAT INCREASETH THAT WHICH IS NOT HIS! HOW LONG? AND TO HIM THAT LADETH HIMSELF WITH THICK CLAY!

NOTE: This Scripture says that the CHURCH and its LEADERSHIP will publicly DENOUNCE THE ***DELIVERER 182 PERSON,*** and say that ***HE*** claims to be that which ***HE*** is not; and they shall ask ***GOD,*** how long will ***HE*** allow this MAN to say these things without being punished for it? They will further say to one another; this MAN proclaims ***HIMSELF*** to be THE ***HOLY SPIRIT,*** but ***HE*** is just another man who claims to be someone ***HE*** is not, and JESUS CHRIST is the HEIR to the EARTH, and not ***HIM*** as ***HE*** has so proclaimed. But those who will say these things will be BLASPHEMING THE ***HOLY SPIRIT; FOR THE EARTH AND ALL OF CREATION IS HIS, AND HE CAN GIVE IT UNTO WHOMSOEVER HE WILL!*** JESUS CHRIST said that everything BELONGS to HIS ***FATHER,*** and HIS ***FATHER*** has GIVEN it unto HIM, and that HIS ***FATHER*** will show that which has been GIVEN to HIM unto YOU!

Reference:

John 16:13 HOWBEIT WHEN HE, THE SPIRIT OF TRUTH, IS COME, HE WILL GUIDE YOU INTO ALL TRUTH: FOR HE SHALL NOT SPEAK OF HIMSELF; BUT WHATSOEVER HE SHALL HEAR, THAT SHALL HE SPEAK: AND HE WILL SHOW YOU THINGS TO COME.

John 16:14 HE SHALL GLORIFY ME: FOR HE SHALL RECEIVE OF MINE, AND SHALL SHEW IT UNTO YOU.

John 16:15 ALL THINGS THAT THE FATHER HATH ARE MINE: THEREFORE SAID I, THAT HE SHALL TAKE OF MINE, AND SHALL SHEW IT UNTO YOU.

Once those of the CHURCH and its LEADERSHIP have DENOUNCED THE ***DELIVER 182*** openly to the public, all HELL will break loose upon the EARTH, and the next FOUR Scriptures denote that which shall come upon them who have BLASPHEMED THE ***HOLY SPIRIT***, and have placed the UNFORGIVABLE SIN upon their SOULS.

Habakkuk 2:7 SHALL THEY NOT RISE UP SUDDENLY THAT SHALL BITE THEE, AND AWAKE THAT SHALL VEX THEE, AND THOU SHALT BE FOR BOOTIES UNTO THEM?

Habakkuk 2:8 BECAUSE THOU HAST SPOILED MANY NATIONS, ALL THE REMNANT OF THE PEOPLE SHALL SPOIL THEE; BECAUSE OF MEN'S BLOOD, AND FOR THE VIOLENCE OF THE LAND, OF THE CITY, AND OF ALL THAT DWELL THEREIN.

Habakkuk 2:9 WOE TO HIM THAT COVET AN EVIL COVETOUSNESS TO HIS HOUSE, THAT HE MAY SET HIS NEST ON HIGH, THAT HE MAY BE DELIVERED FROM THE POWER OF EVIL.

Habakkuk 2:10 THOU HAST CONSULTED SHAME TO THY HOUSE BY CUTTING OFF MANY PEOPLE, AND <u>HAST SINNED AGAINST THY SOUL</u>.

NOTE: The last FOUR Scriptures not only tells those who have BLASPHEMED THE ***DELIVERER 182*** of what is going to happen to them, it also says by their FALSE LEADERSHIP, they have caused themselves and the congregation to be CUTOFF. This means that the Leadership of the Church and those who follow after them are ALL going to HELL, ***SAITH THE LORD.***

The Scriptures of Habakkuk then go on to ask, how could anyone be so foolish as to make such a fatal mistake? For the Scriptures clearly WARN them against making such a MISTAKE and SINNING against ***THE LORD* of *HOSTS.***

> ***Habakkuk 2:11 FOR THE STONE SHALL CRY OUT OF THE WALL, AND THE BEAM OUT OF THE TIMBER SHALL ANSWER IT.***

NOTE: The Scripture says that the WARNING in the SCRIPTURES is so clear, even the BEAMS within the WALL have heard it, so why haven't they who have READ them taken heed to the WARNING?

> ***Habakkuk 2:12 WOE TO HIM THAT BUILDETH A TOWN WITH BLOOD, AND STABLISHETH A CITY BY INIQUITY!***

NOTE: This is a WARNING to ALL who have SINNED against ***GOD*** by establishing cultures and religions through BLOODSHED and LIES.

> ***Habakkuk 2:13 BEHOLD, IS IT NOT THE LORD OF HOSTS THAT THE PEOPLE SHALL LABOUR IN THE VERY FIRE, AND THE PEOPLE SHALL WEARY THEMSELVES FOR VERY VANITY?***

NOTE: The Scripture again WARNS the people about their BLASPHEMY against THE ***DELIVERER 182,*** by saying, don't they realize they are SINNING against ***THE LORD of HOSTS,*** and ***HE*** will CONDEMN them to HELLFIRE for their SINS? It further says, the people have fallen prey to their own VANITY by committing SINS that can never be FORGIVEN.

The following Scriptures then go on to say that there isn't any EXCUSE for the peoples ERRORS, for the *WORD of* ***GOD*** is EXPLICIT in its WARNINGS.

The Scriptures further WARN of the punishment that will be LEVIED on those who falsely teach the *WORD of* ***GOD,*** whose teaching has caused MANY SOULS to be lost.[1]

Footnote 1: GOD holds each and every person ACCOUNTABLE to themselves. If a person has decided to believe in what the Church teaches rather than them READING the HOLY BIBLE for themselves; if the Church has taught them WRONGLY, then both they and the Church hierarchy will be held RESPONSIBLE for the ERRORS. The BLAME cannot be passed from one to the other, for both have ERRED!

Habakkuk 2:14 FOR THE EARTH SHALL BE FILLED WITH THE KNOWLEDGE OF THE GLORY OF THE LORD, AS THE WATERS COVER THE SEA.

Habakkuk 2:15 WOE UNTO HIM THAT GIVETH HIS NEIGHBOR DRINK, THAT PUTTEST THY BOTTLE TO HIM, AND MAKEST HIM DRUNKEN ALSO, THAT THOU MAYEST LOOK ON THEIR NAKEDNESS.

NOTE: These WARNINGS are directed to them who FALSELY teach the *WORD of* ***GOD***, CORRUPTING OTHERS by their FALSE TEACHING. This is the BLIND leading the BLIND, and SOON both them who follow and them that lead will REALIZE their ERRORS. However, it will then be too late, and SHAME shall be upon them both.

Habakkuk 2:16 THOU ART FILLED WITH SHAME FOR GLORY: DRINK THOU ALSO, AND LET THY FORESKIN BE UNCOVERED: THE CUP OF THE LORDS RIGHT HAND SHALL BE TURNED UNTO THEE, AND SHAMEFUL SPEWING WILL BE ON THY GLORY.

NOTE: This is the PUNISHMENT for them who believe, teach and follow after the FALSE PROPHET'S DOCTRINE. This applies to any Pastor, Priest, Minister, or Church Leader standing at the pulpit without the PROPER ANOINTING, and also to their CONGREGATIONS. The Scripture says that once their FALSE DOCTRINE has been REVEALED, the ***WRATH of the LAMB*** will be upon them, and JESUS CHRIST will disown and SPIT upon them.

Habakkuk 2:17 FOR THE VIOLENCE OF LEB'-A-NON SHALL COVER THEE, AND THE SPOIL OF THE BEASTS, WHICH MADE THEM AFRAID, BECAUSE OF MEN'S BLOOD, AND FOR THE VIOLENCE OF THE LAND, OF THE CITY, AND OF ALL THAT DWELL THEREIN.

NOTE: This Scripture refers to the Middle East and its ongoing VIOLENCE and how that VIOLENCE will spread throughout the world during the GREAT TRIBULATION. The Scripture says, most of the world, starting with the

Middle East will sit in ruins, and become a nest of wild men, seeking the blood of other religious cultures. The entire world will fall prey to the Middle East violence, referred to in the Scripture as "The Violence of Lebanon". These are the terrorist acts that are now prevalent throughout the world, and the Scripture says these acts will continue to worsen.

The Scripture then asks the CHURCH being led by the FALSE PROPHET, and the other false religions of the world; did they think they could profit by their FALSE TEACHINGS and LIES and get away with it, ***SAITH THE LORD***? These teachers of LIES have now become SERVANTS to them, and have FALLEN from the GRACE of ***GOD*** through their own falsities.

> ***Habakkuk 2:18 WHAT PROFITETH THE GRAVEN IMAGE THAT THE MAKER THEREOF HATH GRAVEN IT; THE MOLTEN IMAGE, AND A TEACHER OF LIES, THAT THE MAKER OF HIS WORK TRUSTETH THEREIN, TO MAKE DUMB IDOLS?***

> ***Habakkuk 2:19 WOE UNTO HIM THAT SAITH TO THE WOOD, AWAKE; TO THE DUMB STONE, ARISE, IT SHALL TEACH! BEHOLD, IT IS LAID OVER WITH GOLD AND SILVER, AND THERE IS NO BREATH AT ALL IN THE MIDST OF IT.***

NOTE: THE LORD sees the FALSE PROFIT and those of false religions as the IDOLS of yesteryear; as the DUMB STONE that is VOID of LIFE but yet having the appearance of nobility because it is covered with gold and silver. Saying by its noble appearance, "SEE I AM GODLY AND ABLE TO TEACH THE *WORD of* ***GOD***", all the while TEACHING LIES!

In the FINAL Scripture of the 2nd Chapter of Habakkuk (2:20), ***GOD*** WARNS ALL to be very CAUTIOUS and maintain SILENCE while in the PRESENCE of THE ***DELIVERER 182. THIS IS SHILOH, GOD'S HOLY TEMPLE.*** The Scripture WARNS that the WORDS spoken to ***HIM*** or about ***HIM*** should be few and cautious ones, for by those WORDS YOU WILL BE JUDGED!

> ***Habakkuk 2:20 BUT THE LORD IS IN HIS HOLY TEMPLE: LET ALL THE EARTH KEEP SILENCE BEFORE HIM.***

THE DELIVERER'S DESCRIPTION According to Isaiah

As discussed in "Revealing The Bible's Truth", the GOSPELS are not error free. Except for the Gospel According to John, which hasn't any errors in it other than the spelling of some names, the Gospels of Matthew, Mark and Luke do indeed contain errors. One of the errors so noted is that which can be found in the 12th Chapter of Matthew, where Matthew references Scripture taken from the 42nd Chapter of the Book of Isaiah, relating it to JESUS CHRIST. Matthew did this in error, because the Scriptures he so cited applied to THE ***DELIVERER 182*** and not to JESUS.

Due to the similarities between JESUS and THE ***DELIVERER 182*** (as previously mentioned in this Chapter), the clergy routinely confuses the TWO, (when those of the clergy realize there are TWO MESSIAHS) and there was no exception regarding this confusion when it came to the Disciple Matthew. You were told previously that the major differences between JESUS and THE ***DELIVERER 182,*** is that JESUS came to SAVE the world; whereas THE ***DELIVERER 182*** COMES to JUDGE the world, and its UNBELIEVERS (the GENTILE). And furthermore, even though JESUS was EMPOWERED to JUDGE the world if HE so desired, HE chose not to.

Reference:

> ***John 12:46 I AM COME A LIGHT INTO THE WORLD, THAT WHOSOEVER BELIEVETH ON ME SHOULD NOT ABIDE IN DARKNESS.***
>
> ***John 12:47 AND IF ANY MAN HEAR MY WORDS, AND BELIEVE NOT, I JUDGE HIM NOT: FOR I CAME NOT TO JUDGE THE WORLD, BUT TO SAVE THE WORLD.***

As WE go into the 42nd Chapter of the Book of Isaiah, WE will identify the various differences between JESUS and THE ***DELIVERER 182*** to CONFIRM that the Scriptures refer to THE ***DELIVERER MESSIAH,*** and not to JESUS, THE SAVIOR MESSIAH.

> ***Isaiah 42:1*** *BEHOLD* ***MY SERVANT,*** *whom I uphold; MINE ELECT, in whom MY SOUL DELIGHTETH;* ***I HAVE PUT MY SPIRIT UPON HIM: HE*** *shall bring forth JUDGMENT to the GENTILES.*

NOTE: The 1st Scripture of the 42nd Chapter of Isaiah immediately IDENTIFIES that the ***ONE*** spoken of in it, has COME to JUDGE the UNBELIEVERS and FALSE BELIEVERS, referred to in the Scripture as the GENTILES.

> ***Isaiah 42:2 HE*** *shall not cry, nor lift up, nor cause* ***HIS VOICE*** *to be heard in the street.*

NOTE 1: This Scripture further IDENTIFIES the ***PERSON*** spoken about as being different than JESUS, for JESUS did CRY and was lifted up, and PREACHED PUBLICLY throughout the land. JESUS' VOICE was heard in the streets, and in the countryside, and in the synagogues, and HE was LIFTED UP (HIS CRUCIFIXION). JESUS also did publicly CRY with regard to HIS friend Lazarus' death, whereas THE ***DELIVERER 182 WILL NOT CRY, AS THE SCRIPTURE SO STATES.***

Reference:

> ***John 3:14 AND AS MOSES LIFTED UP THE SERPENT IN THE WILDERNESS, EVEN SO MUST THE SON OF MAN BE LIFTED UP.***
>
> ***John 11:35*** *JESUS WEPT.*

NOTE 2: Furthermore, Habakkuk, 42:2, notes that the ***PERSON*** spoken of in the Scripture will not cry nor will ***HE*** be HUMILIATED as JESUS was HUMILIATED during HIS trial and crucifixion (being LIFTED UP). The Scripture also says that this ***PERSON*** will not PREACH openly throughout the land as JESUS had done ("nor cause ***HIS VOICE*** to be heard in the street"). However it does say that THE ***DELIVERER 182*** WILL JUDGE the UNBELIEVERS and the FALSE BELIEVERS (bring forth JUDGMENT to the GENTILES), by the LAWS given to MOSES on Mount Sinai, and by the TESTIMONY GIVEN by JESUS CHRIST!

> ***Isaiah 42:3*** *A BRUISED REED shall* ***HE*** *not BREAK, and the SMOKING FLAX shall* ***HE*** *not QUENCH:* ***HE*** *shall bring forth JUDGMENT unto TRUTH.*

NOTE: Unlike JESUS, this ***PERSON*** will not be looking to change anything about the people, the CHURCH or its beliefs; because ***HE*** will COME to simply JUDGE THEM as they are, and for who they are; in accordance with the LAWS and TRUTHS so NOTED in the ***HOLY*** Scriptures.

> ***Isaiah 42:4 HE*** *shall not fail nor be discouraged, till* ***HE*** *have SET JUDGMENT in the EARTH: and the isles shall wait for* ***HIS*** *LAW.*

NOTE: The Scripture states, this ***PERSON*** cannot fail in ***HIS*** MISSION, nor can ***HE*** be discouraged from performing it. It further says that the ISLES (meaning, the BRIDE of CHRIST and the EARTH) have been SPIRITUALLY waiting for ***HIS*** LAW (TRUTHS) to come and for the JUDGMENT of the EARTH to be SET.

BEAUTY and BANDS; JESUS CHRIST and THE DELIVERER 182

The Prophet Zechariah was given VISIONS of the coming MESSIAHS whom he called in the Scriptures the BRANCH and the TWO ANOINTED ONES. Zechariah sees the MESSIAH as being TWO PEOPLE and not just one as the CHURCH so often teaches. The TWO ANOINTED ONE'S (the MESSIAHS) referred to in the Scriptures of Zechariah are differentiated and IDENTIFIED in the 11th Chapter of the Book of Zechariah; with ONE being called "BEAUTY" and the OTHER being called "BANDS".

There are several places prior to the identification of the MESSIAHS in the 11th Chapter, where Zechariah so notes in the Scriptures that there are TWO ANOINTED ONE'S, even though he refers to BOTH in a singular form, as being the "BRANCH". The first mentioning of the BRANCH comes in the 8th verse of the 3rd Chapter and WE want to remind you that the WORD, "MESSIAH" means the "ANOINTED ONE", as does the WORD, CHRIST, however, the WORD, CHRIST, only applies to JESUS.

> ***Zechariah 3:8*** *Hear now, O Joshua the High Priest, thou and thy fellows that sit before thee; for they are men wondered at: for, BEHOLD,* ***I WILL BRING FORTH MY SERVANT THE BRANCH.***

> ***Zechariah 3:9*** *For BEHOLD the STONE that I have laid before Joshua; upon ONE STONE shall be* ***SEVEN EYES:*** *BEHOLD I will engrave the graving thereof,* ***SAITH THE LORD of HOSTS,*** *and I will REMOVE the INIQUITY of that land in ONE DAY.*

> ***Zechariah 3:10** In that DAY, **SAITH THE LORD of HOSTS,** shall ye call every man his neighbor under the VINE and under the FIG TREE.*

NOTE: These last three Scriptures IDENTIFY the FIRST BRANCH, the ONE who will be referred to later on in the Scriptures as "BEAUTY", this is JESUS CHRIST. In Revelation 5:6 it is so noted that THE ***LAMB of GOD*** has SEVEN HORNS and SEVEN EYES. The FIRST BRANCH represents only ONE HALF of the LAMB of ***GOD***, and this is why by Scripture only the SEVEN EYES are mentioned, omitting the SEVEN HORNS. This Scripture also supports that which JESUS CHRIST had said, regarding HIM being the CORNERSTONE of CHRIST, the STONE that the BUILDERS REJECTED. JESUS was the FIRST STONE laid for the FOUNDATION of the CHURCH of CHRIST, therefore making HIM the CORNERSTONE of the ***TEMPLE of GOD.*** JESUS is the ONE who ANCHORS the FAMILY of CHRIST together as BROTHER and SISTER, and this is why it is said in the Scripture that every MAN of the VINE (CHRIST) shall be called NEIGHBORS.

The next time "THE BRANCH" is mentioned in the Book of Zechariah, is in the 12th verse of the 6th Chapter, and this "BRANCH" is THE ***DELIVERER 182,*** THE ONE who BUILDS on the CORNERSTONE that was laid BEFORE ***HIM.***[2]

> ***Zechariah 6:12** And speak unto him, saying, **THUS SPEAKETH THE LORD of HOSTS,** saying, **BEHOLD THE MAN WHOSE NAME IS THE BRANCH; AND HE SHALL GROW UP OUT OF HIS PLACE, AND HE SHALL BUILD THE TEMPLE OF THE LORD:***

> ***Zechariah 6:13 EVEN HE SHALL BUILD THE TEMPLE OF THE LORD; AND HE SHALL BEAR THE GLORY, AND HE SHALL SIT AND RULE UPON HIS THRONE; AND THE COUNSEL OF PEACE SHALL BE BETWEEN THEM BOTH.***

Footnote 2: In days of old, family members lived one next to the other, and most often one's neighbor would be a brother or a sister. "That DAY" referred to in the Scripture, is the DAY the SACRIFICE was made at the "Cross of Crucifixion", the DAY when the SINS of the WORLD were FORGIVEN, for them PARTAKING in the SACRIFICE.

NOTE: The first Scripture referenced above refers to THE ***DELIVERER 182***, the REPRESENTATIVE of THE ***HOLY SPIRIT of GOD*** who is THE ***SEVEN SPIRITS of GOD*** that BUILDS the ***TEMPLE of THE LORD*** attaching the remaining stones to the CORNERSTONE (JESUS CHRIST). This is done through ***HOLY SPIRIT*** BAPTISM. The Scripture says it is THE ***DELIVERER 182*** who RECEIVES the GLORY and passes that GLORY down to ***HIS*** SON, JESUS CHRIST. This is why the Scripture of 6:13 says, "***THE COUNSEL OF PEACE SHALL BE BETWEEN THEM BOTH***", thus RECOGNIZING that there are TWO BRANCHES, the TWO ANOINTED ONES, the MESSIAHS, "THEM BOTH", THE SAVIOR and THE ***DELIVERER 182***.

It may also be noted, once the FOUNDATION of the TEMPLE has been laid, the footprint of the TEMPLE has been established. Therefore, THE ***DELIVERER 182*** merely SETS the STONES to be LAID onto the FOUNDATION, once they have all been gathered together. If THE ***DELIVERER 182*** finds a STONE that will not fit into its PROPER PLACE, ***HE*** then CASTS that STONE aside. ***HE*** neither COLLECTS the STONES nor does ***HE*** SELECT them, ***HE*** simply SETS them into their proper places and makes use of the STONES GIVEN to ***HIM***.

The 11th Chapter of the Book of Zechariah specifically IDENTIFIES the TWO ANOINTED ONES, the BRANCH, by NAME. The ONE called "BEAUTY" is JESUS CHRIST, and the ONE CALLED "BANDS", is THE ***DELIVERER 182. GOD*** in the Scriptures refers to the TWO ANOINTED ONES, as being TWO STAVES, and these TWO STAVES represent the staves that carried the ARK of the COVENANT.

Reference:

> ***Exodus 37:4*** *And he made STAVES of Shit'-tim wood, and overlaid them with GOLD.*
>
> ***Exodus 37:5*** *And he put the STAVES into the rings by the sides of the ARK, to bear the ARK.*

BEAUTY and BANDS:

> ***Zechariah 11:7 AND I WILL FEED THE FLOCK OF THE SLAUGHTER, EVEN YOU, O POOR OF THE FLOCK. AND I TOOK UNTO ME <u>TWO STAVES</u>; THE ONE I CALLED <u>BEAUTY</u>, AND THE OTHER I CALLED <u>BANDS</u>; AND I FED THE FLOCK.***

NOTE: This is the IDENTIFICATION of the TWO MESSIAHS. ***GOD,*** calls the FIRST, BEAUTY (JESUS), and the LAST, ***GOD*** calls BANDS (THE ***DELIVERER 182***).

> ***Zechariah 11:10 AND I TOOK MY STAFF, EVEN BEAUTY, AND CUT IT ASUNDER, THAT I MIGHT BREAK MY COVENANT WHICH I HAD MADE WITH ALL THE PEOPLE.***
>
> ***Zechariah 11:11 AND IT WAS BROKEN IN THAT DAY: AND SO THE POOR OF THE FLOCK THAT WAITED UPON ME KNEW THAT IT WAS THE WORD OF THE LORD.***

NOTE: These Scriptures foretell of the COMING of JESUS CHRIST (BEAUTY) to BREAK the OLD COVENANT made with the Jews, and make a NEW COVENANT that also applied to the GENTILE; referred to in the Scripture as "the POOR of the FLOCK". The Scripture also states that JESUS CHRIST, BEAUTY, is the *WORD of* ***GOD*** sent down from HEAVEN in the FORM of a MAN, and that the HOLY BIBLE is the CONFIRMATION that the MAN, JESUS, is CHRIST ("*so the poor of the flock that waited upon* ***ME*** *knew that it was the WORD of* ***THE LORD.***").

Reference:

> ***Malachi 3:16 Then they that feared THE LORD spake often to one another: and THE LORD hearkened, and heard it, and a BOOK of REMEMBRANCE was WRITTEN before HIM for them that feared THE LORD, and thought upon HIS NAME.***
>
> ***Malachi 3:17 AND THEY SHALL BE MINE SAITH THE LORD of HOSTS, IN THAT DAY WHEN I MAKE UP MY JEWELS; AND I WILL SPARE THEM, AS A MAN SPARETH HIS OWN SON THAT SERVETH HIM.***

Breaking the OLD COVENANT:

> ***Zechariah 11:12 AND I SAID UNTO THEM, IF YE THINK GOOD, GIVE ME MY PRICE; AND IF NOT, FORBEAR. SO THEY WEIGHED FOR MY PRICE THIRTY PIECES OF SILVER.***
>
> ***Zechariah 11:13*** *And* ***THE LORD*** *said unto to me,* ***CAST IT UNTO THE POTTER: A GOODLY PRICE THAT I WAS PRISED AT OF THEM.*** *And I took the THIRTY PIECES of SIL-*

*VER, and cast them to THE **POTTER** in the HOUSE of **THE LORD.***

NOTE: The last two Scriptures are PROPHECY of the BETRAYAL of JESUS CHRIST by Judas Iscariot. The Pharisees paid Judas THIRTY PIECES of SILVER to tell them of JESUS' whereabouts on the night of the LAST SUPPER. Then after Judas had realized what he had done, he tried to give them back their money, but the Pharisees refused to take it for they said that there was BLOOD upon it, and Judas cast the money onto the floor of the TEMPLE and went and hanged himself. The Pharisees then took the THIRTY PIECES of Silver and used it to buy some burial ground for strangers, in a place called "THE POTTER'S FIELD". This PROPHECY was WRITTEN about JESUS by Zechariah approximately FIVE HUNDRED and SIXTY YEARS before JESUS' COMING.

Reference:

Matthew 27:3 *Then Judas, which had BETRAYED HIM, when he saw that he was CONDEMNED, repented himself, and brought again the THIRTY PIECES of SILVER to the Chief Priests and Elders.*

Matthew 27:4 *Saying, I have SINNED in that I have BETRAYED INNOCENT BLOOD. And they said, What is that to us? see thou to that.*

Matthew 27:5 *And he cast down the pieces of silver in the TEMPLE, and departed, and HANGED himself.*

Matthew 27:6 *And the Chief Priests took the SILVER PIECES, and said, It is not lawful to put them into the treasury, because it is the PRICE of BLOOD.*

Matthew 27:7 *And they took counsel, and bought them the POTTER'S FIELD, to bury STRANGERS in.*

NOTE: When Matthew wrote these Scriptures, he was unaware of Zechariah's PROPHECY of the EVENT; for he would have so noted those particular Scriptures of Zechariah in his GOSPEL to CONFIRM the PROPHECY. The HOLY BIBLE as you so know it today was compiled 1611 years after the DEATH and RESURRECTION of JESUS CHRIST. Matthew wrote his GOS-

PEL 65 years after JESUS' RESURRECTION and only small portions of the OLD TESTAMENT were available to him. The books available to Matthew at that time were namely the Book of Isaiah, the FIVE BOOKS of MOSES and Chronicles of the Kings, three of the FIVE BOOKS of Psalms, and except for the Book of Jeremiah, Matthew only had bits and pieces of the other books of the Sixteen WRITING PROPHETS. Matthew had only the 13th and 14th Chapters of the Book of Zechariah and not the book in its entirety, and so notes the 13th Chapter of Zechariah in the 31st verse of the 26th Chapter in his GOSPEL. After the RESURRECTION of JESUS CHRIST, the Jews made it very difficult for the FOLLOWERS of JESUS to obtain the HOLY SCRIPTURES, which they had in their possession. This is why ***GOD*** had King James compile and PUBLISH the HOLY BIBLE, thus making the *WORD of **GOD*** readily available to the people, and no longer under the control of the Jews.

THE SENDING FORTH of BANDS:

Zechariah 11:14 THEN I CUT ASUNDER MINE OTHER STAFF, EVEN BANDS, THAT I MIGHT BREAK THE BROTHERHOOD BETWEEN JUDAH AND ISRAEL.

NOTE: The BREAKING of the BROTHERHOOD between JUDAH and ISRAEL represents the SEPARATION between Judaism (JUDAH) and CHRISTIANITY (ISRAEL). THE ***HOLY SPIRIT*** BAPTISM refused by those of Judaism is a MANDATE for the CHURCH of JESUS CHRIST. When the Jews refused BAPTISM, this caused a SEPARATION to occur in the two FAITHS, even though BOTH FAITHS BELIEVED in the SAME ***GOD***. It must be REMEMBERED that THE ***DELIVERER 182*** comes FIRST in the ***SPIRIT*** and then in the FLESH. Those who have not RECEIVED ***HIM*** SPIRITUALLY through BAPTISM cannot RECEIVE ***HIM*** at all. The reason Zechariah refers to the TWO ANOINTED ONES in a SINGULAR FORM (the BRANCH) is because one must RECEIVE both JESUS CHRIST and ***HOLY SPIRIT*** BAPTISM to be COMPLETE in CHRIST. If you receive JESUS (the LIVING WATERS), and not the BAPTISM HE brings with ***HIM***, you're in an incomplete SPIRITUAL STATE and are UNSAVED, ***SAITH THE LORD of HOSTS.*** One must be BAPTIZED in THE ***HOLY SPIRIT*** to be SAVED!

Reference:

John 3:5 JESUS** answered, **VERILY, VERILY, I SAY UNTO THEE, EXCEPT A MAN BE BORN OF WATER AND OF SPIRIT, HE CANNOT ENTER INTO THE KINGDOM OF GOD.

The LAST SHEPHERD, BANDS:

Zechariah 11:15** And **THE LORD** said unto me, **TAKE UNTO THEE YET THE INSTRUMENTS OF A FOOLISH SHEPHERD.

NOTE: This is ***THE LORD'S*** WARNING to Zechariah for them who follow after the FALSE PROPHET'S doctrine, adhering to their religion rather than OBEYING the *WORD of **GOD!*** This applies to any religion that either DEFILES or DENIES the MANDATE of ***HOLY SPIRIT*** BAPTISM.

Zechariah 11:16 FOR, LO, I WILL RAISE UP A SHEPHERD IN THE LAND, WHICH SHALL NOT VISIT THOSE THAT BE CUT OFF, NEITHER SHALL SEEK THE YOUNG ONE, NOR HEAL THAT THAT IS BROKEN, NOR FEED THAT THAT STANDETH STILL: BUT HE SHALL EAT THE FLESH OF THE FAT, AND TEAR THEIR CLAWS IN PIECES.

NOTE: This Scripture tells about ***GOD'S*** SENDING FORTH of ***BANDS***, THE ***DELIVERER 182.*** It says that THE ***DELIVERER*** will not look to CONVERT anyone to CHRISTIANITY, or help the NEW CHRISTIAN (the YOUNG ONE) along the right path; nor will ***HE*** try to CHANGE one's position in regard to their belief, albeit KNOWING that their beliefs are WRONG. THE ***DELIVERER 182, BANDS,*** will neither try to PREACH CHRISTIANITY to the UNBELIEVERS nor to the FALSE BELIEVERS. However, ***HE*** will JUDGE the CHURCH and those leading the CHURCH for their RIGHTEOUSNESS, and DESTROY them who have MISLED the CHURCH and have profited by their FALSE TEACHINGS!

Zechariah 11:17 WOE TO THE IDOL SHEPHERD THAT LEAVETH THE FLOCK! THE SWORD SHALL BE UPON HIS ARM, AND UPON HIS RIGHT EYE: HIS ARM SHALL BE CLEAN DRIED UP, AND HIS RIGHT EYE SHALL BE UTTERLY DARKENED.

NOTE: This is a WARNING to any Pastor, Priest, Minister, or CHURCH Leader, who has MISLED the CHURCH for any REASON. This applies to both them who have done so knowingly, and to them who have done so unknowingly! ***THE LORD*** says whether it should be by IGNORANCE or by GREED, the PUNISHMENT and PAIN will be the SAME! ***FOR THE***

WRATH of GOD SHALL COME UPON THEM, SAITH THE LORD of HOSTS, AND MY DELIVERER SHALL JUDGE AND DELIVER MY WRATH UPON THEM!

> ***Micah 5:14 AND I WILL PLUCK UP THY GROVES OUT OF THE MIDST OF THEE: SO WILL I DESTROY THY CITIES.***
>
> ***Micah 5:15 AND I WILL EXECUTE VENGEANCE IN ANGER AND FURY UPON THE HEATHEN, SUCH AS THEY HAVE NOT HEARD.***

EVENTS TRIGGERED by THE DELIVERER'S PRESENCE

There are TEN MAJOR EVENTS that will be TRIGGERED by THE ***HOLY SPIRIT*** after ***HE*** takes on the CARNAL FORM of THE ***DELIVERER 182;*** however, the final SEVEN EVENTS will occur at the TIME of ***HIS*** DEPARTURE from the EARTH.

The FIRST EVENT occurring is the LAMB'S BREAKING of the FIRST SEAL. This is the TIME when the ***AUTHORITY*** of THE ***HOLY SPIRIT*** is HANDED DOWN to JESUS CHRIST, the ***LAMB of GOD,*** so noted in the 5th and 6th Chapters of the Book of Revelation. This is also the TIME when THE ***HOLY SPIRIT*** takes on a CARNAL FORM as THE ***DELIVERER 182*** and goes forth into BATTLE against EVIL. This is indicated in the Scriptures by the sending out of the WHITE HORSEMAN to CONQUER and GATHER TOGETHER the CHOSEN, called, the "BRIDE of CHRIST" for the FIRST RAPTURE.

During the TIME of the gathering of the "BRIDE", both the SECOND and the THIRD SEALS are BROKEN. Once the SECOND SEAL is BROKEN, this sends forth the RED HORSEMAN and he takes PEACE from the EARTH. This is the TIME when VIOLENCE spreads throughout the world, starting first in the Middle East as explained in Habakkuk 2:17 (covered previously in this Chapter). This VIOLENCE will take on several forms; domestic atrocities, wars and rumors of wars, terrorist acts and the corruption of governments. There will also be NATURAL DISASTERS occurring routinely throughout the world and divisions amongst families and friends. This state of the world will continually worsen on through to the END TIME!

When the THIRD SEAL is BROKEN, the BLACK HORSEMAN of the APOCALYPSE will be RELEASED upon the EARTH, and this will cause shortages to occur throughout the world. There will be shortages in food, water, fuel, and shelter from the extreme changes in the weather patterns. There will also be many birth defects in the children being born throughout the world. The Book of Ecclesiastes WARNS against having children during the time when the WEATHER and SEASONS of the EARTH begin to change unpredictably and falter.

Reference:

> ***Ecclesiastes 11:4*** *He that observeth the wind shall not sow; and he that regardeth the clouds shall not reap.*
>
> ***Ecclesiastes 11:5*** *As thou knowest not what is the way of the SPIRIT, nor how the bones do grow in the womb of her that is with child: even so thou knowest not the WORKS of* ***GOD*** *who maketh all.*

The SHORTAGES of the necessities of life will be widespread and will occur very quickly, and only the SAVED, the "BRIDE", the "TRIBULATION SAINTS", and the wealthy, will be unaffected by them. Heinous acts of cannibalism will be widespread in the eastern world due to the famine and starvation of them living in those countries. Parents will start eating their own children, and the dead bodies of the starved will be eaten rather than buried or burned, because the fields will no longer bring forth a harvest, nor will the trees bear fruit, and the animals will decrease in their numbers and diminish ***SAITH THE LORD.***

All these things START, once the CHURCH has DENOUNCED THE ***DELIVERER 182,*** prior to the TWO WITNESSES of the OLD COVENANT coming forward. Once THE ***DELIVERER*** leaves the EARTH, the TWO WITNESSES will carry on for ***HIM*** until ***HE*** RETURNS, to SET JUDGMENT and POUR OUT the FURY and the ***WRATH of GOD*** upon the EARTH.

Six months after the BREAKING of the THIRD SEAL, the FIRST TRUMPET will be SOUNDED. At that time, THE ***DELIVERER 182*** and 10,400,000 PEOPLE (the BRIDE) will DEPART the EARTH in RAPTURE. Listed below is the final SEVEN EVENTS TRIGGERED by the PRESENCE of THE ***DELIVERER 182*** taking place at the SOUNDING of the FIRST TRUMPET:

1. The CHURCH (THE BRIDE of CHRIST) RECEIVES RAPTURE.
2. THE ***HOLY SPIRIT*** leaves the earth (as the ***182 PERSON***).
3. THE GREAT TRIBULATION BEGINS!
4. The TWO WITNESSES are awakened in the earth and

START their MINISTRIES.

5. The TRIBULATION SAINTS are MARKED and SEALED.
6. A meteor shower hits the earth causing one-third of it to be deprived of sunlight.
7. The ANGEL MICHAEL cast Lucifer (the Devil) down to the earth.

Chapter 14
Hardships

JESUS said in John 16:33, in this world you will have TROUBLE, but don't let that bother you; for JESUS said HE had LEARNED how to overcome the PROBLEMS HE must encounter, and wants you to know that YOU CAN TOO! What did JESUS mean when HE said this, for HE gave no further explanation of the matter?

How to deal with your worldly problems and the troubling times ahead will be the topic of discussion in this Chapter. ***THE LORD*** wants ME to teach you by Scripture exactly what JESUS had LEARNED in regard to your DEALING with the TROUBLING TIMES ahead.

Starting with JESUS' BAPTISM and the BEGINNING of HIS MINISTRY, the PROBLEMS and TROUBLE JESUS encountered compounded daily. HE was heckled, accused of being a liar and a drunk, the Jews attempted to stone HIM whenever HE would publicly SPEAK, and continually tried to arrest HIM in an attempt to take HIS LIFE. When all the while, all JESUS did was to HELP OTHERS having TROUBLE, and would not allow HIS own TROUBLE to keep HIM from it. What is being said here is, although JESUS' problems were bothersome to HIM, they didn't hinder nor keep HIM from what HE was sent to do, because ***GOD*** would not allow that to HAPPEN! And, by JESUS' KNOWING that ***THE LORD*** would not let ANYTHING keep HIM from HIS WORK, HE stayed FOCUSED on it and IGNORED HIS OWN PROBLEMS, because HE KNEW that ***GOD*** would tend to them for HIM.

There can't be found anywhere in the HOLY SCRIPTURES where ***GOD*** promises to keep you out of TROUBLE, even though ***HE*** PROMISES to PROTECT YOU in a time of TROUBLE. If you are not SAVED but are WORTHY of being SAVED, ***GOD*** will allow Lucifer or one of his delegates to attack you, much like what ***HE*** allowed Satan to do to Job. And, although Job endured HARDSHIPS, pain and suffering, ***GOD*** got Job through it and back onto his feet; and made Job a BETTER MAN because of it! ***GOD*** uses HARDSHIPS to build CHARACTER, and exposes you to them so you might learn how to overcome and defeat EVIL. NO PAIN, NO GAIN!

On the other hand, if you are SAVED, ***GOD*** will not allow the DEVIL to come near to you. Neither Lucifer nor one of his villains can personally harm you in anyway. However the DEVIL can still create HARDSHIPS for you by attacking a loved one and causing you grief by proxy. This CONFIRMS JESUS' STATEMENT, that in this world there is TROUBLE, and while in this world there are not any exceptions to HIS STATEMENT. However, ***GOD*** says that ***HE*** will get you through your time of TROUBLE, and ***PERSONALLY*** see to your safety.

> ***Isaiah 43:1 BUT NOW THUS SAITH THE LORD THAT CREATED THEE, O JACOB, AND HE THAT FORMED THEE, O ISRAEL, FEAR NOT: FOR I HAVE REDEEMED THEE, I HAVE CALLED THEE BY THY NAME; THOU ART MINE.***
>
> ***Isaiah 43:2 WHEN THOU PASSEST THROUGH THE WATERS, I WILL BE WITH THEE; AND THROUGH THE RIVERS, THEY SHALL NOT OVERFLOW THEE: WHEN THOU WALKEST THROUGH THE FIRE, THOU SHALT NOT BE BURNED; NEITHER SHALL THE FLAME KINDLE UPON THEE.***

NOTE: This is ***GOD'S*** PROMISE of PROTECTION when ONE encounters HARDSHIPS! ***GOD*** does not say, ***HE*** will not expose you to HARDSHIPS, ***HE SAYS, HE WILL GET YOU THROUGH THEM.***

A good example of HARDSHIPS the SAVED may encounter, is what I just experienced myself. I received a call from my ex-wife recently and she informed ME that my sixteen-year old daughter had been taken into the hospital emergency room with severe abdominal pain, and the doctors were running tests on her to see what was causing it. I was told that the pain was so severe she had to be given morphine to subdue it.

After getting off the phone, I immediately asked ***THE LORD*** what was wrong with her and was simply told to let her doctors do what they will recommend doing. Even the Angels couldn't help ME in regard to MY dealing with the situation, and one Angel said to COMFORT ME, maybe it is only a severe case of abdominal gas. But I knew deep in my heart that it was more than just gas pains. It was very difficult for ME to UNDERSTAND why ***GOD*** was allowing this to happen. I can say both BOLDLY and TRUTHFULLY that there isn't a person upon the EARTH that is CLOSER to ***GOD*** than ***I AM,*** and yet I was encountering emotional pain, and wished it were I rather than my daughter suffering her physical pain.

But ***THE LORD SAID, MY SON, HAVE FAITH IN ME, FOR THERE IS NOTHING THAT I CANNOT OVERCOME. AND I SAID, FATHER, PLEASE DON'T TAKE HER FROM ME. AND GOD SAID, "SHE WILL BE FINE TRUST IN ME", "FOR IF SHE IS NOT, THEN I WOULD BE A LIAR, AND I CANNOT LIE".***

Once at the hospital and at her bedside along with her Mother, Grandmother, and her two Aunts, ***THE LORD*** told ME that my daughter was suffering from appendicitis, and that the doctor was going to recommend surgery to remove her appendix. ***GOD*** said that I should follow the doctor's advice and allow the surgery, and that ***HE*** would see to her safety and recovery. Shortly thereafter the doctor came out and said what ***THE LORD*** had said he would say.

The operation went off without a hitch, and unlike many of the other appendectomies where they remove the appendix and are still uncertain as to whether or not it was the appendix causing the problem; in this case they were certain that the appendix was bad. My daughter within eighteen hours after her surgery was home, and other than feeling a little sore from the surgery, doing well. Within seven days, she had fully recovered and was back to her old self again.

Compounding Hardships

As previously mentioned, JESUS' HARDSHIPS compounded daily and worsened with TIME. However, in each and every situation JESUS encountered, ***GOD*** got HIM through them, even DEATH! ***THE LORD*** says that the world is now in TROUBLING TIMES, and henceforth the TROUBLE will worsen to a point of mass-hysteria. ***THE LORD*** says that the world will see TROUBLE, the likes of which it has never seen before, even from its BEGINNING to this TIME.

Once THE ***HOLY SPIRIT*** (as THE ***DELIVERER 182***) leaves the EARTH, and the GREAT TRIBULATION begins, ***HOLY SPIRIT*** BAPTISM will cease, and the many left behind will no longer be able to be BAPTIZED in the SPIRIT of ***GOD***. However; there will still be HOPE for the HOPELESS ***SAITH THE LORD;*** for those seeking BAPTISM will RECEIVE the ***SEAL of the LIVING GOD*** for their PROTECTION in lieu of SPIRITUAL BAPTISM.

This ***SEAL*** will be TRANSPARENT and not visible to the human eye, somewhat like a SPIRITUAL BUBBLE that will encapsulate the PERSON RECEIVING it, and will act like an impervious shield, shielding ONE from the forces of EVIL. ***THE LORD*** has told ME that ONE bearing the ***SEAL*** could stand in the midst of an atomic explosion and not be harmed by it. However, they bearing the ***SEAL*** will still endure HARDSHIPS**,** for they will bear witness to the calamities experienced by those people around them not having the ***SEAL.***

> ***Psalm 91:7*** *A thousand shall fall at thy side, and ten thousand at thy right hand; but it shall not come nigh thee.*

> ***Psalm 91:8*** *Only with thine eyes shalt thou BEHOLD and SEE the reward of the WICKED.*

In the EYES of ***GOD*** only the SAVED are WORTHY, and the UNSAVED belong to this world, a world, which has been JUDGED by THE ***DELIVERER 182*** and found to be EVIL and CORRUPT. There will be MANY of the UNSAVED seeking the COMFORT and PROTECTION of the SAVED, and the SAVED will have COMPASSION for them. When the calamities of the GREAT TRIBULATION befalls the UNSAVED in the presence of the SAVED, and they can only observe and not do anything about the calamities, those HARDSHIPS will be most difficult to endure.

When the SAVED hear the cries of the UNSAVED, begging for ***GOD*** to let them die, but they cannot die for death has fled from them, the burden of grief from seeing the pain and suffering of the UNSAVED will be nearly unbearable. But the SAVED will overcome and endure. There will be MANY of the UNSAVED that will have loved ones that are SAVED, and while the one will suffer the physical pain, the other SEEING will suffer the emotional pain. This is similar to what I had encountered with my daughter's illness, being helpless and seeking ***GOD'S*** MERCY, having only MY FAITH in ***GOD*** to cling to, and knowing that the outcome rests in ***GOD'S HANDS.***

The physical and EMOTIONAL PAIN that WE have just spoken of is expressed throughout the Scriptures of the Book of Revelation. EVERYONE who has been left upon the EARTH to endure the GREAT TRIBULATION will experience this GRIEF, so PRAY that YOU are not ONE of them who has been LEFT BEHIND! However, there will be a TIME when all the pain and suffering will cease, and ***GOD*** will mend all broken hearts, and any MEMORY of PAIN and SUFFERING will be wiped away.

> ***Revelation 21:4*** *And* ***GOD*** *shall wipe away all tears from their eyes; and there shall be no more death, neither sorrow, nor crying, neither shall there be any more pain: for the former things are PASSED AWAY.*

Isaiah 35:10 *And the ransomed of* ***THE LORD*** *shall return, and come to ZION with songs and everlasting joy upon their heads: they shall obtain joy and gladness, and sorrow and sighing shall flee away.*

TRUSTING in GOD

It is easy for a person to say that they TRUST in ***GOD,*** but do they really? JESUS CHRIST TRUSTED in ***GOD*** over HIS entire life on EARTH, as HE does in HEAVEN. All the way through to HIS LAST BREATH, JESUS TRUSTED IN ***GOD*** and ***GOD*** never BETRAYED JESUS' TRUST. But to TRUST in something you cannot see with your eyes and touch with your hands can be most DIFFICULT ***SAITH THE LORD.***

GOD, in this world, can only be seen as WORDS in a BOOK, and the BOOK is called the HOLY BIBLE. The MESSAGE contained in all THREE BOOKS I have written for ***THE LORD*** is the SAME, "READ THE HOLY BIBLE"! The MESSAGE is clear and so very IMPORTANT; because only through the SCRIPTURES can ***GOD*** be seen in this world, and only through the SCRIPTURES can ***GOD*** be TRUSTED, for ***HE*** will adhere to ***HIS WORD!***

When things are going good for the people, most of them rarely give ***GOD*** a second thought, however, when things turn SOUR and TROUBLE comes upon the people, they are QUICK to turn to ***THE LORD*** for COMFORT and HELP. It has always been this way ***SAITH THE LORD, AND THIS IS WHY THERE SHALL BE A GREAT TRIBULATION, TO GET THE PEOPLES ATTENTION!***

ONE must be most familiar with the HOLY SCRIPTURES, because in the TROUBLING TIMES ahead only by ONE'S TRUST in ***GOD*** can they both ENDURE and SURVIVE the HARDSHIPS of the TROUBLING TIMES. ***GOD*** expects them BELONGING to ***HIM*** to CLING to the SCRIPTURES in a TIME of TROUBLE, and TRUST in ***HIM*** to do as the SCRIPTURES say ***HE WILL DO. GOD CAN BE HELD ACCOUNTABLE TO HIS WORD, SO ONE MUST KNOW HIS WORD BEFORE HE CAN HOLD GOD ACCOUNTABLE TO IT!***

Using SCRIPTURE for GUIDANCE

The FORTY-FOUR BOOKS of the HOLY BIBLE are woven together by a SINGLE SCARLET THREAD, and although at times it may seem as though there are contradictions in the BIBLE, there are not! Only to the UNLEARNED will there be apparent contradictions in the HOLY BIBLE, because they do not UNDERSTAND the SCRIPTURES and the world holds them hostage to their own foolish wisdom.

Only through ***HOLY SPIRIT*** BAPTISM can the SCRIPTURES be UNDERSTOOD, and this is why there will be 144,000 TRIBULATION SAINTS during the GREAT TRIBULATION to INTERPRET the SCRIPTURES for the people. This is because at the TIME of the GREAT TRIBULATION there will be no more BAPTISM ***SAITH THE LORD,*** and if it weren't for the HELP of the TRIBULATION SAINTS, ALL of the people left on the EARTH would PERISH with it.

For every situation encountered in the GREAT TRIBULATION there is a COUNTERMEASURE for it, and that COUNTERMEASURE lies somewhere in the HOLY SCRIPTURES. The COUNTERMEASURE may lie in a PSALM or PROVERB, in the GOSPELS or the BOOKS of PROPHECIES. It may lie in one of the stories of the OLD TESTAMENT or in the FIVE BOOKS of MOSES, but rest assured, the COUNTERMEASURE is there!

During the GREAT TRIBULATION the HOLY BIBLE will be the most VALUED weapon for ONE'S DEFENSE, for it is THE ROD of IRON that all nations will be ruled by. The HOLY BIBLE will provide the TACTICS and the rules of ENGAGEMENT for the SAVED, and only by SCRIPTURE can the ENEMY be DEFEATED ***SAITH THE LORD.***

Only ***GOD*** knows at this time the list of them intended to be left behind, and they are MANY (6,000,000,000 PEOPLE), so it is MOST IMPORTANT that ALL be PREPARED. Even THE ***DELIVERER 182*** knows only a few of the 10,400,000 who have been CHOSEN to be the BRIDE and accompany ***HIM*** in RAPTURE, while the balance of the BRIDE (93,600,000 PEOPLE) remain in PARADISE until the SOUNDING of the SEVENTH TRUMPET. And, of the 10,400,000 that will be taken in RAPTURE, there are only 800,000 that will be over the age of NINETEEN YEARS OLD.

If the world knew what I KNOW, there wouldn't be ONE PERSON not having a HOLY BIBLE in their POSSESSION, specifically the King James 1611 Authorized Version, for the other translations are WORTHLESS ***SAITH THE LORD;*** for they are the work of the DEVIL and will MISGUIDE YOU! The HOLY SCRIPTURES will be YOUR GUIDE and SAFE PASSAGE through the GREAT TRIBULATION, so every WORD must be as it was WRITTEN by King James in 1611, omitting ALL of the Epistles from it; for they will cause your DEMISE as they have caused the CHURCH'S DEMISE!

Prepare for HARDSHIP

If or when you might hear that PEOPLE (mostly CHILDREN) have simply vanished from off the EARTH, know that the FIRST RAPTURE has occurred. There will be no WARNING SIGNS precluding the RAPTURE, for it will come as a THIEF in the NIGHT, without WARNING. The CHURCHES will tell their congregations that is was not the RAPTURE, and refuse to believe that it was, because only a very few will be taken from the congregations of the CHURCHES. However, shortly thereafter, it will be most apparent to them that THEY HAD BEEN LEFT BEHIND!

Only the TRIBULATION SAINTS and the TWO WITNESSES will KNOW for certain their DESTINY, while all the others are in DOUBT and wonder whether or not their NAMES are WRITTEN in the LAMBS BOOK of LIFE. For the WORTHY, this is a time when they will leave their CHURCH and turn toward the TRIBULATION SAINTS for their GUIDANCE, for the TRIBULATION SAINTS will be the CHURCH. However, there will be many who will stay within the congregations of their churches and be taught to worship the DEVIL and the BEAST (the Antichrist) by the FALSE PROPHET, these are the DAMNED!

> ***Revelation 13:8*** *And all that dwell upon the EARTH shall worship him, whose NAMES ARE NOT written in the BOOK of LIFE of the LAMB slain from the foundation of the world.*

> ***Revelation 13:9 IF ANY MAN HAVE AN EAR, LET HIM HEAR.***

Chapter 15
COMING DOWN with VENGEANCE

Psalm 73:19 *How are they brought into DESOLATION, as in a MOMENT! They are utterly CONSUMED with TERRORS.*

Psalm 73:20 *As a dream when one awaketh; so,* ***O LORD,*** *when THOU AWAKEST, THOU SHALT DESPISE THEIR IMAGE.*

The HOLY BIBLE tells you throughout its SCRIPTURES that the FEAR of ***THE LORD*** is the beginning of WISDOM. This means that every living person on the EARTH should RECOGNIZE that there is a ***GOD*** and that ***HE*** is to be both FEARED and RESPECTED. ***GOD*** is to be RESPECTED because ***HE*** is the SOVEREIGN POWER over all of EXISTENCE, and ***HE*** is to be FEARED for what ***HE*** can do to you.

Many people FAIL to RECOGNIZE ***GOD*** because ***HE*** is SLOW TO ANGER, and they CONFUSE ***HIS*** PATIENCE that of which is forbearance, with WEAKNESS or LACK of CONCERN! ***GOD*** allows certain things that are worthy of PUNISHMENT to happen, with the appearance of no penalty being levied against those who perpetrate the actions. However, I can assure you that no one gets away with anything, even though it may initially appear to be otherwise!

Some people even believe that ***GOD*** overlooks some things they do, that they themselves know to be unrighteous, because ***HE*** is either too busy or considers the acts to be too petty for ***HIS*** involvement. THIS IS A FOOLISH BELIEF, for ***GOD*** is aware of all things that transpire, and no UNRIGHTEOUS ACTIONS will go UNPUNISHED ***SAITH THE LORD***. It is not a question of "IF" there will be a PUNISHMENT LEVIED, but rather "WHEN" will the PUNISHMENT be LEVIED on them who perpetrate the UNRIGHTEOUS ACTS!

These days I hear routinely on the news about someone somewhere wanting to REMOVE the ***NAME of GOD,*** or something making reference to ***GOD,*** from the schools, the workplace, and public domain. This is the work of SA-

TAN and of them DESTINED to spend their ETERNITY with him. When confronted with their EVIL DEEDS, many would say, "What should I fear; is ***GOD*** going to kill me"? But I can tell these people that ***GOD*** rather than killing them will cause them to live, even though they will beg for DEATH and this will be only the BEGINNING of their SORROWS.

Some of these people haven't any FEAR of ***GOD*** because they are to STUPID to FEAR ***GOD***, while others fail to recognize ***HIM*** because they HATE ***GOD***, just like their father, Lucifer hates ***GOD***. However, if they were allowed to SPEAK to the others before them who also failed to FEAR ***GOD*** and are in HELL because of it, some of them would be a bit more cautious in their accusations against ***GOD.***

Many people would like to believe there are going to be warning signs that will allow them time to REPENT of their DEEDS. But I can tell you that other than the THREE BOOKS that I have WRITTEN for ***THE LORD***, the WARNING SIGNS they seek have come and gone. These things that are about to COME upon the EARTH, will come fast and furiously, without further WARNING. And, many of the evil perpetrators will PRAY for FORGIVENESS, but ***THE LORD*** will turn ***HIS BACK*** to them as they had once too often TURNED their backs to ***HIM***, and will not hear their PRAYERS, nor will ***HE*** forgive them of their SINS.

JESUS CHRIST warned of these TIMES and told those who would HEAR HIS WORDS to be PREPARED, because these things would come in an INSTANT, leaving no time for preparation after they start to come.

> ***Mark 13:35 WATCH YE THEREFORE: FOR YE KNOW NOT WHEN THE MASTER OF THE HOUSE COMETH, AT EVEN, OR AT MIDNIGHT, OR AT THE COCKCROWING, OR IN THE MORNING:***

> ***Mark 13:36 LEST COMING SUDDENLY HE FIND YOU SLEEPING.***

> ***Mark 13:37 AND WHAT I SAY UNTO YOU I SAY UNTO ALL, WATCH.***

NOTE: The "MASTER of the HOUSE" spoken of in the Scripture refers to THE ***DELIVERER 182, GOD'S ELECT,*** THE ***HOLY SPIRIT.*** The Scripture

WARNS ALL to be PREPARED, for when ***HE COMES, HE COMES AS A THIEF IN THE NIGHT, WITHOUT PRIOR WARNING. AND, WHEN HE COMES, HE COMES WITH DELIVERANCE FOR THE WORTHY IN HIS RIGHT HAND, AND WITH THE VENGEANCE OF GOD FOR THE WICKED IN HIS LEFT! THERE WILL BE WEEPING AND GNASHING OF TEETH SAITH THE LORD.***

Punishment LEVIED by GOD

Up until the TIME of the COMING of THE ***DELIVERER 182, GOD*** has LEVIED PUNISHMENT on INDIVIDUALS, FAMILIES, and even NATIONS that failed to FEAR ***HIM,*** but not on the WORLD as a whole. Once the BRIDE of CHRIST is taken in RAPTURE, the remaining SIX BILLION on the EARTH will HIDE from ***GOD*** like WORMS in HOLES, for ***GOD*** will PUNISH the EARTH in its ENTIRETY. Only the TRIBULATION SAINTS and those RECEIVING the ***SEAL*** of the ***LIVING GOD*** will ***HE*** SPARE from ***HIS WRATH.***

> ***Micah 7:16*** *The NATIONS shall see and be CONFOUNDED at all their MIGHT: they shall lay their hand upon their mouth, their ears shall be deaf.*

> ***Micah 7:17*** *They shall lick the dust like a serpent, they shall move out of their holes like WORMS of the EARTH: they shall be AFRAID of* ***THE LORD*** *our* ***GOD,*** *and shall FEAR because of* ***THEE.***

Man's VANITY will bring about his own GRIEF, because his VANITY has caused him to FAIL in his RECOGNITION that ***THE LORD*** is ***GOD!*** The PAIN, SUFFERING, and HUMILITY that JESUS CHRIST endured at the CROSS will be "CHILDS PLAY" in regard to what the WICKED and the UNSAVED will RECEIVE for their PUNISHMENT. The crimes that man will impose upon man will be raised exponentially as compared to the crimes of the past, with even slow death while enduring great pain being sought after more than survival. Death will be seen as a BLESSING from ***GOD.*** This will be a TIME of HELL on EARTH, and any form of DEATH will be considered a BLESSING, for life will be HELL!

Things will only WORSEN with TIME!

Once HELL is opened and allowed access to the EARTH, those of HELL will bring HELL with them to the EARTH. For a FIVE-MONTH period of TIME after HELL is OPENED, no one on the EARTH will be allowed to DIE, and will be made to SUFFER beyond IMAGINATION.

Revelation 9:1 *AND the FIFTH ANGEL SOUNDED, and I saw a STAR fall from HEAVEN unto the EARTH: and to HIM was given the KEY of the BOTTOMLESS PIT.*

Revelation 9:2 *And HE OPENED the BOTTOMLESS PIT; and there arose smoke out of the PIT, as the smoke of a great furnace; and the sun and the air were darkened by reason of the smoke of the PIT.*

Revelation 9:3 *And there came out of the smoke LOCUSTS upon the EARTH: and unto them was given power, as the SCORPIONS of the EARTH have power.*

Revelation 9:4 *And it was commanded them that they should not hurt the grass of the EARTH, neither any green thing, neither any tree; but only those men which have not the* ***SEAL of GOD*** *in their foreheads.*

Revelation 9:5 *And to them it was given that they should not KILL them, but that they should be TORMENTED FIVE MONTHS: and their TORMENT was as the TORMENT of a SCORPION, when he striketh a man.*

Revelation 9:6 *And in those days shall men SEEK DEATH, and shall not find it; and shall desire to DIE, and DEATH SHALL FLEE FROM THEM.*

After HELL is OPENED and those of HELL allowed to move freely about the EARTH, with each coming day will come more EVIL; making the day before better than the present day. All upon the EARTH will KNOW that the HORROR of tomorrow will be WORSE than the HORROR of today.

Instituting the MARK of the BEAST

Once the FIRST VIAL of the ***WRATH of GOD*** is POURED OUT upon the EARTH, the "Mark of the BEAST" will be instituted, and this EVENT marks the FINAL TWENTY-ONE MONTHS of the GREAT TRIBULATION. This will be a TIME when one can neither buy nor sell anything without first receiving the Mark of the BEAST either upon their RIGHT HAND or on the FOREHEAD.

The Mark required to buy or sell can only be received by them who have PUBLICLY DENOUNCED ***GOD,*** and have PUBLICLY DECLARED Lucifer and the Antichrist as being god. Anyone receiving this Mark will have SEALED their FATE in HELL, and the TRIBULATION SAINTS will have WARNED them remaining on the EARTH, prior to their RAPTURE, against taking the Mark. The RAPTURE of the TRIBULATION SAINTS and the GUESTS of the WEDDING SUPPER also takes place at the POURING OUT of the FIRST VIAL of the ***WRATH of GOD.***

No one left on the EARTH after the TRIBULATION SAINTS have RECEIVED RAPTURE can be SAVED and RECEIVE ETERNITY. However, there is still a chance for some of them remaining on the EARTH to enter the MILLENNIUM by being MARTYRS in the NAME of ***GOD***, upholding the TESTIMONY of JESUS CHRIST, and refusing to take the Mark of the BEAST.

Martyrs for GOD:

After refusing to take the Mark of the BEAST, the Antichrist will then have them refusing, BEHEADED; and by their own blood (rather than the BLOOD of the LAMB) they will be allowed to ENTER into the MILLENNIUM PERIOD. Even though the MARTYRS will partake in the ONE THOUSAND YEARS of HEAVEN on EARTH with CHRIST REIGNING over the EARTH, they will not RECEIVE ETERNITY, and will RETURN to the DUST of the EARTH at its CONCLUSION.

There will be some of them who were allowed to enter the MILLENNIUM to live once more on the EARTH. Although they had returned to the DUST of the EARTH at the MILLENNIUM'S CONCLUSION, those of them who had SERVED ***GOD*** well during the MILLENNIUM will be REWARDED for their SERVICE. These people will be allowed to live again in the NEXT WORLD, as GENTILES, and RECEIVE a SECOND CHANCE to be SAVED. This is their FINAL CHANCE to be ONE in CHRIST, for if they FAIL again, they will not be given a THIRD opportunity. And, if after their SECOND CHANCE they again were to martyr themselves as they had done before, after their SECOND MILLENNIUM PERIOD has expired, they will EXPIRE and be NO MORE! However, they will not suffer the SECOND DEATH (HELL), they will simply be no more!

> ***Revelation 20:4*** *And I saw THRONES, and they sat upon them, and JUDGMENT was given unto them: and I saw the SOULS of them that were BEHEADED for the witness of JESUS, and for the WORD of* ***GOD,*** *and which had not worshipped the BEAST, neither his IMAGE, neither had received his MARK upon their FOREHEADS or in their HANDS; and they LIVED and REIGNED with CHRIST a THOUSAND YEARS.*

> ***Revelation 20:5*** *But the rest of the dead lived not again until the THOUSAND YEARS were finished. This is the FIRST RESURRECTION.*

> ***Revelation 20:6*** *BLESSED and HOLY is he that hath part in the FIRST RESURRECTION: on such the SECOND DEATH hath no power, but they shall be PRIESTS of* ***GOD*** *and of CHRIST, and shall REIGN with* ***HIM*** *a THOUSAND YEARS.*

Identification:

Those receiving the Mark of the BEAST will be tattooed with an IDENTIFICATION NUMBER that will be prefixed with the NUMBER 666, and that NUMBER must be visible at all times. They will also have a microchip implanted in them that bears the number as well, and the microchip will act as a locating device. The tattoo must be displayed on the right hand or on the forehead of the one bearing the number of the BEAST, and that person's number will track any transactions regarding the selling or buying of anything. The microchip will provide a means of tracking that individual's every move, and will locate the person anywhere on the EARTH within one meter of their actual location.

The DEVIL, the Antichrist, or any of his delegates will know at a glance who has or hasn't the Mark and where those having the Mark are at, at all times. Those who are caught without the Mark by either trying to buy or sell something will be brought before the Antichrist along with their families. These people will then be offered the Mark in a publicly televised event, and must publicly DENOUNCE ***GOD*** before receiving it. Those accepting the Mark, afterwards enjoy a ceremonial banquet as honored guests of the BEAST, and are given a videotape of them kneeling before the BEAST and worshipping him as god during the event.

However, of those refusing to take the Mark, their heads of household will be made to watch as their entire families are BEHEADED in front of them, then they as well will be BEHEADED and this is also televised worldwide. After the institution of the "Mark of the BEAST", all crimes against the Antichrist will be punishable by death, and the only form of government execution will be, decapitation by guillotine.

These events will take place daily, and all of the news networks will be made to cover the events. Everyone owning a television will be required by law to watch the event take place, and a tally of the IDENTIFICATION NUMBERS missing the telecast of the event will be given to the Antichrist. Then those without the proper excuses for missing the event will themselves take part in the next event, taking place on the following day.

None can be trusted:

There will be bounty money offered to them that turn over to the authorities the names or ID NUMBERS of them either not having the Mark, or those who have the Mark that are violating the law set forth by the Antichrist. No one will be able to trust another; not a father nor a son, a wife or a daughter, a brother nor a sister, aunts, uncles nor cousins; there won't be any friends; and none can be trusted. A man's enemies will be those of his own household; and many families having the Mark will separate themselves from each other, in fear of being sold out to the Antichrist by another family member for the bounty.

Worshipping the BEAST and the GOD of FORCES:

People will no longer openly criticize anything the government might do, for if they were to be reported for doing so, whether bearing the Mark or not, they would be put to death. Everyday at six o'clock in the evening, all the people will be required to gather before a television set and worship the BEAST (Antichrist) and the DEVIL whom the Antichrist calls the "GOD of FORCES".

> ***Daniel 11:38*** *But in his estate shall he honour the GOD of FORCES: and a god whom his fathers knew not shall he honour with gold, and silver, and with precious stones, and pleasant things.*

> ***Daniel 11:39*** *Thus shall he do in the most strong holds with a strange god, whom he shall acknowledge and increase with glory: and he shall cause them to rule over many, and shall divide the land for gain.*

The six o'clock worship session will be televised throughout the world, and in the poorer areas of the world where there aren't many televisions, the people will gather at their local churches to see the telecast, and local Officials throughout the world will verify and record who attends the service. This telecast will be a live event and based on local Jerusalem time, where the telecast will originate. So the times will vary throughout the world depending on what time zone one might be in at the time of the telecast, however the telecast must be viewed live.

NO RIGHTS:

Except for the Officials of the Government, everyone else will be stripped of his or her RIGHTS, not even having the right to live. The Government will dictate everything to everybody; when one may eat or sleep, where they may work, and even how much money they are allowed to have in their possession. At anytime during the day or night a Government Official may enter a home and remove from it whomsoever they desire for what ever reason, and that family member may or may not be returned.

Homosexuality will be the preferred life style and heterosexuals will be treated as Breeders and Second Class Citizens. At the age of ten, children being born to the Breeders will be the property of the State and can be used by the State as they so please. Some will be given to the BEAST or the DEVIL in sacrifice, even after the two are cast into HELL, while the other children may be used as workers of any sorts, or for entertainment purposes. The Roman Style Government set forth by the BEAST and the DEVIL will continue on throughout the MILLENNIUM PERIOD.

Earth During the MILLENNIUM:

The EARTH will continue during the MILLENNIUM and repopulate from the 104,000,000 survivors to 7,000,000,000 people over the one thousand years. These people will live normal life spans (60–80 years) outside of the NEW JERUSALEM and will continue in the same government format set forth by the BEAST and the DEVIL, even though the BEAST and the DEVIL had been CAST into HELL at the start of the MILLENNIUM.

Fertility and libido drugs will be given to the people over the age of ten to improve their sexual activity and the rate of childbirth during the one thousand years. Although cloning will be tried, the effort will fail due to hormone imbalances causing the clones to have gross deformities and premature death. Furthermore, the clones will be incapable of reproduction, because neither the male's sperm nor the females reproductive system will function properly and provide childbirth.

Due to the failure in cloning, the Government will mandate fornication between the male and female humans. The females will be required to bear children continually up to the age of 60, and the males will continually father the children up until their time of death. The EARTH will take on the likeness of SODOM and GOMORRAH, and there will be MANDATORY fornication periods everyday.

The Government will continually create more powerful libido drugs for the men, however the women will start dying at a very young age from the fertility drugs, because many of them will die while giving birth to several children at a time. Nearing the END of the MILLENNIUM and when the population approaches the seven billion mark, due to the lack of women in the world and the overwhelming sexual desire of the men, homosexual activities will run amuck throughout the world.

The END of the WORLD:

Five months prior to the END of the MILLENNIUM, the DEVIL again will be loose upon the EARTH, and over the FIVE MONTHS will seize control of it. He will then gather all seven billion of its inhabitants together and convince them to swarm the CITY of NEW JERUSALEM and take it by force. They will then encircle the GREAT CITY housing CHRIST and the BEHEADED SOULS, and once they do, ***GOD*** will DESTROY both them and the WORLD that they live in, and CAST the DEVIL back into the LAKE of FIRE whose FLAME cannot be QUENCHED.

> ***Revelation 20:7*** *And when the THOUSAND YEARS are EXPIRED, Satan shall be loosed out of his prison,*
>
> ***Revelation 20:8*** *And shall go out to DECEIVE the nations which are in the four quarters of the EARTH, GOG and MA'-GOG, to gather them together to BATTLE: the number of whom is as the sand of the sea.*

Revelation 20:9 *And they went up on the breadth of the EARTH, and compassed the CAMP of the SAINTS about, and the BE-LOVED CITY: and FIRE came down from* ***GOD*** *out of HEAVEN, and DEVOURED them.*

Revelation 20:10 *And the DEVIL that DECEIVED them was CAST into the LAKE of FIRE and BRIMSTONE, where the BEAST and the FALSE PROPHET are, and shall be TORMENTED day and night for ever and ever.*

Chapter 16

GOD'S COMMANDMENTS and LAWS

MOSES, while on Mount Sinai for FORTY-DAYS and FORTY-NIGHTS, was given ***GOD'S*** COMMANDMENTS and LAWS regarding both MORAL and SPIRITUAL BEHAVIOR. HE was also INSTRUCTED on how the ARK of the COVENANT and the TABERNACLE were to be fabricated, and given the RULES governing the Priests CONDUCT and what APPAREL they must wear while being in the ***PRESENCE of GOD.***

MOSES was given these COMMANDMENTS and LAWS in GREAT DETAIL for HIM and the people to follow, and TOLD; if the people in anyway VIOLATED ***GOD'S*** COMMANDMENTS, LAWS, or RULES of CONDUCT, those in VIOLATION while being in the ***PRESENCE of GOD*** would be CONSUMED by FIRE. However, if ***GOD'S*** COMMANDMENTS or LAWS were VIOLATED elsewhere, and not in the ***PRESENCE of GOD,*** the perpetrators of the VIOLATIONS were then to be considered UNCLEAN and UNFIT to be in the ***PRESENCE of GOD;*** because they had now SINNED against ***GOD.*** The UNCLEAN were not allowed back into ***GOD'S PRESENCE*** until they had received ATONEMENT (FORGIVENESS) for their SIN and made CLEAN by the ATONEMENT, and the ATONEMENT came only by OFFERING to ***GOD*** a BLOOD SACRIFICE. MOSES was also given the SPECIFICS on how the SACRIFICE was to be offered, and told if the SACRIFICE were to be IMPROPERLY OFFERED, those making the OFFERING would also be CONSUMED by FIRE. Furthermore, if the UNCLEAN were to come back into the ***PRESENCE of GOD*** prior to ATONEMENT, they as well would be CONSUMED by FIRE.

NOTE: The UNHOLY cannot be in the ***PRESENCE*** of the ***HOLY,*** so therefore, once SIN (the UNHOLY) comes into the ***PRESENCE of GOD*** (THE ***HOLY***), CONSUMMATION by THE ***HOLY*** takes place. This is a PURIFICATION PROCESS that occurs INSTANTANEOUSLY like a CHAIN REACTION. This can be compared to trying to mix any foreign particle with PURE ENERGY. Once the particle comes in contact with the ENERGY it is CONSUMED by the ENERGY, because ENERGY can only mix with ENERGY of the SAME LIKENESS.

None of the LAWS or RULES given to MOSES had exceptions to them, and this was made quite clear to MOSES. There weren't any ALTERNATIVES to ***GOD'S*** COMMANDMENTS, LAWS, or RULES of CONDUCT, all were to be specifically followed without ERROR! It was KEY to MOSES' UNDERSTANDING that ONE must be FREE from SIN to exist while being in the ***PRESENCE of GOD,*** and ***GOD'S*** COMMANDMENTS, LAWS, and RULES of CONDUCT determined a person's STATE of SIN. Any VIOLATION of ***GOD'S LAWS*** brought SIN upon the perpetrator, and if any person so DESIRED to COME INTO the ***PRESENCE of GOD***, that PERSON MUST BE FREE FROM SIN!

THE LORD has TOLD ME that only the SINLESS may ENTER into HEAVEN, being FREE from any SIN whatsoever. This is to say that even a SINGLE SIN upon a person's SOUL will deny that person's access to HEAVEN. After considering what ***THE LORD*** had TOLD ME, I became somewhat CONFUSED, because I know of NO ONE ever on this EARTH, EXCEPT for JESUS CHRIST, who hadn't SINNED or had not exposed themselves to SIN.

THE LORD then explained to ME how BAPTISM in THE ***SPIRIT of GOD*** INSTANTANEOUSLY and CONTINUALLY CLEANSES SIN. Once a PERSON is BAPTIZED, and that BAPTISM is CONFIRMED in HEAVEN, that PERSON'S SINS are CONSUMED; much like what happens to SIN when being in the ***PRESENCE of GOD.*** The PERSON then takes on the LIKENESS of CHRIST, the SON of ***GOD,*** being the LAMB without BLEMISH and SINLESS! While on the EARTH and in the presence of SIN, the COUNSELING against SIN and the CLEANSING of IT is ONGOING. The MOMENT the SOUL is exposed to SIN, the SIN is INSTANTANEOUSLY CONSUMED by THE ***HOLY SPIRIT of GOD,*** for that PERSON is now ***GOD'S DOMAIN,*** and SIN cannot exist in ***GOD'S DOMAIN!***

This may be a bit confusing to you, as it was to ME when ***THE LORD*** had FIRST TOLD ME of it; but once a PERSON is SAVED by BAPTISM in THE ***HOLY SPIRIT of GOD,*** that PERSON can no longer RETAIN SIN, for the SIN is CONSUMED at the very INSTANT the SOUL is EXPOSED to it; much in the same way that SIN is CONSUMED while in the ***PRESENCE of GOD.***

The WONDERFUL GIFT of ***HOLY SPIRIT*** BAPTISM, given by the GRACE of ***GOD,*** comes only as a RESULT of JESUS' willingness to DIE for the SINS of the WORLD upon the CROSS of CRUCIFIXION. JESUS came and lived a SINLESS LIFE on EARTH to be the SACRIFICIAL LAMB, without a BLEMISH, who was OFFERED to ***GOD*** for the ATONEMENT of the SINS of the WORLD. ONCE the ATONEMENT is RECEIVED through the BLOOD of the ***LAMB of GOD,*** that ATONEMENT is EVERLASTING, because with the ATONEMENT comes ***HOLY SPIRIT*** BAPTISM in the ***NAME of GOD;*** and that PERSON then becomes ***GOD'S DOMAIN!***

SEALING Versus BAPTISM

As previously explained in this BOOK, once THE ***DELIVERER 182*** leaves the EARTH with the BRIDE of CHRIST in the FIRST RAPTURE, BAPTISM in the ***SPIRIT of GOD*** CEASES and the ***SEAL*** of the ***LIVING GOD*** is GIVEN in lieu of BAPTISM. And, although the ***SEAL*** provides PROTECTION for the ONE RECEIVING it against EVIL, unlike BAPTISM in the SPIRIT, the ***SEAL*** does not CONSUME SIN! Therefore, after the ***SEAL*** has been RECEIVED, the person receiving it will more than likely have SIN upon their SOUL, and even though they are MARKED by the ***SEAL*** as to BELONGING to ***GOD,*** they are not SAVED, for they are not yet SINLESS.

These PEOPLE however will RECEIVE ***HOLY SPIRIT*** BAPTISM once in the MILLENNIUM and in their NEW FORM of FLESH. This change in physical anatomy is explained in "Revealing The Bible's Truth" in the Chapter titled "End or BEGINNING?" which should be READ to further your UNDERSTANDING of the phenomena. Once in the MILLENNIUM, the WEDDING GUESTS received from off the EARTH who were taken out of the GREAT TRIBULATION (not the ones RECEIVED from PARADISE, for they had already RECEIVED BAPTISM), will RECEIVE ***HOLY SPIRIT*** BAPTISM. The BAPTISMS for this GROUP will take place during the first few years of the MILLENNIUM, and those without BAPTISM will be SEGREGATED from them who are BAPTIZED while they are in their UN-BAPTIZED STATE.

This isn't meant to be any form of punishment for these PEOPLE, but is rather done to PROTECT them against being CONSUMED by THE ***HOLY SPIRIT,*** who will see them as SIN in the PRESENCE of the HOLY. However; once they are SAVED and have RECEIVED ***HOLY SPIRIT*** BAPTISM, they too may MINGLE with whosoever they DESIRE, and will be FREE to MOVE about within the CITY of NEW JERUSALEM; that of which will be a WORLD within a world, more so than a CITY within a world.

NEW JERUSALEM will be 1377 miles in it's LENGTH, WIDTH, and HEIGHT, and will sit ABOVE and be CENTERED on, where the old City of Jerusalem once sat.

Zechariah 14:9** And **THE LORD** shall be KING over ALL the EARTH: in that day shall there be **ONE LORD,** and **HIS NAME ONE.

***Zechariah 14:10** All the land shall be turned as a plain from Ge'-ba to Rim'-mon south of JERUSALEM: and it shall be LIFTED UP, and inhabited in HER PLACE, from Benjamin's Gate, unto the place of the First Gate, unto the Corner Gate, and from the Tower of Ha-nan'-e-el unto the King's winepresses.*

***Zechariah 14:11** And MEN shall DWELL in it, and there shall be no more utter destruction; but JERUSALEM will be SAFELY INHABITED.*

GOD'S LAWS and STATUTES

JESUS said that HE did not COME to change the LAW, but rather to FULFILL it. HE said, not any part of the LAW could be changed until the LAW had been adhered to and abided by during the EARTH'S LIFECYCLE.

Matthew 5:17 THINK NOT THAT I AM COME TO DESTROY THE LAW, OR THE PROPHETS: I AM NOT COME TO DESTROY, BUT TO FULFILL.

Matthew 5:18 FOR VERILY I SAY UNTO YOU, TILL HEAVEN AND EARTH PASS, ONE JOT OR ONE TITTLE SHALL IN NO WISE PASS FROM THE LAW, TILL ALL BE FULFILLED.

In these Scriptures JESUS is saying while on the EARTH, the LAWS and the STATUTES given to MOSES still all apply, regardless of time passing. This means WITHOUT EXCEPTION, every COMMANDMENT, STATUTE, PRECEPT, or RULE governing the SPIRITUAL and MORAL BEHAVIOR of MANKIND must be ENFORCED and ADHERED to by ANYONE expecting to go to HEAVEN! This furthermore means that no person is AUTHORIZED to CHANGE, MODIFY, MANIPULATE or DISREGARD ***GOD'S*** COMMANDMENTS, LAWS, STATUTES and PRECEPTS as they are WRITTEN into the TORAH (the Five Books of MOSES). JESUS makes this VERY CLEAR in the

Scriptures, and WE want to point out to you some DISCREPANCIES in MAN'S interpretation of ***GOD'S LAWS.***

GOD'S TEN COMMANDMENTS are given in the 20th Chapter of the Book of Exodus and then again in the 5th Chapter of the Book of Deuteronomy. These COMMANDMENTS given to MOSES apply in both the NEW and OLD COVENANTS that ***GOD*** made with ***HIS*** PEOPLE. Whereas the OLD COVENANT was based solely on the LAW, the NEW COVENANT is based on FAITH that abides within the LAW. However in either case the LAW still applies; and this is what JESUS had meant when HE said that HE hadn't come to change the LAW, but rather to FULFILL it. For now, only by FAITH can the LAW be FULFILLED.

Therefore, if a PERSON wants to stay in the GOOD GRACE of ***GOD,*** even though not BAPTIZED yet in the ***SPIRIT of GOD***, that PERSON must HONOR and OBEY ***GOD'S*** COMMANDMENTS, LAWS, STATUTES, and PRECEPTS. Then if that PERSON were to VIOLATE any of ***GOD'S*** COMMANDMENTS, LAWS, STATUTES, or PRECEPTS, REPENT and SEEK ATONEMENT (FORGIVENESS) by PRAYER in the NAME of JESUS CHRIST.

WE want to list for YOU the TEN COMMANDMENTS and make certain that YOU UNDERSTAND ***GOD'S*** WORD; for each and every time one of these COMMANDMENTS is VIOLATED in any way, SIN has come upon YOUR SOUL. This is also TRUE regarding ***GOD'S*** LAWS, STATUTES and PRECEPTS; for YOU have SINNED when you VIOLATE them as well, and IGNORANCE is NO EXCUSE ***SAITH THE LORD!***

THE FIRST COMMANDMENT:

THOU SHALT HAVE NO OTHER gods BEFORE ME!

NOTE: This COMMANDMENT says that NO PERSON or OBJECT should be more important to YOU than ***GOD;*** and that YOU should not allow ANYTHING or ANYBODY to come between ***HIM*** and YOU; and that YOU MUST always RECOGNIZE ***GOD*** as being the SOVEREIGN and SUPREME POWER over all that EXISTS!

THE SECOND COMMANDMENT:

THOU SHALT NOT MAKE UNTO THEE ANY GRAVEN IMAGE, OR ANY LIKENESS OF ANY THING THAT IS IN HEAVEN ABOVE, OR

THAT IS IN THE EARTH BENEATH, OR THAT IS IN THE WATER UNDER THE EARTH:

THOU SHALT NOT BOW DOWN THYSELF TO THEM, NOR SERVE THEM: FOR I THE LORD THY GOD AM A JEALOUS GOD, VISITING THE INIQUITY OF THE FATHERS UPON THE CHILDREN UNTO THE THIRD AND FOURTH GENERATION OF THEM THAT HATE ME;

AND SHEWING MERCY UNTO THOUSANDS OF THEM THAT LOVE ME, AND KEEP MY COMMANDMENTS!

NOTE: This COMMANDMENT says that no IMAGES whatsoever should be WORSHIPPED or allowed to be in a "PLACE of WORSHIP". It refers to ANY manmade OBJECTS; including CRUCIFIXES, STATUES made to resemble any HEAVENLY or earthly BEINGS of any sorts that are PERCEIVED to be HOLY OBJECTS by the MAKERS and the KEEPERS of them. It further says; ***GOD*** will hold anyone who does WORSHIP any GRAVEN OBJECTS of any sorts, ACCOUNTABLE for doing so, and they and their FAMILIES will be CURSED out to the FOURTH GENERATION. ***GOD*** further says in this COMMANDMENT, that ***HE*** will show MERCY to those who LOVE ***HIM*** and HONOR and OBEY ***HIS COMMANDMENTS, WHEREAS HE WILL CURSE THEM THAT DO NOT!***[1]

THE THIRD COMMANDMENT:

THOU SHALT NOT TAKE THE NAME OF THE LORD THY GOD IN VAIN; FOR THE LORD WILL NOT HOLD HIM GUILTLESS THAT TAKETH HIS NAME IN VAIN!

NOTE: This COMMANDMENT should be treated like a DOUBLE EDGED SWORD; for if VIOLATED in one way it is a FORGIVABLE SIN, however if the VIOLATION consists of a BLASPHEMY against THE ***HOLY SPIRIT of GOD,*** it becomes an UNFORGIVABLE SIN, ***SAITH THE LORD.*** In the former state, this would be a person's using ***GOD'S NAME*** CONTEMPTIBLY, such as to scorn someone; this is FORGIVABLE. However in the latter state, this would be to say that ***GOD*** had said something, when he had

Footnote 1: It may also be noted that even though ***THE LORD*** told Ezekiel that ***HE*** would not hold the fathers accountable for the son's actions, nor the sons accountable for the father's actions; ***HE*** will hold an entire family accountable out to the FOURTH GENERATION, if the father of the family were to VIOLATE ***HIS*** 2nd Commandment.

NOT; this is an UNFORGIVABLE SIN, ***SAITH THE LORD!*** ONE should be MOST CAUTIOUS when using ***THE LORDS NAME,*** for if it is PERCEIVED to be BLASPHEMOUS by THE ***HOLY SPIRIT*** the perpetrator of the BLASPHEMY has SEALED their FATE in HELL!

THE FOURTH COMMANDMENT:

REMEMBER THE SABBATH DAY, TO KEEP IT HOLY. SIX DAYS SHALT THOU LABOUR, AND DO ALL THY WORK: BUT THE SEVENTH DAY IS THE SABBATH OF THE LORD THY GOD: IN IT THOU SHALT NOT DO ANY WORK, THOU, NOR THY SON, NOR THY DAUGHTER, THY MANSERVANT, NOR THY MAIDSERVANT, NOR THY CATTLE, NOR THY STRANGER THAT IS WITHIN THY GATES:

FOR IN SIX DAYS THE LORD MADE THE HEAVEN AND THE EARTH, THE SEA, AND ALL THAT IN THEM IS, AND RESTED THE SEVENTH DAY: WHEREFORE THE LORD BLESSED THE SABBATH DAY, AND HALLOWED IT!

NOTE: JESUS clarified this COMMANDMENT to the Jews because they had misunderstood it; and ***THE LORD*** wants ME to further clarify it! ***GOD*** HALLOWED the SEVENTH DAY unto ***HIMSELF,*** and said it was to be a DAY of REST! The COMMANDMENT says that any work for personal gain is FORBIDDEN, for both YOU and them who are under your control. However, if something urgently needs to be attended to, and is not something that can be put off, nor is it something for personal gain; these things can be done on the SABBATH ***SAITH THE LORD. GOD IS STILL GOD ON THE SABBATH EVEN THOUGH IT BE HIS DAY OF REST; AND HE TENDS TO THOSE THINGS NEEDING HIS ATTENTION, WHETHER IT BE THE SABBATH OR NOT. YOU MAY AS WELL DO THE SAME; PROVIDING THAT THE WORK CANNOT BE PUT OFF, OR IS DONE IN THE SERVICE OF GOD, AND NOT FOR PERSONAL GAIN! THE LORD*** says that SATURDAY is the SEVENTH DAY, the SABBATH, and ***HIS*** HOLY DAY, and says that the CHURCHES ROUTINELY VIOLATE THIS COMMANDMENT!

THE FIFTH COMMANDMENT:

HONOUR THY FATHER AND THY MOTHER: THAT THY DAYS MAY BE LONG UPON THE LAND WHICH THE LORD THY GOD GIVETH THEE.

NOTE: GOD says that a SON or a DAUGHTER should both HONOR and be HOPEFUL that BOTH PARENTS have a LONG and fruitful LIFE. The COMMANDMENT further says that ***GOD*** has GIVEN both the PARENTS and the CHILDREN their PROPERTIES, and the CHILDREN will receive the parent's PROPERTIES in due time. It says that the children should not look towards an early inheritance but rather towards a long and prosperous life for their PARENTS.

THE SIXTH COMMANDMENT:

THOU SHALT NOT KILL!

NOTE: This COMMANDMENT says that NO PERSON has the right to take ANOTHER'S LIFE, except in a time of war or in the DEFENSE of ONE'S SELF or their FAMILIES, or for the PROTECTION of the INNOCENT. The law does not justify the overriding of this COMMANDMENT! Therefore, KILLING ONE for the punishment of any CRIME is a VIOLATION of this COMMANDMENT, ***SAITH THE LORD!***

THE SEVENTH COMMANDMENT:

THOU SHALT NOT COMMIT ADULTERY!

NOTE: This COMMANDMENT says that both the HUSBAND and the WIFE should hold the MARRIAGE COVENANT between them SACRED, allowing NO PERSON to come between them, departing from the MARRIAGE by death only.

THE EIGHTH COMMANDMENT:

THOU SHALT NOT STEAL!

NOTE: This COMMANDMENT states that ONE should not take for THEM SELF that which belongs to ANOTHER, and this INCLUDES CHEATING one out of their BELONGINGS as well, for CHEATING is merely another form of STEALING!

THE NINTH COMMANDMENT:

THOU SHALT NOT BEAR FALSE WITNESS AGAINST THY NEIGHBOUR!

NOTE: This COMMANDMENT says that ONE should not LIE nor FALSELY ACCUSE another under any circumstances, and that ***GOD*** will hold you ACCOUNTABLE for UNTRUTHFUL WORDS.

THE TENTH COMMANDMENT:

THOU SHALT NOT COVET THY NEIGHBOUR'S HOUSE, THOU SHALT NOT COVET THY NEIGHBOUR'S WIFE, NOR HIS MANSERVANT, NOR HIS MAIDSERVANT, NOR HIS OX, NOR HIS ASS, NOR ANY THING THAT IS THY NEIGHBOUR'S.

NOTE: This COMMANDMENT says that ONE should not be ENVIOUS of the holdings of ANOTHER, regardless of what the holdings may be; and be THANKFUL for what the ***GOOD LORD*** has GIVEN both you and those who are around you!

All TEN of the COMMANDMENTS are STRAIGHT FORWARD and haven't any loopholes in them. Any PERSON looking to SERVE and HONOR ***GOD,*** MUST HONOR, OBEY, and UPHOLD all TEN of ***GOD'S COMMANDMENTS,*** and allow neither MAN'S law or RULES to OVERRIDE or OUTWEIGH them. By LOVING and SERVING ***GOD, HE*** WILL SEE TO YOUR NOT VIOLATING ***HIS LAWS***, FOR BY FAITH SHALL YOU UPHOLD THEM!

GOD'S LAW versus Political Correctness

During the time that the Kings ruled over Judah and Israel, ***GOD*** provided each and every King with at least one Prophet. Whereas the King served the nation and its people, the Prophet served only ***GOD,*** and ***GOD*** gave the Kings the Prophets for a very specific reason. Whereas the King would look to the people's approval of his actions to maintain their support of him, the Prophet served only ***GOD*** and didn't care what the people thought of him. Whenever a King would make a declaration or decree that either disregarded or violated one of ***GOD'S LAWS,*** the Prophet would tell the King of his wrongdoing, and if the King were a just King, he would correct his course of action so it coincided and was in agreement with ***GOD'S LAWS.***

Throughout the OLD TESTAMENT, the BIBLE tells of how the Kings who had listened to the Prophets and stayed within ***GOD'S LAWS*** prospered, and how those Kings who did not listen to the Prophets and violated ***GOD'S LAWS*** had continually failed! These stories are put into the BIBLE to TEACH YOU that the success or failure of a nation of people is in direct proportion to either the success or failure of that nation's leadership in following ***GOD'S LAWS.***

When READING the BIBLE STORIES it is made CRYSTAL CLEAR that once ***GOD'S LAWS*** were abandoned or set aside to accommodate the King's laws or the people's wishes, that King and nation underwent chaos and into an immediate downfall. This phenomenon has happened routinely throughout the history of the world, and will continue to happen up until the TIME of the END! Whenever a nation's leadership places its laws above ***GOD'S LAWS*** or circumvents ***GOD'S LAWS*** to satisfy POLITICAL CORRECTNESS (the will of the people), that nation and its people are DOOMED, ***SAITH THE LORD, FOR I WILL SEE TO ITS DESTRUCTION!***

THE LORD wants ME to list some of the COMMON PRACTICES that VIOLATE ***HIS LAWS,*** and GIVE the Scripture that IDENTIFIES those VIOLATIONS.

Legalized Abortion:

THE LORD says, at the TIME of CONCEPTION, both a SPIRIT and a SOUL have been given to the CHILD within the WOMB; and the CHILD becomes a LIVING SOUL. Any premature removing of the CHILD from the WOMB for the purpose of causing the DEATH of the CHILD is a VIOLATION of ***GOD'S SIXTH COMMANDMENT.***

Exodus 20:13 THOU SHALT NOT KILL.

Legalized Capital Punishment:

THE LORD says, in the NEW COVENANT established by JESUS CHRIST, NO CRIME is WORTHY of DEATH, for JESUS CHRIST DEFEATED DEATH! Punishment by DEATH for a CRIME was abolished with the ABOLISHMENT of the OLD COVENANT ***SAITH THE LORD THY GOD, AND NO MAN HATH THE RIGHT TO TAKE ANOTHER'S LIFE!***

Exodus 20:13 THOU SHALT NOT KILL.

The Legalization and Embracement of Homosexuality:

THE LORD says that HOMOSEXUALITY is an ABOMINATION unto ***HIM,*** and even though in the NEW COVENANT Capital Punishment has been abolished, if there were a crime worthy of Capital Punishment, it would be the act of HOMOSEXUALITY; for neither MAN nor WOMAN should participate in such an act ***SAITH THE LORD.*** By either of the GENDERS participating in the HOMOSEXUAL ACT, they have DEFILED the SANCTITY of MARRIAGE that ***GOD*** holds SACRED between the MAN and the WOMAN.

> ***Leviticus 20:13*** *If a MAN also lie with MANKIND, as he lieth with a WOMAN, both of THEM have committed an ABOMINATION: they shall surely be put to death; their blood shall be upon them.*

The Removal of *GOD'S NAME* from the Public Domain:

THE LORD says, WHOMSOEVER shall REMOVE ***GOD'S NAME*** from ANYPLACE where ***HIS NAME*** shall RESIDE; ***THEIR NAMES AS WELL SHALL BE REMOVED FROM THE LAMBS BOOK OF LIFE!*** This is a VERY SERIOUS OFFENSE, because this is a BLASPHEMY against THE ***HOLY SPIRIT of GOD, WHOM RESIDES WHERE EVER THE NAME OF GOD RESIDES.***

> ***Matthew 12:32 AND WHOSOEVER SPEAKETH A WORD AGAINST THE SON OF MAN, IT SHALL BE FORGIVEN HIM: BUT WHOSOEVER SPEAKETH AGAINST THE HOLY GHOST, IT SHALL NOT BE FORGIVEN HIM, NEITHER IN THIS WORLD, NEITHER IN THE WORLD TO COME.***

> ***Matthew 10:28 AND FEAR NOT THEM WHICH KILL THE BODY, BUT ARE NOT ABLE TO KILL THE SOUL: BUT RATHER FEAR HIM WHICH IS ABLE TO DESTROY BOTH SOUL AND BODY IN HELL.***

Chapter 17
The Survivors

After the CONCLUSION of the GREAT WAR and the Battle at the Valley of Me-gid'-don (Armageddon), the DEVIL, the BEAST and the FALSE PROPHET are cast into HELL, and HELL is once more shut up and sealed off from the EARTH. The Book of Daniel tells you that this happens ONE THOUSAND TWO HUNDRED and NINETY DAYS after the SOUNDING of the FIRST TRUMPET.

The POURING out of the FIRST VIAL of the ***WRATH of GOD*** that happens TWENTY-ONE MONTHS after the FIRST TRUMPET SOUNDS, MARKS the setting up of the "ABOMINATION that makes DESOLATE" in the TEMPLE of ***GOD*****,** and the "MARK of the BEAST".

It also MARKS the MIDPOINT of the GREAT TRIBULATION and the FINAL TWENTY-ONE and one-half MONTHS of the ONE THOUSAND TWO HUNDRED and NINETY DAY (FORTY-THREE MONTH) GREAT TRIBULATION PERIOD. After the GREAT TRIBULATION has ended, there is yet a FORTY-FIVE DAY PERIOD of time in which the balance of them who had been either wounded during the GREAT WAR, or afflicted by the PLAGUES brought on by the GREAT TRIBULATION who hadn't yet died, will die. The world's population at the conclusion of the FORTY-FIVE DAY PERIOD of DEATH will be 104,000,000 people in total.

NOTE: Although there appears to be a conflict in the Scriptures of the Book of Daniel when being compared to the Scriptures of the Book of Revelation, as to the length of TIME in which the GREAT TRIBULATION PERIOD takes place, there isn't a CONFLICT. The Book of Daniel says the GREAT TRIBULATION goes on for a ONE THOUSAND TWO-HUNDRED AND NINETY-DAY PERIOD, whereas the Book of Revelation (Revelation 12:6) says that it goes on over a ONE THOUSAND TWO-HUNDRED AND SIXTY-DAY PERIOD. The TIME in which the GREAT TRIBULATION takes place is actually ONE THOUSAND TWO-HUNDRED AND SEVENTY-EIGHT DAYS, and Daniel simply rounded that number up, whereas the Apostle John rounded it down. The GREAT TRIBULATION happens over a THREE and ONE-HALF

YEAR PERIOD of TIME. When using the Jewish calendar this comes out to be 1260 days, and this is what the Apostle John based the three and one-half years on. The Prophet Daniel added in one extra 30-day month to allow for the error in the Jewish calendar and this is why there is a 30-day discrepancy in time between the two. This is why the PERIOD of GREAT TRIBULATION is also expressed elsewhere in both the Scriptures of Daniel and in the Book of Revelation as being a TIME, and TIMES, and a HALFTIME, rather than being expressed in a number of DAYS.

Those who survive the GREAT TRIBULATION and the FORTY-FIVE DAYS of death after its CONCLUSION are referred to in the Book of Daniel, as being BLESSED.

> ***Daniel 12:11*** *And from the time that the daily sacrifice is taken away, and the ABOMINATION that maketh DESOLATE set up, there shall be a THOUSAND TWO HUNDRED and NINETY DAYS.*

> ***Daniel 12:12*** *Blessed is he that waiteth, and cometh to the THOUSAND THREE HUNDRED and FIVE and THIRTY DAYS.*

The BLESSED are the SURVIVING people of the GREAT TRIBULATION who are spared by ***GOD*** to re-populate the EARTH during the ONE-THOUSAND-YEAR long MILLENNIUM PERIOD of HEAVEN on EARTH. Of the 104,000,000 survivors, 77,000,000 of them will be from the United States of America, and will be people who had lived primarily in the mid-western states. The eastern seaboard and the west coast of the United States were completely DESTROYED during the GREAT WAR, leaving only a few people alive, however, the mid-western states was not hit nearly as hard and there were many survivors.

Aside from those in the Continental United States who had survived, there remain 27,000,000 other people who are scattered throughout the world, with neither a Jew nor an Arab among them. Nearly all of the 104,000,000 survivors are of the GENTILE, with only a very few being of the Canaanite Seed (less than 10,000). Over a ten-year span of time, nearly all of the 27,000,000 who are scattered throughout the world will migrate to the United States of America to live, and a World Government will be formed there that will follow the same doctrine of government that had been instituted by the DEVIL and BEAST during the GREAT TRIBULATION.

Any form of religion will be banned from society by the government, because them remaining on the EARTH will blame the EARTH'S DESTRUCTION on its previous religious culture. However, these people OUT of FEAR will still WORSHIP ***GOD*** on ***HIS*** HOLY DAYS, even though they HATE ***HIM*** and any type of religious order. At the conclusion of the GREAT TRIBULATION, ***GOD*** COMMANDS them left on the EARTH to come up to JERUSALEM and WORSHIP on the 13th Day of October, and to also HONOR ***HIS*** other SABBATHS regardless of where they may be on the SABBATHS.

GOD WARNS the people left on the EARTH, that if anyone were to not WORSHIP ***HIM*** or acknowledge ***HIS*** HOLY DAYS, those failing to OBEY ***HIM*** will be CONSUMED by FIRE, a FIRE that will come down from HEAVEN. ***GOD*** further WARNS the communities of the EARTH as well as the individuals, that if they were to FAIL to ENFORCE ***HIS COMMANDMENTS*** and allow anyone of that community to DISOBEY ***HIM***, the whole community would be CURSED, and hardships would be LEVIED on them along with the individual who had DISOBEYED.

> ***Zechariah 14:16*** *And it shall come to pass, that every one that is left of ALL the NATIONS which came against JERUSALEM shall even go up from year to year to WORSHIP the KING,* ***THE LORD of HOSTS,*** *and to keep the FEAST of TABERNACLES.*

> ***Zechariah 14:17*** *And it shall be, that whoso will not come up of ALL the families of the EARTH unto JERUSALEM to WORSHIP the KING,* ***THE LORD of HOSTS,*** *even upon them shall be no RAIN.*

> ***Zechariah 14:18*** *And if the family of Egypt go not up, and come not, that have no RAIN; there shall be the PLAGUE, wherewith* ***THE LORD*** *will smite the HEATHEN that come not up to keep the FEAST of TABERNACLES.*

THE PLAGUE:

> ***Zechariah 14:12*** *And this shall be the PLAGUE wherewith* ***THE LORD*** *will smite all the people that have fought against JERUSALEM; Their FLESH shall CONSUME away while they stand upon their feet, and their EYES shall CONSUME away in their holes, and their TONGUE shall CONSUME away in their mouth.*

NOTE: The last Scripture explains what will happen to them who fail to

WORSHIP ***GOD*** and recognize ***HIS SABBATHS*** during the MILLENNIUM. However, the same Scripture also explains what happens to them who come up to fight against the CITY of NEW JERUSALEM at the CONCLUSION of the MILLENNIUM PERIOD.

All the people of the world will be required once a year to come up to the CITY of NEW JERUSALEM to HONOR and WORSHIP ***THE LORD of HOSTS,*** on the DAY of the FEAST of TABERNACLES held on the 13th DAY of October. This is the same DAY that ***GOD*** had COME DOWN to ME in the year of 1997. This HOLY DAY had been previously celebrated on the 15th day of October by the Jews, and was called the Day of Booths as well as the FEAST of TABERNACLES. However, ***THE LORD*** has told ME that it should have ALWAYS been on the 13th DAY of OCTOBER and not on the 15th DAY as so stated by MOSES (Leviticus 23:34), to CELEBRATE the BIRTH of JESUS CHRIST who was BORN on the 13th DAY of OCTOBER!

NEW JERUSALEM

As previously explained in this BOOK, the CITY of NEW JERUSALEM is more like a WORLD within a world rather than a CITY within a world. This is said in this way, because the CITY of NEW JERUSALEM will be a THREE DIMENSIONAL CITY existing in a FOUR DIMENSIONAL WORLD; having a MAGNIFICENT PROPORTION to it; being 1377 miles (144,000 furlongs) in length, 1377 miles (144,000,000 furlongs) in width, and 1377 miles (144,000 furlongs) in height, and not having a TIME DIMENSION within its CONFINES.

The CITY of NEW JERUSALEM will hover above the location where the original City of Jerusalem once sat, and ALL of the occupants of the EARTH will be made to come up to the GATES of the CITY once a year on the FEAST of TABERNACLES to HONOR ***GOD.***

During the first few years after the GREAT TRIBULATION there will be some people who will refuse to OBEY and will not come up to JERUSALEM as they had been so COMMANDED, for the FEAST of TABERNACLES. Nor will they HONOR ***THE LORD'S SABBATHS.*** However, once the others see before their very eyes, what ***GOD*** does to these people for their DISOBEDIENCE, all thereafter will OBEY as COMMANDED out of FEAR!

Although they are not allowed ACCESS to the CITY, nor could they enter even if they were allowed to, (for the CITY is SUSPENDED in air and ONE must ASCEND to enter), food from the FEAST is brought outside of the CITY'S GATES to the HEATHEN; so they too might eat of the FOOD prepared for the FEAST in HONOR of ***GOD.***

As mentioned earlier, TIME is nonexistent in NEW JERUSALEM and nothing ages once within the CITY GATES. There is a MATURING process for all things that grow, but once maturity is reached, the process stops. This is also true for the PEOPLE within the CITY of NEW JERUSALEM; for once they have MATURED to the EQUIVALENCY of THIRTY-THREE YEARS of AGE, they age no further during the BALANCE of the ONE THOUSAND YEARS. Mothers and Fathers will appear to look the same age as their Grandparents and Great Grandparents and as their Children, once the children have reached their MATURITY.

ALL living within the CONFINES of the CITY, MAN and animal alike, will no longer process their food as they had previously done while being on EARTH in FLESH. They now will CONSUME their FOOD in its entirety, therefore leaving no waste byproduct resulting from the FOOD behind, as they had once done in their previous form of FLESH. The NEW form of FLESH RECEIVED by ALL of the INHABITANTS of NEW JERUSALEM will be the same FLESH that ADAM and EVE once had, up until the TIME they were made to leave the GARDEN of EDEN. Prior to their being CAST OUT of the GARDEN, ***THE LORD*** changed ADAM and EVE'S ANATOMY, making it the same as the GENTILE who processed food rather than CONSUMING it. It is the food waste byproduct that became the breeding ground for bacteria, thus causing illness and death to occur in the body of flesh. The BODY of FLESH originally given to ADAM and EVE had an intended life expectancy of ONE THOUSAND YEARS.

This is why as TIME progressed, the Scriptures show a decline in how long people lived, with none living to the ONE THOUSAND YEAR life expectancy originally intended for ADAM and EVE. Both bacteria and time caused the body of flesh to degrade and die. Once outside of the GARDEN, neither ADAM nor EVE lived out their entire life spans, with only Methuselah coming close to it by living to the age of 969, however still falling short of the ONE THOUSAND YEARS, by THIRTY-ONE YEARS.

Not only did the food waste byproduct cause illness and death to occur prematurely, the DIMENSION of TIME when introduced to the PHYSICAL BEING outside of the GARDEN of EDEN, caused the physical body to age and deteriorate. Then as TIME PROGRESSED so did the AGING PROCESS progress, with the life expectancy declining continually down through the generations. During the TIME of DAVID, people were living to be between the ages of seventy or eighty years old, and life spans continued to decline by generation after DAVID. With the exception of some of the Disciples, most people died in their fifties and sixties during the time of JESUS and in their forties and fifties up until the late 1800's. Then with the advent of medicines, most specifically antibiotics, life spans started to increase with the ability to fight infection caused by bacteria. Life spans are now about the same as they were during the TIME of DAVID due to these medicines. However the aging process continues to hasten with time and even though people now live a little longer, they now age faster than the previous generations.

The World Outside of NEW JERUSALEM

During the first one hundred years of the MILLENNIUM, many of the damaged earth structures are rebuilt. However due to a shortage in manpower and the many contaminated areas of the world as a result of radiation fallout, the rebuilding of the structures is slow and takes place primarily in what was once the central United States. Due to the birthrate being low, and the population only increasing by one percent per decade, the New World Government approves the process of human cloning.

At first, the cloning of human beings appeared to be going well, however over a period of time, the clones developed a hormone imbalance causing them to have deformities in their internal organs, ultimately causing premature death of the clone. It was also found that the clones could not reproduce and give birth, even when the male or female clone copulated with a normal person. The sperm of the male clone was impotent and the female clone's ovaries failed to function as a normal woman's would. Many experiments were tried, such as DNA matching for the clones to see if a clone could mate with another clone of the same DNA structure, but all attempts failed and no offspring could be produced. The use of clones for vital organ donors was also abandoned, because the hormone imbalance of the clone made their internal organs unsuitable for transplanting.

After sixty years of the cloning effort, the cloning program was abolished, and the government made a law regarding mandatory child bearing by anyone being able to conceive and bear a child. This was done in an effort to increase the population to a level of manpower that was needed for the rebuilding of the earth.

An all out effort was done in the research and development of libido and fertility drugs, and the public was mandated by law to not only take the drugs, but to have daily sexual intercourse with at least three different partners per day. After two hundred years of mandated childbirth by the government, marriage became obsolete and was abolished by law. The Government Leaders told the people that the obligation made by their marriage vows conflicted with the government's laws regarding multiple partner copulation, and that marriage was now illegal and could no longer be practiced in any form whatsoever!

The government then formed breeding centers, and women by law had to bear children annually up to the age of sixty. The men were also required by law to visit the breeding centers two hours per day (or as long as it would take to fertilize three women), everyday, and their term of commitment for breeding was life long, starting at the age of twelve.

Anyone caught violating any of the laws was put into labor camps for some period of time, with the time varying depending on the violation, and capital punishment was abolished altogether. This was done because the world's population was so low it couldn't afford to loose any of its subjects. At that time its population was under 300,000,000 people, even after two hundred and fifty years of forced breeding.

Three hundred years into the MILLENNIUM, research centers of the government develop a libido drug and treatment program using various steroids and synthetic hormones for men. This treatment will allow men at any age the ability to ejaculate up to six times daily, having the sperm count and potency levels of a nineteen year old male. They also develop a fertility drug for the women enabling them to have no fewer than three children at a time, and over the next one hundred years the population of the world increases to nearly 1,000,000,000 people.

However, due to the fertility drugs, some women start to die while giving birth to multiple children at one time. So the Government then decides to dilute the fertility drug, but finds that the drug still remains in the women's systems even after they had been taken off of it. During the next fifty years, although the population of the world has increased to nearly 1.5 billion, the ratio of men to women starts to increase. Nearly 60% of the world's population at this time is now men, even though the birthrate of both males and females is still nearly equal.

To counter this imbalance between the male and female population, the government signs into law a mandate requiring, all males at the age of ten years old must be turned over to the government. The government then selects which males may be used for breeding or for any of the various jobs the government deems appropriate for them.

All free enterprise had been abolished at the onset of the NEW WORLD GOVERNMENT, as it so called itself, and all merchandising, manufacturing, or servicing of any type was owned, regulated, and controlled by the State. The government then placed the people as it saw fit into the various job categories, with similar job responsibilities given similar pay for an equivalent category of work. All banking became abolished, and no person was allowed to have in his or her possession more money (credits) than what could be earned by his or her wages for three months. Excess money (credits) was to be handed over to the local officials and kept in a community fund for the betterment of the community. Whoever was caught failing to disclose or to hand over their excess money (credits) to the community fund, were then no longer paid their wage by the government, and were put on government welfare programs which provided only the bare essentials to live. The balance of the wage they had previously earned was then disbursed to the community fund.

Five hundred years into the MILLENNIUM the population had grown to be nearly 3,000,000,000 people, however only a little over one-third of them were females, and this lack of females caused the men to turn to homosexuality. The libido drug program was then halted for the men, but the centuries of the men taking the drug had caused the males to genetically inherit and maintain the same excessive sexual behavior that was originally produced by the drugs.

The government then decided to no longer allow women to work at any job, and signed into law a decree that said: anyone caught using a woman for any type of work whatsoever would be put to death for it. Hence, once again the government enacted Capital Punishment as a deterrent to crime. The women were then kept at the breeding centers and were no longer allowed to be out within the general population, and only the male breeders had access to them. This caused the homosexual activity of the men to further increase and by the end of the seven hundredth year of the MILLENNIUM the men had come to prefer homosexuality to heterosexuality. The population during the seven hundredth year had now increased to be slightly over 4,750,000,000 people, and the female content of the population had also increased to equal 45% of the overall populous.

Due to the overwhelming numbers of homosexual men, the government began to embrace homosexual behavior, and the government took on the form of Sodom and Gomorrah. There were televised events of homosexual acts being routinely broadcasted by the State ran channels and women were rarely seen on any of its broadcasted shows. It was commonplace to see homosexual behavior between men on the city streets, and near to the end of the nine hundredth year of the MILLENNIUM, one of the highest paying jobs for the government, was that of a breeder, because most men detested having sex with a woman, and demanded a great deal of money to do so.

During the nine hundredth year, women were once again allowed to leave the breeding centers. However, the men were not receptive to them and the women would gather together in groups by themselves, and they also participated in homosexuality. The population was now nearing the 7,000,000,000 mark, and the government no longer took an interest in further population growth.

With the breeding and birthing centers now being nearly abandoned, very few children were being born at the end of the nine hundredth year and the EARTH'S POPULATION was stymied at 7,000,000,000.

During the ONE THOUSAND YEAR long MILLENNIUM, government technology in all areas of science was now at a level of one thousand times greater than it had been at the start of the MILLENNIUM. Objects could be broken down to the molecular level and transported by riding on radio waves from one place to another, and even time travel had been successfully achieved. Then during the last five months of the MILLENNIUM, the DEVIL was released once again from HELL and immediately thereafter took back control of the EARTH.

He convinced the people that they no longer had to WORSHIP ***GOD*** or obey ***HIS COMMANDMENTS,*** as they had done over the past nine hundred and ninety-nine years. He said that he would protect them from ***GOD,*** and that he was now their ***GOD*** as he had been in the past during the GREAT TRIBULATION. The people believed Lucifer because they hated ***GOD,*** and Lucifer performed many miracles and demonstrated his great power before them, and the people worshipped him.

On October the 13th when it became time again for the people to go up to the CITY of NEW JERUSALEM to WORSHIP ***GOD*** during the FEAST of TABERNACLES, the DEVIL devised a plan. The people were told to bring with them the Time Travel Equipment he had them modify to accommodate the masses of people, and once the GATES of the CITY were OPENED to bring out the food for the FEAST, they were to activate the equipment. Lucifer told the people, that once they were within the time warp provided by the Time Travel Equipment, they could ascend into the CITY, and that even ***GOD*** could not keep them from entering the CITY and taking it by force once they were in the time warp.

However ***GOD*** knew ***HIS*** ENEMIES (GOG and MA'-GOG) every move, and once the 7,000,000,000 of them encompassed the CITY of NEW JERUSALEM, FIRE came down from ***GOD*** out of HEAVEN and CONSUMED each and every one of them. Lucifer was then again taken captive and cast back into HELL where he must reside until the next generation of the EARTH, when NOAH once more releases him from the ARK into the NEW EARTH.

Revelation 20:7 *And when the thousand years are expired, SATAN shall be loosed out of his prison.*

Revelation 20:8 *And shall go out to DECEIVE the NATIONS which are in the four quarters of the EARTH, GOG and MA'-GOG, to gather them together to BATTLE: the number of whom is as the sand of the sea.*

Revelation 20:9 *And they went up the breadth of the EARTH, and COMPASSED the CAMP of the SAINTS about, and the BELOVED CITY: and FIRE came down from* ***GOD*** *out of HEAVEN, and DEVOURED them.*

Revelation 20:10 *And the DEVIL that DECEIVED them was CAST into the LAKE of fire and BRIMSTONE, where the BEAST and the FALSE PROPHET are, and shall be tormented day and night for ever and ever.*

Chapter 18

LIFE within the CITY WALLS

In the last Chapter WE told you about the "Survivors" who live during the MILLENNIUM outside of the CITY of NEW JERUSALEM. These people live out normal life spans (60-80 years) and repopulate the world over the ONE THOUSAND YEAR MILLENNIUM PERIOD. Other than their being made to HONOR ***GOD'S SABBATHS,*** the people of the world primarily live under the law of the land, which is dictated to them by the government; whose laws deny ownership and marriage, and routinely violate ***GOD'S LAWS*** regarding MORALITY.

In this Chapter WE shall talk about them who LIVE within the CITY WALLS of NEW JERUSALEM and LOVE and WORSHIP ***GOD,*** unlike them that live outside of the CITY and worship ***GOD*** only out of FEAR! It was previously told to you that the CITY of NEW JERUSALEM was much more like a WORLD within a world rather than being a city within a world, and that within the CONFINES of the CITY TIME is irrelevant, because the DIMENSION of TIME does not exist within the CITY.

We can therefore distinguish between the TWO WORLDS by their differences in PHYSICAL DIMENSIONS. The world outside of NEW JERUSALEM is much like the world you live in now, having FOUR PHYSICAL DIMENSIONS, "LENGTH", "WIDTH", "HEIGHT", and "TIME". The WORLD housing the CITY of NEW JERUSALEM however does not have a TIME DIMENSION, thus making all within the CONFINES of the CITY "TIMELESS", albeit still having the other THREE PHYSICAL DIMENSIONS of "LENGTH", "WIDTH", and "HEIGHT".

The world outside of the CITY has both a night and a day, and the light of that world comes from the sun during the daylight hours, and from the moon in the evening. It is the rising of the sun and the going down of it that governs the element of TIME within the world outside of the CITY, and with every cycle of the sun one day is SPENT. The sun acts much like a ticking clock and the measurement of TIME is relative to the EARTH'S MOVEMENT about the sun. Therefore, if the EARTH were to stay fixed about the sun and never turn its backside to it, the side facing the sun would remain in DAYLIGHT, whereas its backside would remain in DARKNESS. In either of the TWO CASES of the EARTH being fixed about the sun, by neither spinning on its own axis or orbiting around the sun, TIME would become a CONSTANT rather than a VARIABLE, and therefore irrelevant.

The CITY of NEW JERUSALEM is not dependant on the sun for its LIGHT, for the LIGHT of ***GOD*** provides its LIGHT, and furthermore, the LIGHT of ***GOD*** does not cycle as does the light from the sun and it REMAINS CONSTANT throughout ETERNITY. The Scriptures throughout the HOLY BIBLE speak of this phenomenon and although it may be somewhat difficult for you to grasp at this time, the CONCEPT of "IRRELEVANT TIME" is REAL!

> ***Isaiah 60:19*** *The SUN shall no more be thy LIGHT by day; neither for brightness shall the MOON give LIGHT unto thee: but* ***THE LORD*** *shall be thine EVERLASTING LIGHT, and thy* ***GOD*** *thy GLORY.*

> ***Isaiah 60:20*** *Thy SUN shall no more go down; neither shall thy MOON withdraw itself: for* ***THE LORD*** *shall be thine EVERLASTING LIGHT, and the days of thy MOURNING shall be ENDED.*

> ***Revelation 22:5*** *And there shall be NO NIGHT there; and they need no candle, neither light of the SUN; for* ***THE LORD GOD*** *giveth them LIGHT: and they shall REIGN for EVER and EVER.*

Therefore, the ONE THOUSAND YEAR MILLENNIUM PERIOD can be viewed as being ONE SINGLE DAY, with that DAY being ONE THOUSAND YEARS LONG when compared to the number of the cycles of the sun taking place during that ONE DAY! The Apostle Peter UNDERSTOOD the CONCEPT of "IRRELEVANT TIME", and although I rarely make references to the Epistles, because they are not the *WORD of* ***GOD,*** I will cite one verse taken from the 2nd Epistle of Peter, to verify that Peter UNDERSTOOD the CONCEPT of "IRRELEVANT TIME"!

> ***2 Peter 3:8*** *But, beloved, be not ignorant of this one thing, that one day is with* ***THE LORD*** *as a THOUSAND YEARS, and a THOUSAND YEARS as ONE DAY.*

Hopefully you can see that the Scriptures match what WE have told you thus far about the CITY of NEW JERUSALEM; being a WORLD of its own and TIMELESS, while it yet exists within in a world governed by time. There is a reason why ***THE LORD*** makes the CITY TIMELESS, for if ***HE*** did not, ***HE*** wouldn't be fulfilling THE LORD'S PRAYER. THE LORD'S PRAYER says: "Thy KINGDOM COME, thy WILL be DONE, on EARTH as it is in HEAVEN"! Therefore, by HEAVEN being TIMELESS, the CITY of NEW JERUSALEM, being representative of HEAVEN on EARTH, must also be TIMELESS!

There is yet another oddity to be discussed about the CITY of NEW JERUSALEM that has already been mentioned in this BOOK but not yet EX-PLAINED. You were told earlier that the CITY of NEW JERUSALEM hovers above the land where the city of old Jerusalem had once sat; and there are SEV-ERAL very SPECIFIC reasons as to why the CITY'S locale must be in that very place, but for now WE will discuss only ONE of those REASONS.

The Scriptures given in the HOLY BIBLE are ***GOD'S DIVINE WILL,*** and JESUS CHRIST said also in HIS PRAYER to ***THE LORD;*** "THY ***WILL*** BE DONE", thus meaning ALL SCRIPTURE must be FULFILLED. The Prophet Zechariah says in the 12th Chapter of his Book of Prophecy, that JERUSALEM will be inhabited in its OWN PLACE, therefore necessitating the CITY of NEW JERUSALEM'S LOCALE.

> ***Zechariah 12:6*** *In that day will **I** make the governors of Judah like an hearth of FIRE among the wood, and like a torch of FIRE in a sheaf; and they shall DEVOUR all the people round about, on the right hand and on the left: and JERUSALEM shall be INHABITED AGAIN in HER OWN PLACE, even in Jerusalem.*

This last Scripture explains why the CITY of NEW JERUSALEM must be located on the EARTH where it had once been, however it does not explain why the CITY must hover above that location rather than its sitting on the EARTH. First of all, one must UNDERSTAND that the CITY of NEW JERUSALEM is not a STRUCTURE that had been constructed on the EARTH, but rather a STRUCTURE that was CONSTRUCTED in HEAVEN and brought down to the EARTH. This is explained in the book of Revelation.

> ***Revelation 21:2*** *And I John saw the HOLY CITY, NEW JERUSA-LEM, coming down from **GOD** out of HEAVEN, prepared as a BRIDE adorned for her HUSBAND.*

The CITY of NEW JERUSALEM both descends from HEAVEN at the BEGINNING of the MILLENNIUM, and ASCENDS back to HEAVEN at the CONCLUSION of the MILLENNIUM; therefore FULFILLING ***GOD'S PROMISE*** by Scripture, of the COMING of HEAVEN to the EARTH (Thy ***KINGDOM*** COME). Furthermore, by the CITY being a STRUCTURE of HEAVENLY CONSTRUCTION and UNCHANGEABLE by TIME, if it were to be setting upon the EARTH rather than HOVERING above it, it would be the same as if one were to set the foundation of an earthly house upon a major fault line. The house would eventually move off its foundation, for the EARTH forever changes with TIME!

GOD'S PEOPLE, ISRAEL

There are 7,000,000,000 PEOPLE that live within the CITY'S WALLS, and these PEOPLE are called ISRAEL, and the CITY itself is called ZION, ***GOD'S*** HOLY MOUNTAIN and NEW JERUSALEM. Of the 7,000,000,000, there are THREE CATEGORIES of PEOPLE. The first GROUP is called the EARTH ANGEL, and these are Angels who had come down from HEAVEN to serve a DIVINE PURPOSE for ***GOD*** while on EARTH. During each LIFE CYCLE of the EARTH (7,000 years), 500,000,000 Angels come down to the EARTH, with the bulk of them coming after the RESURRECTION of JESUS CHRIST (over the last 2,000 years).

Except for SIX ANGELS, the ANGEL in HEAVEN hasn't a GENDER, so each Angel must come twice to the EARTH, once as a male, and once as a female. Therefore, the ONE BILLION Angels that ENTER the MILLENNIUM leave it being FIVE HUNDRED MILLION complete ANGELS rather than ONE BILLION Angels with GENDER. During the MILLENNIUM these Angels cohabitate with their other half just like the WEDDING GUESTS and the BRIDE of CHRIST do with their SOUL MATES. Then at the CONCLUSION of the MILLENNIUM, the TWO GENDERS of EARTH Angels RECOMBINE as they once were in HEAVEN and ASCEND as a COMPLETE ANGEL back into HEAVEN.

The SECOND CATEGORY of PEOPLE living within NEW JERUSALEM is called CHRIST, and CHRIST consists of 4,000,000,000 people. Within CHRIST there are TWO different GROUPS of PEOPLE, ONE GROUP is called the BRIDE of CHRIST and the OTHER is called the WEDDING GUESTS, or GUESTS of the WEDDING SUPPER. Of the 4,000,000,000 in CHRIST, only 104,000,000 of them are of the BRIDE of CHRIST, and the remaining 3,896,000,000 are all of the WEDDING GUESTS. At the CONCLU-

SION of the MILLENNIUM, both the BRIDE and the WEDDING GUESTS ASCEND in CHRIST to HEAVEN. Both GROUPS in CHRIST keep their GENDER while in HEAVEN and reside with their SOUL MATE throughout ETERNITY.

The THIRD CATEGORY of PEOPLE in NEW JERUSALEM is called the "BEHEADED SOULS". There are 2,000,000,000 "BEHEADED SOULS", all of which are of the GENTILE that enter into the MILLENNIUM with the EARTH ANGEL and CHRIST; however, none of these people ever ascends beyond the EARTH PLANE. At the CONCLUSION of the MILLENNIUM these people return to the DUST of the EARTH, with some of them given a second chance at life. Those of the "BEHEADED SOULS" who had excelled in their SERVICE to ***GOD*** during the MILLENNIUM will be given a SECOND chance to become ONE in CHRIST. In the next REGENERATION of the EARTH, they will be born once more in the FLESH and given the opportunity to be SAVED by being BAPTIZED in the ***SPIRIT of GOD.***

NOTE: All of the "BEHEADED SOULS" come from the GENTILE and are them that had never been BAPTIZED in the ***SPIRIT of GOD,*** but had MARTYRED themselves in the NAME of ***GOD*** and in the TESTIMONY of JESUS CHRIST. This is not to be confused with the many religious fanatics who had killed innocent people and claimed to be doing so in the NAME of ***GOD (ALLAH),*** for they ALL have since went to HADES; and after JUDGMENT will be CAST into HELL! It must also be REMEMBERED that a MARTYR must give his or her life in BOTH the ***NAME of GOD,*** and in the TESTIMONY of JESUS CHRIST; so one cannot martyr his or herself if they do not BELIEVE in JESUS! ALL of the "BEHEADED SOULS" come after the RESURRECTION of JESUS CHRIST (over the last 2,000 years), with the VAST MAJORITY of the "BEHEADED SOULS" coming out of the GREAT TRIBULATION.

In summary: 7,000,000,000 PEOPLE ENTER the MILLENNIUM and LIVE within the CITY of NEW JERUSALEM during the ONE THOUSAND YEARS of HEAVEN on EARTH. Then of the 7,000,000,000, 2,000,000,000 return to the DUST of the EARTH, 4,000,000,000 ASCEND to HEAVEN in CHRIST, and 1,000,000,000 EARTH Angels UNITE and ASCEND as 500,000,000 COMPLETE ANGELS in HEAVEN.

The CITY'S Architecture

The CITY of NEW JERUSALEM is like no other city on the EARTH, because there are THIRTEEN LEVELS to it. In measurement from the 1st LEVEL to the 2nd LEVEL there is a ONE HUNDRED FOURTEEN and THREE QUARTER MILES of elevation to it, and as the CITY ASCENDS, its perimeter decreases. Then from the 2nd LEVEL to the 3rd, there is also another ONE HUNDRED FOURTEEN and THREE QUARTER MILES of elevation, and its perimeter further decreases from that of the 2nd LEVEL and this continues on throughout the remaining LEVELS of the CITY. If you can visualize the CITY and see as it raises and declines in its perimeter, you should see that it forms a GIGANTIC PYRAMID, somewhat like a MOUNTAIN rising up out of the SEA. This is why ***GOD*** refers to ***HIS HOLY CITY*** as ZION, a GREAT MOUNTAIN that RISES UP ABOVE ALL of the STRUCTURES on EARTH.

NOTE: To the onlookers that live outside of ZION, NEW JERUSALEM appears to be a CITY having a WALL that rises up out of sight and visually appears to have no end to it. However, the government of them living outside of the CITY knows by its satellite imagery that the CITY is in the form of a PYRAMID and from the BASE to its TIP it reaches 1377 MILES into space.

Likening to HEAVEN, people LIVE at varying LEVELS within the CITY (the PYRAMID) and there are both high-speed elevators and escalators that can shuttle the PEOPLE within the CITY to the various LEVELS and do so rather quickly. However, only the FIRST SIX LEVELS can be ACCESSED by MAN, and the SEVENTH LEVEL and above is RESERVED for only the ANGEL and those of the BRIDE of CHRIST.

The CITY appears to them within it like being a COMPLETE WORLD, for within the CITY there are parks, forests, lakes and streams, and every imaginable beauty that exists on the EARTH; having not a single defect in any of its beautiful sights. Every LEVEL has its own UNIQUE BEAUTY in architecture and landscape and all LEVELS differ from the other LEVELS in their architecture and landscape.

Each and every PERSON within the CITY has a place of residence, and each residence is in the form of a mansion. The sizes of the mansions increase as the LEVEL increases within the CITY, and from the 4th LEVEL and above the mansions are more like estates having sizable parcels of land accompanying them.

NOTE: When ***THE LORD*** had first told ME about the CITY of NEW JERUSALEM (ZION), I had initially thought it would be somewhat over crowded when housing 7,000,000,000 people in 1377 miles. But as ***THE LORD*** further explained to ME the CITY'S ARCHITECTURE, I could see how there would be an abundance of room within the CITY because of its

MULTIPLE LEVELS. When all of the first SIX LEVELS of the CITY are added together to accumulate the ground space, it is equivalent to the surface area of the EARTH.

Activities within the CITY

In the first THREE YEARS of the MILLENNIUM responsibilities will be assigned to each and every PERSON. Also during these THREE YEARS, those of the WEDDING GUESTS who had been ***SEALED*** rather than BAPTIZED will RECEIVE their BAPTISM in THE ***SPIRIT of GOD,*** and the CELEBRATION of the BAPTISMS are MAGNIFICENT, they go on for SEVEN DAYS at a time.

There will be a CONTINUAL TEACHING of ***GOD'S*** WORD that will be TAUGHT in accordance with the LEVEL of ANOINTING RECEIVED at BAPTISM. Even at the ENTRY LEVEL of LEARNING, each PERSON will be able to UNDERSTAND ***GOD'S*** WORD to at least the FOURTH LAYER within the HOLY Scriptures. This means that at the lowest level of UNDERSTANDING, ONE will be able to SEE the PAST, the PRESENT, the FUTURE, and at least ONE LAYER further into the GOSPELS and REVELATION of JESUS CHRIST.

Each PERSON will be taught how to UTILIZE the SKILL they had been GIVEN by THE ***HOLY SPIRIT*** at the TIME of their BAPTISM. The SKILLS GIVEN to each PERSON will be at the MASTER LEVEL of that CRAFT, whether it be in carpentry, art, music, architecture, or the creation of anything. Each MASTER CRAFTSMAN will be UNIQUE in what HE or SHE does, with no TWO being alike in their STYLE of CRAFTS. Everyone will be PRODUCTIVE and be COMPLETELY satisfied in what they do, and each and every day will be BETTER than the DAY BEFORE, and that shall never change ***SAITH THE LORD of HOSTS.***

Every single INDIVIDUAL will have the opportunity to SPEAK ONE on ONE with JESUS CHRIST, whenever and as often as they so desire; for JESUS possesses OMNI-PRESENCE and can be in all PLACES at ALL TIMES. There will be at the very onset of the MILLENNIUM, a FEAST HONORING the GLORIFICATION of JESUS CHRIST by HIS ***FATHER,*** THE ***HOLY SPIRIT***, making JESUS the REIGNING KING and ***GOD*** over ALL the EARTH. This FEAST and CELEBRATION will go on for SEVENTY-SEVEN DAYS in HONOR of CHRIST, ***THE LORD*** and SAVIOR of the EARTH.

The "BEHEADED SOULS" in the MILLENNIUM

Unlike those of CHRIST who are BAPTIZED in the ***SPIRIT of GOD,*** to be able to SERVE in the TEMPLE of ***GOD***, the "BEHEADED SOULS" must be SANCTIFIED. They will neither have a SOUL MATE nor are they allowed to move about the CITY and will be confined to the SEVENTH LEVEL where they will be given residency. Rather than mansions, the "BEHEADED SOULS" will live on the TEMPLE grounds in MONASTERIES, and will be as the LEVITE PRIESTS were in the days of old.

The PRIESTS (the BEHEADED SOULS) will tend to the needs of the TEMPLE and be SERVANTS to the ANGELS of the SEVENTH LEVEL. Their duties will vary in their SERVICE to ***GOD,*** and they will be allowed to share in the various FEASTS and CELEBRATIONS while yet remaining in their own domain. The PRIESTS cannot leave the SEVENTH LEVEL, for their SANCTIFICATION remains at the SEVENTH LEVEL, and movement elsewhere would cause their DEMISE by FIRE CONSUMPTION. This is similar as to what would happen to the UN-BAPTIZED if they were to move outside of their SANCTUARY prior to their BAPTISM.

TIME IRRELEVANCY

For the PEOPLE within the CITY CONFINES, TIME becomes IRRELEVANT, because the TIME DIMENSION does not exist within the BOUNDARIES of the CITY. This means that although time still passes, the effects of TIME are no longer relevant to ALL within the CITY. The ONE THOUSAND YEAR long MILLENNIUM will feel to the OCCUPANTS of the CITY, like ONE THOUSAND YEARS; however nothing will AGE as a result of the ONE THOUSAND YEARS passing, thus rendering TIME IRRELEVANT.

In the BOOK titled, "The ROD of IRON", it was explained how all things within a TIME CONTINUUM continually change as a result of TIME PASSING, and the effect caused by TIME is called AGING. Without a TIME CONTINUUM, such as it is within the CITY CONFINES, even though time still passes for a measurement of duration, nothing changes as a result of that passing time.

This phenomenon occurs as a result of being in the ***PRESENCE of GOD,*** for ***GOD*** and ***HIS DOMAIN*** is TIMELESS! As ***GOD*** is not subject to CHANGE with TIME, neither is ANYBODY or anything within ***GOD'S DOMAIN*** subject to CHANGE with TIME. Although time is still used for a means of measurement of DURATION, whether the elapsed time is an INSTANT or an ETERNITY, ALL things within the ***PRESENCE of GOD*** remain as they were prior to that duration of time.

Throughout the Scriptures of the HOLY BIBLE, ***GOD*** uses TIME for an INDICATOR of DURATION between certain EVENTS taking place. This is done to merely provide a sequence in which the EVENTS take place and not done necessarily to provide an absolute measurement of TIME. The Scriptures say in the BEGINNING, ***GOD CREATED*** ALL that EXISTS in SIX DAYS, and ***HE*** rested on the SEVENTH DAY. However, elsewhere in the Scriptures it also states that one-day to ***GOD*** can be ONE THOUSAND YEARS, or ONE THOUSAND YEARS, one day!

Earlier in this BOOK WE pointed out how there appeared to be a discrepancy in the TIME given for the GREAT TRIBULATION. The Prophet Daniel said that the TIME DURATION for the GREAT TRIBULATION would be ONE THOUSAND, TWO HUNDRED and NINETY DAYS, whereas the Apostle John in the Book of Revelation said it would take place over ONE THOUSAND, TWO HUNDRED and SIXTY DAYS. However WE also POINTED OUT that in both the Books of Daniel, and Revelation, that same duration of time is given as "a TIME, and TIMES, and a HALFTIME". Now this can be INTERPRETED to mean "a YEAR, and TWO YEARS, and ONE-HALF of a YEAR", or simply THREE and ONE-HALF YEARS. But then again it can be INTERPRETED to mean "THREE and ONE-HALF TIMES" some DURATION of TIME, and this would be the MORE ACCURATE INTERPRETATION of the DURATION of TIME!

WE now live in a TIME CONTINUUM and OUR UNDERSTANDING of TIME is important to US; because WE know how TIME AFFECTS things by its AGING them. However, for ONE to TRULY UNDERSTAND the *WORD of* ***GOD***, ONE must SEE TIME as being IRRELEVANT, and having no AFFECT whatsoever on what the Scripture might say. TIME should be seen in the Scriptures as merely representing some DURATION of passing time for SEQUENTIAL PURPOSES, and should not be confused as meaning a specific ALLOTMENT of TIME! For ***GOD*** can make a day be a week, or a week a month, or a month a year, or a year, ONE THOUSAND YEARS, whatever pleases ***HIM*** is what the ALLOTMENT of TIME will be!

In all THREE BOOKS ("Revealing The Bible's Truth", "The ROD of IRON", and Revelation the FOURTH SON), WE have given ELEMENTS of TIME ALLOTMENTS regarding the TRIBULATION and GREAT TRIBULATION PERIODS. WE have done so to relate TIME to the EVENTS taking place, for these EVENTS will take place in a TIME CONTINUUM. This was not done to CONFUSE YOU, but rather to ENLIGHTEN your UNDERSTANDING of the SEQUENCE of the coming EVENTS. However, it must be REMEMBERED that the THREE and ONE-HALF YEARS of the GREAT TRIBULATION, can occur over any THREE and ONE-HALF ELEMENTS of TIME and not necessarily in YEARS. Whether the UNITS of TIME used are in YEARS, DECADES of YEARS, or in CENTURIES is IRRELEVANT to your UNDERSTANDING. However, you can be assured that the outcome from the EVENTS will be as they are WRITTEN in the THREE BOOKS.

> ***Psalm 90:4*** *For a THOUSAND YEARS in thy sight are but as YESTERDAY when it is PASSED, and as a watch in the night.*

LIGHT for the CITY

The sun will provide the light outside of the CITY OF NEW JERUSALEM, whereas ***GOD*** will provide the LIGHT within the CITY. WE have given some of the VARIOUS DESCRIPTIONS of ***GOD*** in all THREE BOOKS I have WRITTEN for ***HIM,*** but it is KEY to UNDERSTAND that ***GOD*** is a PERSON and has a ***PERSONALITY. GOD*** LIVES and has FEELINGS and EXPRESSES ***HIS FEELINGS*** with EMOTION, in much the same way YOU express your feelings. ***GOD*** DELIGHTS in certain things and other things ANGER ***HIM,*** and the HOLY BIBLE gives in GREAT DETAIL what ***GOD*** DELIGHTS in, and also what ***ANGERS HIM!***

GOD is ***HOLY (PURE) SPIRITUAL ENERGY,*** and has the FORM of a ***MAN, FOR GOD CREATED MAN IN HIS OWN IMAGE! GOD*** cannot be LOOKED UPON with the human eye, for the INTENSITY of ***HIS LIGHT*** is so GREAT, it would cause IMMEDIATE DEATH to the ONLOOKER. ***GOD*** is the SOURCE of ALL ENERGY and by ***HIS HOLINESS (PURITY of ENERGY) HE CAN NEITHER BE DIMINISHED IN POWER NOR CAN HIS POWER BE INCREASED, FOR HE IS INFINITE IN HIS HOLINESS!***

GOD can BOTH REGULATE and CHANNEL ***HIS POWER*** to ANYTHING or ANYBODY at ANYTIME; and ***GOD*** uses ***HIS SON, IXOTE*** as the CONDUIT for DISPENSING ***HIS POWER. GOD'S POWER,*** is ***SPIRITUAL POWER (SPIRITUAL ENERGY),*** and this is why ***IXOTE*** is called THE ***HOLY SPIRIT of GOD, FOR IXOTE TRANSFERS GOD'S POWER IN VARYING LEVELS TO WHOMSOEVER OR WHATSOEVER GOD HAS DIRECTED HIM TO.***

THE ***HOLY SPIRIT*** can TRANSFER ***GOD'S POWER*** in such a way that it can either CREATE or DESTROY that which it is TRANSFERRED to. THE

SPIRIT of GOD can be DISPENSED at LEVELS that can be FELT as a CALMING or DISRUPTIVE FORCE with varying levels of INTENSITY and without LIMITATION. This TRANSFERRING of ***GOD'S POWER*** in the POSITIVE FORM is called ANOINTING, and in the NEGATIVE FORM is called ***GOD'S WRATH.***

While in the CITY of NEW JERUSALEM, ***GOD'S POWER*** is seen as ***LIGHT,*** with the SOURCE of that ***LIGHT*** coming from the very TIP of the PYRAMID and then SPREADING and DIMMING as it DESCENDS to the BASE of the PYRAMID; much like a light bulb's light spreads and dims as it descends to the floor of a room. The INTENSITY of ***GOD'S LIGHT*** INCREASES as ONE ASCENDS within the PYRAMID shaped CITY of NEW JERUSALEM, and the HIGHER the LEVEL within the CITY the BRIGHTER the ***LIGHT*** becomes. For instance; if a PERSON resides at the 3rd LEVEL within the CITY, the ***LIGHT*** at the 4th LEVEL would be DAMAGING to them, because they are EXCEEDING their ANOINTING (EMPOWERMENT) by their being at the 4th LEVEL. The same phenomenon occurs in HEAVEN, even though ALL in HEAVEN are in a BODY of LIGHT. This can be equivalent to trying to connect a 110-volt light bulb to a 220-volt power source; the light bulb would become excessively bright for a moment and would then quickly BURN OUT by its exceeding its power rating.

Whereas the sun is the power source for the light of this world, ***GOD*** is the POWER SOURCE for the ***LIGHT*** in NEW JERUSALEM; just as ***HE*** PROVIDES the ***LIGHT*** for the RESIDENTS in HEAVEN, so does ***HE*** for HEAVEN on EARTH.

> ***Psalm 84:11*** *For* ***THE LORD GOD*** *is a SUN and shield:* ***THE LORD*** *will give GRACE and GLORY: no good thing will* ***HE*** *withhold from them that walk uprightly.*

> ***Psalm 84:12*** *O* ***LORD of HOSTS,*** *BLESSED is the MAN that TRUSTETH in THEE.*

Chapter 19
The CONCLUSION

In this Chapter WE will discuss what happens at the CONCLUSION of the MILLENNIUM PERIOD. As previously mentioned in Chapter 17, titled "The Survivors", FIVE MONTHS prior to the CONCLUSION of the MILLENNIUM the DEVIL, Lucifer, escapes from HELL and returns to the EARTH. In that five-month period of time, Lucifer regains control over the people outside of the CITY of NEW JERUSALEM, and DECEIVES them into believing that they can storm the CITY and take it by force. The DEVIL tells the people how they could gain access to the CITY by utilizing their technology for "Time Travel".

However, this effort fails, and as soon as they encompass the CITY, ***GOD*** sends FIRE down from HEAVEN, and the FIRE CONSUMES each and every person alive on the EARTH outside of the CITY WALLS of NEW JERUSALEM. As with the DEVIL always, he speaks in half-truths, for if ***GOD*** would have allowed it, the people's Time Travel equipment would have enabled them to ENTER the CITY in a TIME WARP, but ***GOD*** denied their access!

NOTE: The reason this point of capability is being brought up is to let you KNOW that ***GOD*** has CONTROL over ALL things. It isn't a question as to whether MAN has the capability to do certain things or not, the question is, WILL ***GOD*** ALLOW IT! ***GOD*** has allowed MAN to develop various technologies to further the ability of MANKIND, but when those technologies are used to challenge the WILL of ***GOD,*** in all cases, they will surely FAIL!

Shortly after the people of the EARTH are DESTROYED by FIRE, Lucifer is once again cast down to HELL; and this is where WE will begin our discussion on the CONCLUSION of the MILLENNIUM.

Returning to the DUST of the EARTH

At the CONCLUSION of the ONE THOUSAND YEARS, the BODY made of FLESH GIVEN to ALL within the CITY GATES expires, for it has reached its TERM LIMIT. The physical CITY of NEW JERUSALEM also expires at the

CONCLUSION of the LAST DAY (the MILLENNIUM PERIOD), and ***GOD*** brings DOWN from HEAVEN, the HEAVENLY CITY of NEW JERUSALEM, which is the EASTERN QUADRANT of HEAVEN PROPER, the KINGDOM of JESUS CHRIST. This is not a physical city as the first NEW JERUSALEM was, but rather a KINGDOM in the shape of a PYRAMID being many times greater than its PREDECESSOR in size, and being COMPOSED of LIGHT rather than physical materials.

This KINGDOM is an EVERLASTING KINGDOM, and ALL going forward will ENTER HEAVEN through its EASTERN GATES and RECEIVE a NEW BODY made of LIGHT as they ENTER the KINGDOM, to replace their BODIES of FLESH. The "BEHEADED SOULS" at this time will TERMINATE and DECOMPOSE in an INSTANT, feeling no pain whatsoever, and fall to the BASE of the PHYSICAL CITY STREETS of NEW JERUSALEM as DUST.

These things that happen at the CONCLUSION of the LAST DAY come as no surprise to the OCCUPANTS of the CITY, as they had all been forewarned of what was to take place at the CONCLUSION of the MILLENNIUM. Even the "BEHEADED SOULS" who had been PRIESTS during the MILLENNIUM were told they would return to the DUST of the EARTH, and they THANKED ***GOD*** for ALLOWING them to participate in the PERIOD of HEAVEN on EARTH. Even though the "BEHEADED SOULS knew that some of them would be GIVEN a SECOND chance at life, none of them knew which ones that might be. However they ALL had PEACE within themselves, for they KNEW they would never suffer the SECOND DEATH; which is the DEATH of the SPIRIT and the LOSS of SOUL, they would simply be NO MORE!

ENTERING IN BY THE EAST GATE

ALL entering into the MILLENNIUM did so by way of RAPTURE, and by RAPTURE AGAIN will they ENTER INTO THE KINGDOM of CHRIST, the HEAVENLY JERUSALEM. There are FOUR GATES on the EAST SIDE of the KINGDOM of CHRIST allowing ACCESS to them ENTERING into it. However ONE cannot simply walk through the GATE and into the KINGDOM for it is a KINGDOM COMPOSED of LIGHT, and only LIGHT may ENTER IN.

Therefore a CHANGE in ANATOMY from a PHYSICAL BEING to a LIGHT BEING is necessary, and this CHANGE can only occur by way of RAPTURE. The RAPTURE for the MILLENNIUM PERIOD caused the PHYSICAL BODY to CHANGE into another PHYSICAL BODY of FLESH suitable for a PHYSICAL LIFE of ONE THOUSAND YEARS. The RAPTURE into the KINGDOM of CHRIST will cause the PHYSICAL BODY to TRANSFIGURE into a PERMANENT BODY of LIGHT, suitable to SUSTAIN LIFE throughout ETERNITY.

Once the SPIRIT has been RELEASED from the BODY of FLESH, the EXPERIENCE of FREEDOM from the FLESH is quite PHENOMENAL! It cannot be expressed in terms relating to physical life, but it can be somewhat related to a physical orgasm that is at least one hundred times greater than that experienced during a sexual climax. However, this FEELING NEVER CEASES, whereas a physical climax does.

The LIGHT FORM BEING will be in the EXACT same IMAGE as the PHYSICAL BEING of the MILLENNIUM was, except rather than being in a carbon based physical form, the BODY will be in a NEUTRINO BASED LIGHT FORM. In this FORM of LIGHT, the PERSON of LIGHT can EXPERIENCE EMOTION by TOUCH, and the senses experienced in LIGHT are INFINITELY GREATER than those same experiences in FLESH. The LIGHT BEING, once in the HEAVENLY DOMAIN can move about at will, and can span distances beyond known measurement in an INSTANCE. The velocities of MOVEMENT for the LIGHT BEING extend well beyond the velocities of physical light that which is photon based; for NEUTRINO BASED LIGHT is COMPOSED of PURE ENERGY, that of which can never be DIMINISHED or DISSIPATED by RESISTIVE ELEMENTS. Therefore, nothing in existence can oppose and limit the MOVEMENT or the VELOCITY of the LIGHT BEING while in HORIZONTAL or DOWNWARD MOVEMENT. However, there are LIMITATIONS for the LIGHT BEING'S VERTICAL MOVEMENT in the UPWARD PLANE, being LIMITED by the EMPOWERMENT (ANOINTING) given to the LIGHT BEING at BAPTISM.

As it was during the MILLENNIUM with each PERSON being limited in their access to the vertical levels in the PHYSICAL CITY of NEW JERUSALEM, so is it in the HEAVENLY DOMAIN. For example, if ONE were to RESIDE at the THIRD LEVEL in the HEAVENLY DOMAIN, they would have complete ACCESS to the first THREE LEVELS within HEAVEN, but would not have ACCESS to the FOURTH LEVEL and ABOVE, unless another PERSON RESIDING at one of the HIGHER LEVELS accompanied them. No PERSON of LIGHT can ACCESS a LEVEL above the SIXTH LEVEL, except for the ANGEL and the BRIDE of CHRIST who has ACCESS throughout the DOMAIN'S LEVELS up to the NINTH LEVEL, for above the NINTH LEVEL is the THRONE of ***GOD.*** Everyone in the HEAVENLY DOMAIN are made PERFECT in ***GOD,*** so NO ONE ever violates ***GOD'S LAWS,*** or tries to EX-

CEED their EMPOWERMENT (ANOINTING).

Communication within the HEAVENLY DOMAIN

Although EVERYONE ENTERS into the HEAVENLY DOMAIN by way of the EAST GATE, once in and given RESIDENCY, many will be MOVED into ONE of the other THREE KINGDOMS; for there are FOUR KINGDOMS making up the HEAVENLY DOMAIN (***GOD'S KINGDOM***). It is PREDETERMINED who will RESIDE in which KINGDOM and at what LEVEL they will RESIDE at the TIME of BAPTISM, and ALL will have been INSTRUCTED as to their ULTIMATE DESTINATION while in the MILLENNIUM.

GOD'S PEOPLE will then MOVE into their RESIDENCES in HEAVEN, however, only the ANGEL will RESIDE in the KINGDOM of the WEST, the KINGDOM of THE ***DELIVERER 182. HIS*** KINGDOM is the DOMAIN of the EARTH ANGEL, and THE ***DELIVERER 182*** prefers the ANGEL to MAN, even when the MAN is in a LIGHT FORM. THE ***DELIVERER 182*** is the DIRECT DESCENDANT of THE ***HOLY SPIRIT,*** WHOM also PREFERS the ANGEL to MAN because it was the CREATION of MAN causing ***HIM*** to lose ONE-THIRD of ***HIS*** Angels to Lucifer during his FALL. This is why MAN has only ACCESS to THE ***HOLY SPIRIT*** by way of JESUS CHRIST, because otherwise THE ***HOLY SPIRIT*** would DENY MAN'S ACCESS TO ***HIM.*** THE ***HOLY SPIRIT*** ONLY ACKNOWLEDGES THE PERFECT MAN WHOM ***HE LOVES***, JESUS CHRIST!

Communication in HEAVEN is done by way of both SPEECH and TELEPATHIC TRANSMISSION. One PERSON may speak to another or to GROUPS of PEOPLE at any RESIDENCE within HEAVEN VOCALLY while in their presence, or through THOUGHT WAVES to them who are beyond an audible range. When sending TELEPATHICALLY, each PERSON'S THOUGHT WAVES have a specific SIGNATURE identifying them, and when the TRANSMISSION is RECEIVED by the intended RECIPIENT or RECIPIENTS, they as well send out TELEPATHICALLY an acknowledgment of RECEIPT carrying with it also their SIGNATURE.

The THOUGHT WAVES are channeled for PRIVACY, and only the INTENDED RECIPIENTS can RECEIVE the communiqué. Multiple conversations can take place as so desired and when directing a personal and private MESSAGE to an INDIVIDUAL, the MESSAGE can be BLOCKED from any unintended PEOPLE taking part in the CONVERSATION by ENCRYPTING the MESSAGE to one or more SIGNATURES. This is somewhat like being able to whisper in the intended RECEIVERS ear, even though they might be vast distances away, and the ENCRYPTING of the MESSAGE is called WHISPERING.

All VOCAL and TELEPATHIC COMMUNICATION is done in the ENGLISH LANGUAGE throughout the first NINE LEVELS in HEAVEN. However, any COMMUNIQUÉS made to the ***THRONE ROOM***, either VOCALLY or TELEPATHICALLY must be done in the HEBREWAH LANGUAGE (TONGUES). Those having the ABILITY for DIRECT COMMUNICATION to the ***THRONE ROOM (GOD)*** aren't many, and only at the SIXTH LEVEL and ABOVE does HIGH LEVEL COMMUNICATION take place. Only them having the ANOINTING to both SPEAK and INTERPRET HEBREWAH may communicate DIRECTLY to ***GOD.*** However there are at any of the LEVELS in HEAVEN, "INTERPRETERS" that are mostly ANGELS, who can both SEND to and RECEIVE from the ***THRONE ROOM.***

However, the ANGELS will most certainly scrutinize the MESSAGES being sent to ***GOD,*** ensuring the COMMUNICATION is necessary and that no ONE other than ***GOD*** could PROVIDE an ANSWER. Rarely do such DIRECT COMMUNICATIONS take place to ***GOD*** by ANYONE below the SEVENTH LEVEL, for the EMPOWERMENT of the FOUR SONS, the SERAPHIM allow them the ABILITY to RESOLVE most matters. Furthermore, prior to ***GOD'S*** RECEIVING IT, ANY COMMUNIQUÉ to the ***THRONE ROOM*** MUST BE FIRST APPROVED BY THE ***DELIVERER 182.*** It is ***HE*** who determines what ***GOD*** should or shouldn't HEAR, much like a PRESIDING JUDGE would do in the DETERMINATION of which of the Judges in a courthouse might hear the various courtroom cases. ***GOD*** only INTERVENES when no ONE other than ***HE*** can RESOLVE the MATTER!

The FOUR KINGDOMS

As explained in ALL THREE of the BOOKS WRITTEN for ***THE LORD,*** there are FOUR KINGDOMS making up HEAVEN. The KINGDOM of the NORTH is RULED by KING DAVID, the KINGDOM of the SOUTH is RULED by KING SOLOMON, the KINGDOM of the EAST by KING JESUS CHRIST, and the KINGDOM of the WEST by THE ***DELIVERER 182;*** who is not referred to as being a KING, but rather addressed as ***THE LORD of HOSTS.*** Each of the FOUR KINGDOMS are COMPOSED of LIGHT and are in the SHAPE of a PYRAMID whose TIP is TRUNCATED, and when each of the FOUR KINGDOMS come together from there respective directions they form a CUBE. In the CENTER of the CUBE, where the FOUR TRUNCA-

TIONS come together, a smaller CUBE is formed within the LARGER CUBE and this is called the ***THRONE of GOD.***

The POPULATION in all FOUR KINGDOMS varies; however, all FOUR are IDENTICAL in GEOMETRIC SIZE. The KINGDOM of the EAST is by far the most POPULATED, while the KINGDOM of the WEST is the least POPULATED, for it GROWS by only 500,000,000 in population for each of the EARTH'S LIFECYCLES. Of the 4,000,000,000 NEW SOULS entering into HEAVEN, the KINGDOMS of the NORTH and SOUTH receive 1,000,000,000 each, whereas the KINGDOM of the EAST RECEIVES 2,000,000,000 NEW SOULS.

The TOTAL POPULATION in HEAVEN cannot be NUMBERED for it consists of TRILLIONS of TRILLIONS of SOULS. The scaled down version of NEW JERUSALEM that had been brought down to the EARTH is in DIRECT PROPORTION to the FOUR KINGDOMS in HEAVEN. However, whereas it was 1377 miles from its base to its tip, the HEAVENLY KINGDOM of NEW JERUSALEM is 1377 GALACTIC MILES from its BASE to its TIP, prior to TRUNCATION, that of which is 1/10 of its ALTITUDE. A GALACTIC MILE is the same as ONE MILE raised to the 91st POWER in the TENS SYSTEM of NUMBERING, thus making the SIZE of HEAVEN orders of MAGNITUDE greater than the UNIVERSE.

As a matter of fact, the UNIVERSE is a scaled down version of HEAVEN, and if the size of the UNIVERSE were raised to the 91st POWER, it would be equivalent to the size of HEAVEN. As the UNIVERSE continually GROWS, so does HEAVEN CONTINUALLY GROW in the exact same proportions when raised to the 91st POWER. However, even the UNIVERSE has a LIFECYCLE whereas HEAVEN does not! When the UNIVERSE reaches a diameter where its elasticity overcomes its outward velocity, it FOLDS BACK within itself. Then when the outer walls of the UNIVERSE make contact with its absolute center, the CYCLE of the UNIVERSE RESTARTS again, and the number ratio given to you in relationship to the SIZE of HEAVEN will no longer be pertinent. At this TIME, HEAVEN ceases in its GROWTH and maintains the SIZE it was at the TIME the UNIVERSE had FOLDED BACK.

Even though this FOLDING BACK of the UNIVERSE will occur again, one should not be concerned about this phenomenon, for there will be many more LIFECYCLES of the EARTH before the UNIVERSE FOLDS BACK and RESTARTS. However, when this does occur, as it has in the PAST, the BIBLE STORY will start back in GENESIS CHAPTER ONE, with ***GOD*** CREATING a NEW HEAVEN and EARTH with LIGHT. This is unlike what happens with each of the EARTH'S LIFECYCLES. When the EARTH REGENERATES, the

BIBLE STORY begins in Chapter SEVEN, with NOAH entering the ARK destined for the NEW WORLD and not back at the TIME of ADAM and EVE.

When the UNIVERSE completes its LIFECYCLE, ***GOD*** makes all things NEW AGAIN, whereas when the EARTH completes its LIFECYCLE ***GOD*** RENEWS the FACE of the EARTH rather than RECREATING it, and the UNIVERSE remains intact. When ***GOD*** does CREATE a NEW HEAVEN and EARTH at the CONCLUSION of the UNIVERSE, the PREVIOUS HEAVEN REMAINS UNCHANGED, and continues on throughout ETERNITY. However that HEAVEN has reached its maturity and will grow no further in either size or population.

This is why JESUS CHRIST said that the HEAVENS and the EARTH would pass away (because they do), but HIS WORDS would not pass away (because the BIBLE STORY goes on). Every TIME the UNIVERSE REGENERATES (every SEVEN TRILLION YEARS), a NEW HEAVEN is CREATED, and everything starts back from the BEGINNING, as it was during the initial fall of Lucifer from the GRACE of ***GOD.*** Every TIME the EARTH REGENERATES in its SEVEN THOUSAND YEAR intervals, the BIBLE STORY starts over again with NOAH entering the ARK and not back at the TIME of ADAM and EVE. This is why the BIBLE states that ***GOD*** both RENEWS the EARTH and also CREATES IT, for both happen over and over throughout ETERNITY!

> ***Psalm 104:30*** *Thou SENDEST FORTH thy* ***SPIRIT,*** *they are CREATED: and thou RENEWEST the FACE of the EARTH.*

Chapter 20
The SCRIBE & The GUARDIAN

WE had earlier discussed how the EARTH Angel comes to the EARTH, once as a MAN and once as a WOMAN to serve a DIVINE PURPOSE for ***THE LORD***. However, WE had not as of yet talked about the other Angels who also come to the EARTH, specifically the SCRIBE and the GUARDIAN Angels.

Unlike the EARTH Angel, the SCRIBE and the GUARDIAN remain in a SPIRITUAL FORM and they can neither be seen nor heard, although at times their PRESENCE might be felt. Only after a PERSON has RECEIVED the GIFT of SPIRITUAL DISCERNMENT, GIVEN at the TIME of their BAPTISM, can the SCRIBE or the GUARDIAN be DISCERNED, however this GIFT is rarely GIVEN.

The first person ever to receive a GUARDIAN Angel was CAIN, the brother of ABEL, whom after murdering ABEL was made to leave the family of ADAM and EVE and live amongst the GENTILES. The SCRIBE Angel however was not sent to the EARTH until long after CAIN. They were sent after NOAH had landed in the NEW WORLD, for the world that was DESTROYED by the GREAT FLOOD had never hosted a SCRIBE Angel.

CAIN received a GUARDIAN Angel but not a SCRIBE, for the GUARDIAN was sent to PROTECT CAIN from DEATH prior to his TIME, and to see that he fulfilled his PURPOSE in ***GOD*** on EARTH, albeit it was an EVIL PURPOSE. Furthermore, CAIN hadn't the need for a SCRIBE, for he had been MARKED for HELL at the time of his BIRTH and therefore the recording of his works during his life to be used during a time of JUDGMENT was not necessary, for he had been already JUDGED!

When ***GOD*** told CAIN that he must LEAVE the family of ADAM and EVE, because of his murdering his own brother ABEL, and live elsewhere, CAIN told ***THE LORD*** that he feared for his own life. CAIN had heard of the GENTILES, who roamed the EARTH, and how it was commonplace for a GENTILE to take the life of another. And now, he was being forced to live among them and away from his parent's camp, and CAIN feared being killed by the GENTILE. So

GOD to comfort CAIN, swore VENGEANCE against anyone trying to SLAY CAIN, and placed a MARK upon him.

The MARK that CAIN received was both a physical mark and a SPIRITUAL MARK. The physical mark was in the form of a birthmark that was BLACK, and the mark was placed on CAIN'S forehead, somewhat like a tattoo, having an image of the NUMBERS 666, with the three sixes being rotated about in a circle. The SPIRITUAL MARK that CAIN received came in the form of a GUARDIAN Angel, whom was sent to the EARTH to PROTECT CAIN and to see that he fulfilled his intended days, and neither CAIN nor his father, Lucifer, could detect the presence of the Angel.

> ***Genesis 4:13*** *And CAIN said unto* ***THE LORD,*** *MY PUNISHMENT IS GREATER THAN I CAN BEAR.*

> ***Genesis 4:14*** *BEHOLD, THOU HAST DRIVEN ME OUT THIS DAY FROM THE FACE OF THE EARTH; AND FROM THY* ***FACE*** *SHALL I BE HID; AND I SHALL BE A FUGITIVE AND A VAGABOND IN THE EARTH; AND IT SHALL COME TO PASS, THAT EVERY ONE THAT FINDETH ME SHALL SLAY ME.*

> ***Genesis 4:15*** *And* ***THE LORD*** *said unto him,* ***THEREFORE WHOSOEVER SLAYETH CAIN, VENGEANCE SHALL BE TAKEN ON HIM SEVENFOLD.*** *And* ***THE LORD*** *set a MARK upon CAIN, lest any finding him should kill him.*

These Scriptures indicate the giving to CAIN a GUARDIAN Angel along with a BLACK MARK on his FOREHEAD. The MARK was both a Spiritual and a physical marking for CAIN'S PROTECTION. At that time, other than CAIN, no one else had a GUARDIAN Angel, and it wasn't until after NOAH had entered the NEW WORLD, that HIS children RECEIVED both a GUARDIAN and a SCRIBE Angel to look after them.

The GUARDIAN ensured that NOAH'S CHILDREN and their offspring took every BREATH of LIFE on EARTH that ***THE LORD*** had intended for them to take, and PROTECTED them from premature death; while the SCRIBE documented the BEHAVIOR of NOAH'S three sons and their families over the course of their lives. Neither NOAH nor his wife MEATERAH received a GUARDIAN or a SCRIBE Angel, because they were DELIVERERS and hadn't the need for the Angels to protect, or to document their behavior.

The SCRIBE Angel

The SCRIBE Angel monitored all that NOAH and MEATERAH'S family members had said and done throughout their entire lives, and even recorded their very thoughts. At the time of death, the RECORDS kept by the SCRIBES are put into BOOKS in HEAVEN; and when standing before ***GOD*** in JUDGMENT, the BOOKS are opened and READ to them being JUDGED. The SCRIBE, leaving nothing to memory, RECORDS every detail regarding a person's life; ALL is DOCUMENTED in the BOOKS.

> ***Revelation 20:12*** *And I saw the DEAD, small and great, stand before* ***GOD;*** *and the BOOKS were OPENED: and another BOOK was OPENED, which is the BOOK of LIFE: and the DEAD were JUDGED out of those things which were WRITTEN in the BOOKS, according to their WORKS.*

These RECORDS are MAINTAINED and KEPT in HEAVEN until such a time that the PERSON has either RECEIVED BAPTISM in the ***SPIRIT of GOD*** or stands before ***GOD*** in JUDGMENT. In the case of the BAPTISM, it MUST BE CONFIRMED to ***GOD*** by the ANGEL RAPHAEL before it can be BONA'-FIDE. RAPHAEL is the ANGEL over FIRE and WATER, and the ANGEL of THE ***HOLY SPIRIT of GOD.*** It is RAPHAEL, who WITNESSES THE ***HOLY SPIRIT*** BAPTISM performed by JESUS CHRIST, and CONFIRMS the BAPTISM to ***GOD.***

ONCE the BAPTISM is CONFIRMED and BONA'-FIDE, the RECORDS KEPT by the SCRIBE are then DESTROYED, and the SCRIBE Angel departs from the one he had been assigned to, and RETURNS to HEAVEN. After BAPTISM and CONFIRMATION there isn't any longer a need for a SCRIBE, for that INDIVIDUAL has been JUDGED in CHRIST and FOUND to be INNOCENT, and only the GUARDIAN remains with the SAVED!

The GUARDIAN Angel

ALL THREE SEEDS on the EARTH receive BOTH a SCRIBE and a GUARDIAN Angel, whether they are of the BLESSED SEED, the DAMNED SEED (the CANAANITE) or the SEED of the BEAST (the GENTILE). Each and every person upon the EARTH receives BOTH Angels, until they either die or RECEIVE BAPTISM. The SCRIBE is called the "UNBIASED Angel", because he hasn't any SPIRITUAL CONNECTION whatsoever to the ONE he is ASSIGNED to, and can be compared to a courtroom stenographer who simply notes that which is said or done in the courtroom.

Unlike the SCRIBE, the GUARDIAN can either be SPIRITUALLY CONNECTED (BIASED) or spiritually unconnected (UNBIASED), and the SPIRITUAL CONNECTION between the GUARDIAN and the INDIVIDUAL varies depending on the SEED TYPE. In the case of the BLESSED SEED, the GUARDIAN will be somehow CONNECTED SPIRITUALLY to that PERSON by a HEAVENLY RELATIONSHIP, because the BLESSED SEED has come down from HEAVEN.

The EARTH Angel, having a DIVINE RIGHT to HEAVEN is in a class by itself and hasn't the need of a SCRIBE Angel. However they do indeed RECEIVE a GUARDIAN Angel. For them, their GUARDIAN is always their other HALF, so on EARTH, while in PARADISE, or in HEAVEN, the TWO SPIRITS of the EARTH Angel are always together and are NEVER SEPARATED. This is TRUE even though they have been separated by GENDER, with one GENDER being in the FLESH while the other remains in SPIRIT; they still remain SPIRITUALLY CONNECTED.

The GUARDIAN Angel of the CANAANITE (the DAMNED SEED) is significantly different than the other GUARDIAN Angels and they are called "TRANSPARENT Angels". They have RECEIVED this name because they can neither be seen nor detected by a DEMON or an Angel outside of the REALM of HEAVEN. The "TRANSPARENT Angel" was the first GUARDIAN Angel given to CAIN, and this kind of Angel can either be a GUARDIAN or a SCRIBE in their DUTIES. Although they perform similar functions as the SCRIBE and the GUARDIAN'S do with the other TWO SEEDS, the "TRANSPARENT GUARDIAN" will only protect the body of flesh and not the Spirit, whereas the GUARDIAN for the other TWO will protect both. The "TRANSPARENT GUARDIAN or SCRIBE", will not make any SPIRITUAL CONTACT whatsoever with their host, and merely shadow them to critique their actions and ensure their physical safety over their intended life.

Only the EARTH Angel, when given the GIFT of SPIRITUAL DISCERNMENT can see the "TRANSPARENT Angel", for outside of the HEAVENLY ANGELIC REALM, the "TRANSPARENT Angel" is undetectable. This is even so for the SAINT who has RECEIVED the GIFT of SPIRITUAL DISCERNMENT, for they cannot see the SPIRIT of the "TRANSPARENT Angel" either, even though they can see other SPIRITUAL MATTER!

Other than after reading about it in this BOOK, which he will read; even Lucifer is unaware of the "TRANSPARENT Angel's" existence. He will be most surprised to find out about them, for he had believed his son CAIN'S MARK was the physical black mark that ***GOD*** put upon CAIN'S FOREHEAD, and was not aware that CAIN was being PROTECTED by a "TRANSPARENT Angel".

The GUARDIAN and the SCRIBE given to the GENTILE (the SEED of the BEAST) are both UNBIASED Angels, for the GENTILE is a product of the EARTH, never having a Spiritual Connection to the HEAVENLY REALM. While the SCRIBE documents the actions of the GENTILE, the GUARDIAN protects only the FLESH and not the SPIRIT of the host, much the same as it is with the CANAANITE. However the GENTILE'S GUARDIAN and SCRIBE Angels are not "TRANSPARENT" as are those assigned to the CANAANITE.

However, because the GENTILE can be BAPTIZED in the SPIRIT of ***GOD*** and RECEIVE a SOUL as a result of their BAPTISM, their GUARDIANS after BAPTISM can PROTECT both the FLESH and the SPIRIT of their HOST. This is because after BAPTISM, the GENTILE takes on the LIKENESS of CHRIST, and they too are treated in the same manner as the BLESSED SEED, but only after the SCRIBE Angel has departed from them and returns to HEAVEN, thus MARKING the CONFIRMATION of BAPTISM.

PROTECTION for the "SAVED"

Prior to SAVING, the EMPOWERMENT given to the GUARDIAN is limited to PHYSICAL PROTECTION. This means that a PERSON'S GUARDIAN Angel can only INTERVENE in PHYSICAL MATTERS that are life threatening and untimely in their occurrence. There isn't anything in a physical nature that cannot be overcome by the GUARDIAN Angel, and they are most POWERFUL when unrestrained by ***GOD*** in their actions. It MUST be REMEMBERED that **ALL EMPOWERMENT** comes from ***GOD*,** and when ***HE*** assigns an Angel to a TASK, ***HE PROVIDES*** ALL that is NEEDED to PERFORM that TASK!

After being BAPTIZED, the SAVED RECEIVE both PHYSICAL and SPIRITUAL PROTECTION from their GUARDIANS. And, at that TIME, RAPHAEL, the ANGEL of THE ***HOLY SPIRIT*** OVERSEES those GUARDIANS, whereas prior to BAPTISM, the ANGEL KIEL oversees both the GUARDIANS and the SCRIBES. When on the EARTH, the ANGEL KIEL was known as AARON, the HIGH PRIEST, and was the BROTHER to MOSES and Miriam. KIEL, in HEAVEN, is the CHIEFTAIN to all of the SCRIBES and the GUARDIANS and he oversees them until the TIME of BAPTISM.

Chapter 21
JUDGMENT DAY!

Before WE detail the EVENTS that happen on JUDGMENT DAY, WE want to make it PERFECTLY CLEAR as to who does and WHO DOES NOT stand before ***IXOTE*** in JUDGMENT. First and foremost, the JUDGMENT takes place on the EARTH, and it MUST be UNDERSTOOD that ANYONE who had LIVED and REIGNED with CHRIST during the ONE THOUSAND-YEAR MILLENNIUM PERIOD had already left the EARTH. They had either ASCENDED into HEAVEN or had returned to the DUST of the EARTH prior to the DAY of JUDGMENT. The BEHEADED SOULS that had participated in the MILLENNIUM were returned to the DUST of the EARTH at the CONCLUSION of the MILLENNIUM PERIOD. Therefore neither they nor those of CHRIST need to STAND BEFORE ***THE LORD*** in JUDGMENT.

ANYONE having been BAPTIZED in the ***SPIRIT of GOD*** will not stand before ***GOD (IXOTE)*** in JUDGMENT, and the reason for this is TWOFOLD. FIRST of all, them who had RECEIVED BAPTISM had already been JUDGED in CHRIST for their SINS and were FOUND INNOCENT. SECONDLY, by being BAPTIZED and REBORN in the ***SPIRIT of GOD,*** that PERSON takes on the LIKENESS of CHRIST by VIRTUE of THE ***HOLY SPIRIT of GOD.*** The ***ONE JUDGING*** is ***IXOTE,*** THE ***HOLY SPIRIT of GOD,*** and ***HE NEED NOT JUDGE HIMSELF!***

At the TIME of JUDGMENT, ALL of CHRIST have already left the EARTH and are in HEAVEN, and only them who are to be JUDGED remain intact on the EARTH. Those to be JUDGED are RAISED from the DEAD at the END of the LAST DAY! These are the people who had either slept in the EARTH or them who had been sent to HADES for their EVIL DEEDS at the time of their DEATH. Both of these categories will RECEIVE JUDGMENT.

What WE are telling you probably differs from that which your Church Leaders have told you; but rest ASSURED ALL that WE SAY is of a TRUTH, for WE CANNOT LIE! JESUS CHRIST bore the SINS of the WORLD on the DAY of HIS CRUCIFIXION. This means that HE RECEIVED ALL of the SINS of them who had or will RECEIVE HIM as their LORD and SAVIOR.

Therefore, once being BAPTIZED with HIS BAPTISM in the ***SPIRIT of GOD,*** that PERSON becomes SINLESS FOREVER in the ***EYES of GOD;*** and this is the SIMPLE TRUTH! NONE OF THE SAVED SHALL STAND BEFORE THE ***HOLY SPIRIT of GOD (IXOTE)*** IN JUDGMENT, ***SAITH THE LORD of HOSTS!***

Them of the OLD COVENANT

Some of them that are RAISED from the DEAD will be of the OLD COVENANT. Anyone being of the OLD COVENANT, and this includes the PROPHETS and the SAINTS of the OLD COVENANT, will STAND BEFORE THE ***HOLY SPIRIT*** in JUDGMENT. ALL of the NAMES in the OLD TESTAMENT, with the EXCEPTION of those who were of THE DELIVERER (NOAH, JOSEPH, MOSES, and their THREE WIVES); of the SERAPHIM (ENOCH/DAVID, SOLOMON/ELIJAH/JOHN the BAPTIST); and of the EARTH Angel (DARIUS, CYRUS, and ARTAXERXES) will STAND BEFORE ***THE LORD*** in JUDGMENT. The REASON THE DELIVERER, THE SERAPHIM, and THE EARTH Angels do not, is because they have a DIVINE RIGHT to HEAVEN, therefore rendering JUDGMENT inappropriate. The Prophet Daniel was told that he would STAND in the LOT with the other PROPHETS at the END of the LAST DAY.

> ***Daniel 12:13*** *But go thy way till the END be: for thou shalt rest, and STAND in thy LOT at the END of DAYS.*

NOTE: The ANGEL GABRIEL was telling Daniel in the last Scripture, that Daniel would die and REST in the EARTH until the END of the LAST DAY. Then at that TIME, he would ARISE from the DEAD and STAND in the LOT with the other PROPHETS (the LOT of the WORTHY) to be JUDGED.

As discussed throughout all THREE BOOKS I have WRITTEN for ***THE LORD,*** NO ONE, not even THE ***HOLY SPIRIT*** may ENTER INTO HEAVEN except through JESUS CHRIST, there isn't an alternative; JESUS, is the ONLY WAY IN! Therefore, unless YOU have RECEIVED JESUS CHRIST and HIS BAPTISM, you cannot ENTER into HEAVEN without JUDGMENT, and only the VERY ELECT can PASS that JUDGMENT, by having died without a SIN upon their SOUL.

The LOT of the WORTHY

The LOT of the WORTHY consists of only a few. The LIST obviously includes those who's NAMES are RECORDED as AUTHORS in the *WORD of **GOD,*** and also them of the OLD TESTAMENT who had SERVED as PROPHETS and SAINTS to ***THE LORD.*** However, because they all died prior to the COMING of JESUS CHRIST and at that time there wasn't any PROMISE of FORGIVENESS, ***THE LORD*** had to PROVIDE the WORTHY with SAVING ***GRACE*** without VIOLATING ***HIS OWN*** LAWS.

So ***THE LORD*** said, ***THOSE OF THE OLD COVENANT THAT WERE IN RECEIPT OF THE HOLY SPIRIT, BY WAY OF HIS VIRTUE, WERE ENTITLED BY HIS HOSTING THEM DURING THEIR LIFE, TO BE BLAMELESS FOR THEIR SINS AT THE TIME OF THEIR DEATH. AND EVEN THOUGH THEY MUST STAND BEFORE ME IN JUDGMENT SAITH THE LORD, THE DEBT FOR THEIR SINS SHALL NOT BE UPON THEM!***

The PROMISE of FORGIVENESS comes by VIRTUE of THE ***HOLY SPIRIT***, WHO is RECEIVED by BAPTISM PERFORMED by JESUS CHRIST. The SAINTS and the PROPHETS of the OLD TESTAMENT could not RECEIVE BAPTISM, because CHRIST had not yet COME to the EARTH and DIED for their SINS. After JESUS had come to the EARTH, anyone RECEIVING ***HOLY SPIRIT*** BAPTISM in the NAME of JESUS CHRIST, could act on occasion as a HOST to the ***HOLY SPIRIT***; whereas prior to JESUS' COMING, THE ***HOLY SPIRIT*** HOSTED THEM who were to be PROPHETS and SAINTS. The DECREE made by ***GOD*** said, that in either CASE; whether ONE IS THE HOST TO, or be HOSTED BY THE ***HOLY SPIRIT,*** BOTH WOULD BE SINLESS in the ***EYES of GOD*** by VIRTUE of THE ***HOLY SPIRIT'S PRESENCE.***

The "LOT of the WORTHY" is the FIRST to be JUDGED on JUDGMENT DAY, and they are JUDGED in ONE LOT TOGETHER rather than individually. Immediately after their JUDGMENT, they RECEIVE RAPTURE, and ASCEND in LIGHT through the EAST GATE and into NEW JERUSALEM. After this GROUP has been JUDGED and ASCEND to HEAVEN, HEAVEN IS CLOSED, and no one else may enter into it. Those remaining on the EARTH to be JUDGED, at best, can return to the DUST of the EARTH, and those who do not return to the DUST of the EARTH will be cast into HELL!

JUDGMENT PROCEDURE

I KNOW that the sun does not set on JUDGMENT DAY until ALL to be JUDGED, are JUDGED. I also KNOW that each and every person (after the "LOT of the WORTHY") stands before ***IXOTE*** individually and they are given ample TIME to explain their SINFUL life on EARTH.

The SCRIBE Angel who had been assigned to the one standing in JUDGMENT reads from the book bearing the RECORD of that person's life, and as the book is read aloud before ***GOD,*** the person being tried may rebut that which is being read, or provide an explanation for it. There aren't any time constraints whatsoever placed on the TRIAL TIME, and ***THE LORD of HOSTS*** listens to what is being READ and SAID intensely, and at times will ask the ACCUSED questions.

Every moment of that person's life is read before them, inclusive of even their thoughts. The SCRIBE has DOCUMENTED each and every detail of that individual's life, with nothing being omitted from the RECORD. The ***JUDGE*** tells the ACCUSED, prior to the TRIAL, that IGNORANCE cannot JUSTIFY one's sinful actions; so being unaware they were committing SIN would not excuse or dismiss the SIN.

The ACCUSED is also made aware prior to the TRIAL that his or her DESTINY will be weighed in the BALANCE of the EVIDENCE being presented against them at the time of TRIAL; and that their SENTENCING can be either PERMANENT DEATH or SECOND DEATH. They are TOLD that *WORD of* ***GOD*** will provide the BASIS for the LAW they will be JUDGED against, and that their SIN will be based on their DEVIANCE from the LAW as provided in the *WORD of* ***GOD***.

It is also explained by the ***JUDGE*** what the differences are between the two possibilities of SENTENCING. It is explained that PERMANENT DEATH means that immediately after SENTENCING, the ACCUSED will return to the DUST of the EARTH and will be forever FORGOTTEN. However, if their SENTENCING is that of SECOND DEATH, the ACCUSED will be cast into HELL, and that there are NINE LEVELS of HELL they could be SENTENCED to. The SEVERITY of their SIN will DETERMINE the level of their PUNISHMENT in HELL.

They are told that the DEEPER they are cast into HELL, the more TORMENT and PAIN they will suffer throughout ETERNITY, and that once in HELL they will experience ongoing spiritual death, a death without end. ***NOTE:*** The death of the spirit entails the loss of identity the spirit once had, and in HELL they will be identified by number only and be given the name of THE DAMNED.

During the TRIAL the ACCUSED will stand NAKED before the ***JUDGE,*** the COURT ANGELS and their ACCUSER, Lucifer. The NAKEDNESS they will experience is not just PHYSICAL NAKEDNESS of the FLESH, but it is also NAKEDNESS of the SPIRIT; for if the ACCUSED were to LIE, the LIE would be VISIBLE to all in the COURTROOM; for there shall be no more CLOAK for the LIES ***SAITH THE LORD!***

Each and every person set for JUDGMENT will be tried on the SAME DAY and at the same time. THE ***HOLY SPIRIT,*** having OMNI-PRESENCE, will be ***JUDGE*** over each TRIAL; for ***HE*** can be in ALL PLACES at ALL TIMES. Lucifer as well will act as the PROSECUTOR in each TRIAL, for he also has Omni-Presence in a limited form, and on the EARTH he can be in all places at the same time! The COURT ANGELS (except for the ANGEL RAPHAEL) will be different in each of the TRIALS, for they do not have OMNI-PRESENCE as RAPHAEL has and can attend just one TRIAL at a time. There will be 14,000,000,000 such TRIALS going on at the same time, and each TRIAL will take place where the ACCUSED had last resided, prior to their death. When raised from the grave, or retrieved from HADES (called HELL in the Scriptures), that person will have the same appearance as they had prior to their time of death. Therefore, if one had been bedridden or disabled, they will be bedridden or disabled as they were prior to their death at the time of their TRIAL. However, if one were to die from dismemberment like being killed in an explosion, they will be as they were prior to the explosion, for they will be as they were prior to their death. ALL will be as they were prior to their death!

Carrying OUT the SENTENCE

THE LORD will see that ALL TRIALS are COMPLETED at the SAME TIME, and that ALL SENTENCING will be done for the TWO LOTS, (those of PERMANENT DEATH and those of SECOND DEATH) at the SAME TIME! After SENTENCING the 4,000,000,000 to PERMANENT DEATH, they will be brought before the WHITE THRONE of ***GOD,*** which will HOVER ABOVE the LOT. The LOT will be placed in a circle standing NAKED shoulder to shoulder, being ten thousand persons deep. There will be men, women, and children among them, for not all children are INNOCENT for their actions ***SAITH THE LORD. IXOTE*** will then say, ***"GO, AND BE NO MORE",*** and FIRE will come down from HEAVEN and vaporize the LOT, and they will be NO MORE!

Those being DESTINED for HELL will also be brought NAKED before the WHITE THRONE of ***GOD***, and all 10,000,000,000 of them will also be placed in a circle, being shoulder to shoulder and ten thousand deep. The circumference of the inner circle that the ACCUSED DESTINED for HELL will form will be FIFTY-SIX MILES, and the outer circle will be ONE HUNDRED and EIGHTY-TWO MILES in circumference. ***THE LORD*** will then OPEN the PIT of HELL in the middle of the inner circle, and the HOLE will begin GROWING and WIDEN until the people standing at the innermost part of the circle nearly begin to fall into the PIT.

The ANGEL RAPHAEL will then THROW Lucifer into the pit, and as he falls to the bottom of the PIT, the onlookers will hear the voices of the residents of HELL, and the sound level will be ear deafening in volume. Once Lucifer lands at the bottom of HELL, the circle of HELL will again begin to GROW and those at HELL'S outer perimeter will begin to fall into the PIT. When the people at the outer circle start to hear the screams of the one's falling into the PIT at the inner circle, they not being able to see what is happening, will start pushing towards the inner circle to see. The WALLS of the PIT will be so steep, only them in the first row will be able to see into the PIT, and those behind will continually push towards the PIT to see, until they themselves fall into it.

There will be many people who will try to climb out of the PIT, but the one's falling into it will negate that effort and will knock them back in. EVERYONE in HEAVEN will WITNESS this EVENT, for ***GOD*** wants ALL to SEE the REWARD for the WICKED. After the last of them have fallen into the PIT, the PORTAL in HEAVEN allowing the RESIDENTS in HEAVEN to VIEW ***GOD'S FINAL JUDGMENT*** is SHUT. HELL is SHUT UP as well and the Angel Uriel is once again assigned to her post of guarding the Gates of HELL.

> ***Revelation 20:10*** *And the DEVIL that DECEIVED them was CAST into the LAKE of FIRE and BRIMSTONE, where the BEAST and the FALSE PROPHET are, and shall be TORMENTED day and night for ever and ever.*

> ***Revelation 20:11*** *And I saw a GREAT WHITE THRONE, and* ***HIM*** *that sat on it, from whose* ***FACE*** *the EARTH and heaven fled away; and there was found no place for them.*

Revelation 20:12 *And I saw the DEAD, small and great, STAND BEFORE* ***GOD;*** *and the BOOKS were OPENED: and another BOOK was OPENED, which is the BOOK of LIFE: and the DEAD were JUDGED out of those things which were WRITTEN in the BOOKS, according to their works.*

Revelation 20:13 *And the sea gave up the DEAD which were in it; and DEATH and HELL delivered up the DEAD which were in them: and they were JUDGED every man according to their works.*

Revelation 20:14 *And DEATH and HELL were cast into the LAKE of FIRE. This is the SECOND DEATH.*

Revelation 20:15 *And whosoever was not found written in the BOOK of LIFE was cast into the LAKE of FIRE.*

Chapter 22,

HELL, An ETERNAL Reality

There are many people who believe that there isn't any HELL, and I find this type of belief to be most TROUBLING. If these people believe in ***GOD*** and in HEAVEN they must also believe in HELL, for the HOLY BIBLE speaks of both HEAVEN and HELL. I could cite Scripture after Scripture within the HOLY BIBLE that makes reference to HELL, and the Scriptures referring to HELL outnumber those speaking of HEAVEN by a very wide margin. What saddens ME most about them not believing there is a HELL is that the people refusing to believe in HELL are more than likely DESTINED for it!

HELL is a REALITY, and refusing to believe there is a HELL doesn't make it any less REAL! In this Chapter WE will discuss the world of HELL, its contents, and what ongoing tragedies its occupants must suffer throughout ETERNITY. ***GOD*** REWARDS the GOOD with an ETERNAL LIFE in HEAVEN; however HE also rewards the EVIL with an ETERNAL DEATH in HELL!

For those of you who refuse to believe in either HEAVEN or HELL, you are of the GENTILE (the NON-BELIEVER), and the best that you can wish for, is that after JUDGMENT you might be allowed to return to the DUST of the EARTH and be forever FORGOTTEN. This will be your reward for refusing to BELIEVE, if you are fortunate enough to be of the LOT of the 4,000,000,000 out of the 14,000,000,000 that STAND BEFORE ***GOD*** in JUDGMENT. Only 4,000,000,000 out of the 14,000,000,000 go back into the DUST of the EARTH, and you will be fortunate to be of that LOT. But what if you are among them of the 10,000,000,000 that are cast into HELL? There aren't any APPEALS, nor are there SENTENCE REVERSALS, nor are there AMNESTIES given. ONCE CONDEMNED to the SECOND DEATH, the SENTENCE is ETERNAL, ***SAITH THE LORD of HOSTS.***

The world of HELL

The world of HELL is the exact OPPOSITE of that of NEW JERUSALEM. Whereas NEW JERUSALEM is a LIGHT STRUCTURE in the shape of a GI-

GANTIC PYRAMID, HELL on the other hand is a DARKENED PIT pointed downward in the shape of a gigantic pyramid, with fiery walls made of BRIMSTONE (SULFUR). The heat within HELL is so INTENSE even rock cannot maintain a solid form, so therefore the earth around HELL acts like the WALLS of a GIGANTIC BRAISING FURNACE. The reason the WORD "BRAISING" is used to describe the FURNACE rather than the words "firing or burning" is because BRAISING best describes what happens to them in HELL. The WORD "BRAISING" is defined as being; a SLOW PROCESS of cooking MEAT in a covered container, and this best describes what happens to them in HELL!

As there are NINE LEVELS in HEAVEN, so are there nine levels in HELL, with the GREATEST TORMENT being endured at the ninth level, which is the DEEPEST level, called, SATAN'S THRONE. Whereas those in HEAVEN have the FREEDOM of MOVEMENT within their DOMAIN, those of HELL are RESTRAINED in MOVEMENT, and are CHAINED one to the other. The STENCH of burning flesh, urine and excrement permeates the environment, and screams of terror and pain go on day and night without end. Talking to one another is forbidden; therefore one cannot even share their experience of PAIN with them who are chained to either side of them.

The SECOND DEATH is ETERNAL DYING, and everyday the spirit dies a little more in each of HELL'S OCCUPANTS. The memories of JUDGMENT DAY reside in each one's thoughts, reminding them as to why they are in HELL! The DAMNED find out very quickly that begging for a lesser torment only entices their OWNERS to TORMENT them all the more, so they learn to hold their tongue, even though the PAIN and SUFFERING is increased daily. ALL continually pray to ***GOD*** for DEATH, but DEATH for them will never come.

Each and every person is given a NUMBER for identification, and when his or her CAPTORS (OWNERS) call out that NUMBER, that person knows that it is their time to receive some form of greater punishment. They are then removed from their shackles and taken elsewhere in the PIT by a DEMON to one of the Fallen Ones. The one they are brought before has devised some form of abuse for them to endure before an audience of other Fallen Angels and Demons, and sometimes, even SATAN attends the showing. Each one of the Fallen Angels tries to outdo the other in their mischief; and by knowing that the DAMNED CANNOT DIE, regardless of what they may do to them, the atrocities they perform on those individuals goes beyond imagination.

Almost always the heinous act for the show will have some sort of a sexual connotation to it, for the Fallen Angels and the Demons do not have a gender, and it pleases them to watch some sort of bizarre sexual act. These acts are done on an individual basis and in duos or in groups, and nearly always include the use of FIRE in the sexual act, for they enjoy both smelling and watching the burning of flesh.

The DEVIL uses YOUR MIND

In HELL the DEVIL has complete OWNERSHIP of its OCCUPANTS, and he will use the MINDS of those CAPTIVE to CREATE their own worst FEARS. Whatever a person fears most will be with them in abundance, whether it be the fear of insects, or of heights, or of confinement, or any phobia other than that of the fear of water, for in HELL water cannot be found.

The DEVIL takes great pride in giving one a very pleasant thought that turns out to be a HORROR to them in REALITY. He can make Demons appear to be handsome young men or beautiful women, who will entice the victim into believing they are embracing or having sex with a desirable person. Then once well into the act, the REALITY will be made perfectly clear to them, and they will find that they are embracing a venomous snake or having sex with an animal. Those in HELL learn very quickly not to think of anything they may fear, for the DEVIL will use that very fear against them.

Your Daily Meal

Your OWNERS do not feed you, nor do they give you anything to drink because you CANNOT DIE in HELL. However your memories of eating and drinking have not left you, and you hunger for food and thirst for water. To supplement your hunger and thirst, you will eat your own shit and drink your own piss and will fight one another over it.

The others on either side of you will try to take your excrement or urine from you as it passes from your body, and even though you may never eat food again, the urine and excrement never ceases from passing through you daily. The eating of your own shit and the drinking of your own piss, or that of another, becomes a delicacy, and while you rot in HELL this becomes the only thing you have to look forward to, your daily meal.

The Levels in HELL

Although all the Levels in HELL are HORRIFIC and UNBEARABLE, those in the First Level suffer less than them who are in the Ninth Level. With each descending Level comes greater pain and suffering, being raised exponentially for the declining Level. For those at the First Level, they believe they are at the worst Level and would not believe it if they were told that there could be worse punishment elsewhere in HELL.

Each of the Levels in HELL have a name, and at any Level, those at that Level, are unaware of either a descending or ascending Level beyond where they reside. For instance, one on the Third Level does not know that they are on the Third Level nor do they know that there are further Levels above and below where they reside; however they certainly know that they are in HELL!

Each of the Levels in HELL is self-supporting and none of HELL'S residents are ever taken to another Level, although they may be moved about in the Level they reside. Each Level has its own staff of Demons to TORMENT at a specific threshold of PAIN, and the Demons at any one of the Levels may never leave that Level where they reside, although they may freely move about their own Level. Only the Fallen Angels and Lucifer have freedom to move about HELL as they so desire, and they routinely inspect each Level to make certain the specific THRESHOLD of PAIN for each of that Level's OCCUPANTS is neither exceeded or diminished from that which is specified.

HELL Resides within the EARTH

When Lucifer was cast out of HEAVEN, he was given the EARTH for his dominion, and he is held captive to the EARTH, whether it is in its BOWELS or on its SURFACE. When Lucifer is allowed by ***GOD*** to walk to and fro upon the surface of the EARTH, he is also allowed on occasion ACCESS to the ***THRONE of GOD,*** by way of the METATRON. However, while he is LOCKED UP in the BOWELS of the EARTH (HELL), his ACCESS is DENIED and he must stay and RULE within the boundaries of HELL!

With each and every CYCLE of the EARTH, the population within HELL grows by 10,000,000,000 OCCUPANTS, excluding the number of DEMONS who also grow in population with each CYCLE. When SEVEN CYCLES have been completed and the number of OCCUPANTS in HELL has grown to be 70,000,000,000, HELL is then said to be at its CAPACITY.

Once HELL has reached its CAPACITY, the EARTH in which HELL is housed is then TOTALLY DESTROYED, however, HELL itself is not DESTROYED and it remains intact. At the TIME of the EARTH'S TOTAL DESTRUCTION, HELL is moved to the ABYSS, where it is merged into the preceding HELLS before it. The ABYSS, where HELL then resides permanently, is called HELL PROPER, and HELL PROPER exists throughout ETERNITY, forever growing in its size and population by its receiving 70,000,000,000 new

OCCUPANTS every FORTY-NINE THOUSAND YEARS.

Even when the SEVEN TRILLION-YEAR Life Cycle of the UNIVERSE is completed, and the UNIVERSE RECYCLES, HELL PROPER remains intact. Unlike the NEW HEAVEN that ***GOD*** CREATES at the BEGINNING of the NEW CYCLE of the UNIVERSE, and the starting back of the BIBLE STORY at ADAM and EVE, HELL PROPER continues on and never recycles as does HEAVEN and the EARTH, forever growing in its size and OCCUPANCY.

When the merging of HELL into HELL PROPER takes place, the OCCUPANTS of HELL see no change in it. The MERGER is transparent to those in HELL and the DEVIL himself is unaware that the MERGER has taken place. In each and every HELL before it, Lucifer resides in all by Omni-Presence, and because each HELL is IDENTICAL to the one before it, with only the OCCUPANTS being different; he is unaware that there is more than one HELL. For only by its OCCUPANTS is there a difference in the HELLS, and the OCCUPANTS have lost their identities and are known by only numbers, numbers that have repeated themselves over and over again and again in every HELL, throughout ETERNITY.

As you have been previously told, sometimes ***GOD*** RENEWS the FACE of the EARTH, and sometimes ***HE*** RECREATES it. It should now be obvious to you that with every SEVEN CYCLES of the EARTH (49,000 years), on the SEVENTH CYCLE, ***GOD*** will DESTROY the EARTH in its ENTIRETY, because HELL has reached its CAPACITY. And, with each and every CYCLE of the EARTH, prior to HELL reaching its CAPACITY, rather than DESTROYING the EARTH, the FACE of the EARTH is RENEWED!

Chapter 23
CYCLES

Ecclesiastes 1:9 *The thing that hath been, it is that which shall be; and that which is done is that which shall be done: and there is NO NEW THING under the sun.*

Ecclesiastes 1:10 *Is there any thing whereof it may be said, SEE THIS IS NEW? IT HATH BEEN ALREADY OF OLD TIME, which was before us.*

Ecclesiastes 1:11 *There is NO REMEMBRANCE of former things: neither shall there be ANY REMEMBRANCE of things that are to come with those that shall come after.*

These three Scriptures taken from the Book of Ecclesiastes was WRITTEN by KING SOLOMON, who ***GOD*** had GIVEN the GREATEST WISDOM of any MAN that had ever walked the EARTH; other than JESUS CHRIST, who had GREATER WISDOM than he.

2 Chronicles 1:11 *And* ***GOD*** *said to* ***SOLOMON, BECAUSE THIS WAS IN THINE HEART, AND THOU HAST NOT ASKED RICHES, WEALTH, OR HONOUR, NOR THE LIFE OF THINE ENEMIES, NEITHER YET HAST ASKED LONG LIFE; BUT HAST ASKED WISDOM AND KNOWLEDGE FOR THYSELF, THAT THOU MAYEST JUDGE MY PEOPLE, OVER WHOM I HAVE MADE THEE KING:***

2 Chronicles 1:12 WISDOM AND KNOWLEDGE IS GRANTED UNTO THEE; AND I WILL GIVE THEE RICHES, AND WEALTH, AND HONOUR, SUCH AS NONE OF THE KINGS HAVE HAD THAT HAVE BEEN BEFORE THEE, NEITHER SHALL THERE ANY AFTER THEE HAVE THE LIKE.

Throughout the ages there hasn't been any King or person having both the WISDOM and KNOWLEDGE of SOLOMON nor his equivalent WEALTH. The first three Scriptures cited from the Book of Ecclesiastes talk about the VARIOUS CYCLES of EXISTENCE. The Scriptures tell you that nothing is NEW, for all things that EXIST have been BEFORE, and they are NOW the same as they were BEFORE. The Scriptures further state, when ***GOD*** RECREATES these THINGS, ***HE*** does it in such a way that NO ONE ever realizes the seemingly NEW THINGS are IDENTICAL to the OLD THINGS ***HE*** had once CREATED. The Scripture also says that anyone who had been here before (a REINCARNATE) hasn't any MEMORY (REMEMBRANCE) of a previous life in this world. Each time they come, their life appears to be something new, something they had never experienced before. Neither will they know what will happen next in their life, even though they had done the exact same things BEFORE.

As mentioned in the other two BOOKS, "Revealing The Bible's Truth" and "The ROD of IRON", all KEY EVENTS and KEY PEOPLE playing a role in determining the DIRECTION of the WORLD as it is TODAY, have been in a world that was IDENTICAL to this one, BEFORE. All the Kings and world leaders of yesteryear, whom impacted the direction of the world, continually come back to each and every NEW EARTH to do as they had done before. These KEY PEOPLE are REINCARNATED with each RECYCLING of the EARTH and RETURN to assume the same ROLE they had had in the PREVIOUS WORLD.

The EARTH every SEVEN THOUSAND YEARS is either RENEWED or RECREATED, depending on where it is in its LIFECYCLE. Every SEVEN LIFECYCLES (49,000 years) the EARTH in its ENTIRETY is DESTROYED, and then RECREATED after the COMPLETION of the SEVENTH CYCLE. After the first SIX LIFECYCLES and prior to its SEVENTH CYCLE, the EARTH is RENEWED, and made to be like it was during the TIME when NOAH entered the ARK. However, after its SEVENTH LIFECYCLE, when HELL has reached its CAPACITY at 70,000,000,000 OCCUPANTS, HELL is then moved to HELL PROPER. The EARTH then, that had HOSTED HELL for FORTY-NINE THOUSAND YEARS, is COMPLETELY DESTROYED, leaving not a trace of its existence BEHIND.

Each and every time the EARTH goes through its SEVEN THOUSAND YEAR CYCLE, the NEW EARTH, whether it be RENEWED or RECREATED, starts back in Chapter 7 of the Book of Genesis, and not back at Chapter 1. The BIBLE STORY restarts with NOAH getting into the ARK, and this scenario repeats itself ONE BILLION TIMES.

However, after the EARTH has gone through ONE BILLION LIFECYCLES (7,000,000,000,000 years), the UNIVERSE reaches its CLIMAX and FOLDS BACK within itself, and the BIG BANG happens again, thus forming a NEW UNIVERSE. At the BEGINNING of the NEW LIFECYCLE for the UNIVERSE, the BIBLE STORY then starts back at the very BEGINNING in Chapter 1 of the Book of Genesis, with ***GOD SAYING, "LET THERE BE LIGHT",*** rather than back with NOAH entering the ARK.

Only ***GOD*** KNOWS how many such LIFECYCLES of the EARTH and the UNIVERSE have thus far taken place. ***THE LORD*** has explained the phenomena to ME in this way: ***HE*** told ME if I were to go to the seashore and look at the sand on its beach, would I be able to tell which one of the GRAINS of SAND on the beach was the FIRST, and which one was the LAST? I, of course, told ***THE LORD*** that I wouldn't be able to differentiate between the FIRST and LAST GRAIN of SAND. ***GOD*** then TOLD ME, whereas I could not give the answer, ***HE COULD,*** without any difficulty whatsoever, FOR ***GOD*** IS ALL KNOWING!

From what ***THE LORD*** had TOLD ME, I could gather that the RECYCLING of the EARTH and the UNIVERSE has been going on FOREVER, and that the NUMBER of CYCLES are INFINITE. Therefore only an INFINITE can quantify an INFINITE, and MAN cannot UNDERSTAND that which is INFINITE.

For each of you on the EARTH, it appears as though this is the only WORLD that EXISTS, or that has ever EXISTED; for this is what ***THE LORD*** wants you to believe. ***GOD*** does this so that each CYCLE of the EARTH appears to be the FIRST and ONLY CYCLE of it, and this is TRUE whether the EARTH has been RENEWED or RECREATED, because in appearance they are BOTH the SAME.

GOD can make OLD THINGS look like NEW, and NEW THINGS look like they are OLD. Furthermore, when MAN tries to gage time of EXISTENCE for anything on the EARTH, he fails in his attempts; for ***GOD*** makes the EARTH to appear to be MUCH OLDER than it really is! Depending on where WE are at in our current EARTH LIFECYCLE, the EARTH can be no older than FORTY-EIGHT THOUSAND YEARS, for the ONE THOUSAND YEAR MILLENNIUM is yet to COME for this EARTH.

> **Ecclesiastes 3:14** *I know that, whatsoever* ***GOD*** *doeth, it shall be for ever: nothing can be put to it, nor any thing taken from it: and* ***GOD*** *doeth it, that men should FEAR BEFORE* ***HIM.***

> ***Ecclesiastes 3:15*** *That which hath been is NOW; and that which is TO BE hath ALREADY BEEN; and* ***GOD*** *requireth that which is past.*

NOTE: These Scriptures say that whatsoever ***GOD*** does, it continues on FOREVER! They also say that ***GOD'S*** CREATION CONTINUALLY REPEATS itself throughout ETERNITY (***GOD*** requireth that which is PAST).

With every REGENERATION of the EARTH, only the people playing a KEY ROLE in determining its DIRECTION return to it. These are the people, such as the BIBLICAL CHARACTERS, including JESUS CHRIST, and also the world's leaders who had an impact on world history; as it is so documented today. There will continue to be a Hitler and a Stalin, a Thomas Jefferson and a Leonardo De Vinci, a Mozart and a Rembrandt, a Michael Angelo and a Thomas Edison, and an Einstein; ALL KEY PLAYERS return to LIVE AGAIN so that the HISTORY of the WORLD REPEATS ITSELF!

Even the KEY PLAYERS who had been CAST into HELL return, to live out their lives on the EARTH and to do once more, as they had done before. However, they again will be RAISED and JUDGED at the END of DAYS, and again will be CAST back into HELL to remain throughout ETERNITY, only leaving HELL for brief intervals of life on EARTH.

The HISTORY of the WORLD continually REPEATS ITSELF, like an ongoing stage play, starting with ACT TWO, by NOAH entering the ARK. ACT ONE however, the STORY of ADAM and EVE, only REPEATS its PERFORMANCE, ONCE every SEVEN TRILLION YEARS, when the UNIVERSE RECYCLES!

Other than the MAIN CHARACTERS, everyone else on the EARTH is NEW to the WORLD, for the EARTH is where LIFE BEGINS. ***GOD*** uses the EARTH like a SILVER REFINER'S MELTING POT, and when the SLAG separates from the SILVER, (the GOOD from the EVIL) ***HE*** CLAIMS the SILVER and DUMPS the SLAG.

For anyone RETURNING to the EARTH (other than for JESUS CHRIST), it is a NEW EXPERIENCE to them, for they REMEMBER nothing of the PAST, and their life on EARTH is the SAME as it is for them who are on the EARTH for the FIRST TIME! JESUS was allowed to REMEMBER HIS previous experiences on the EARTH, so HE could TEACH about the KINGDOM of HEAVEN, and HE so states HIS PREVIOUS EXPERIENCES HERE in the Scriptures. JESUS tells HIS Disciples of HIS continual CYCLING from ***GOD*** to the EARTH and then back to ***GOD*** again.

John 16:28 I CAME FORTH FROM THE FATHER, AND AM COME INTO THE WORLD: AGAIN, I LEAVE THE WORLD, AND GO TO THE FATHER.

HEAVEN AND HELL REMAIN

With every CYCLE of the EARTH, HEAVEN grows by 4,500,000,000 and HELL grows by 10,000,000,000. The surface (only) of the EARTH is DESTROYED after each of the first SIX CYCLES and RENEWED to begin its next LIFECYCLE. With every SEVEN CYCLES of the EARTH, HEAVEN grows by 31,500,000,000 and HELL grows by 70,000,000,000, and the EARTH at this JUNCTURE is DESTROYED in its ENTIRETY and then RECREATED to begin its first NEW LIFECYCLE of FORTY-NINE THOUSAND YEARS.

At the TIME of EARTH'S DESTRUCTION, the HELL within EARTH is MOVED from the EARTH to HELL PROPER, the ABYSS. Then after ONE BILLION such SEVEN THOUSAND-YEAR CYCLES of the EARTH have been COMPLETED, the UNIVERSE reaches its CLIMAX, and EVERYTHING in EXISTENCE folds back into ITSELF. Then after FOLDING BACK into a SINGLE POINT of ***LIGHT***, CREATION BEGINS all over AGAIN, starting over at the BEGINNING of the HOLY BIBLE, as it had done before.

At the TIME of the REGENERATION of the UNIVERSE, that which was called HEAVEN during the PREVIOUS TIME of CREATION is FOLDED in with the HEAVENS occurring before it, while yet maintaining its autonomy. The FOUR PYRAMID SHAPED KINGDOMS thus forming a CUBE that was called HEAVEN are then combined with the many other such KINGDOMS, with each KINGDOM being a BUILDING BLOCK forming yet a GREATER PYRAMID. This GREATER PYRAMID is also called NEW JERUSALEM as were the HEAVENS coming into it. This BUILDING of ***GOD'S KINGDOM*** goes on throughout ETERNITY, never ENDING and CONTINUALLY GROWING in both POPULOUS and SIZE.

Having MULTIPLE KINGDOMS that form even a LARGER KINGDOM is why ALL of the ***TRINITY***, THE ***DELIVERER 182*** and JESUS CHRIST have OMNI-PRESENCE. This is because ***GOD*** RULES ALL the KINGDOMS at the SAME TIME. DAVID however and SOLOMON in each of the KINGDOMS of HEAVEN are separate. Each DAVID and SOLOMON of the various KINGDOMS, RULE INDEPENDENTLY of one another, and although they are the SAME in each of the KINGDOMS, they rule over only the KINGDOMS where they RESIDE.

This may be a bit difficult to UNDERSTAND, but while there is only ***ONE TRINITY,*** ONE ***DELIVERER 182***, and ONE JESUS CHRIST, there are a MULTITUDE of KINGS called DAVID and SOLOMON, with each DAVID and SOLOMON being IDENTICAL in every respect to the others. This duplication of DAVID and SOLOMON takes place with every LIFECYCLE and REGENERATION of the UNIVERSE (every SEVEN TRILLION YEARS). This is also why in the TEMPLE of ***GOD*** and at the THRONE of DAVID there were a MULTITUDE of sculptured LIONS and OXEN, thus indicating the MULTITUDES that EXIST of both DAVID (the LION) and SOLOMON (the OX) throughout ETERNITY.

THE LORD'S SABBATHS, GAPS in TIME

Everything NUMBERING SEVEN belongs to ***GOD. GOD*** HALLOWED the SEVENTH DAY and therefore made it ***HIS DAY*** of REST. However, what ***GOD*** calls a DAY is not the SAME as what MAN calls a DAY, for ***HE*** is TIMELESS! ***GOD*** sees equal INCREMENTS of TIME as being a SINGLE DAY, and after SIX of the EQUAL INCREMENTS has PAST, the SEVENTH INCREMENT BELONGS to ***HIM.***

This holds TRUE whether the INCREMENTS are DAYS, WEEKS, YEARS, DECADES, CENTURIES, MILLENNIUMS, and so forth, regardless of what each INCREMENT of TIME may consist of, that SEVENTH INCREMENT of TIME BELONGS to ***GOD.*** You have been TOLD that at the CONCLUSION of the SIX THOUSAND YEARS of the EARTH'S CYCLE, the SEVEN THOUSANDTH YEAR is called the MILLENNIUM, a TIME of HEAVEN on EARTH. This represents ***GOD'S DAY of REST,*** for ***GOD*** shuts the DEVIL and HELL up during this PERIOD of TIME, thus CLAIMING this PERIOD of TIME for ***HIMSELF!***

Therefore, the same scenario HOLDS TRUE for the SEVENTH CYCLE of the EARTH. The FINAL SEVEN THOUSAND YEARS in the EARTH'S LIFECYCLE, ***GOD*** sees as the CONCLUSION of a WEEK, and HALLOWS that SEVENTH CYCLE UNTO ***HIMSELF*** as ***HIS DAY OF REST.*** Therefore, at the CONCLUSION of the SIXTH CYCLE'S MILLENNIUM, ***GOD RESTS,*** and there is a SEVEN THOUSAND-YEAR GAP in TIME before there is a RECREATION of the EARTH. This same scenario holds true for every EQUAL INCREMENT of TIME, even for the SEVEN TRILLIONTH YEAR of the UNIVERSE'S EXISTENCE.

The UNIVERSE FOLDS back into ITSELF at the CONCLUSION of the SIX TRILLIONTH YEAR, and there will be a ONE TRILLION YEAR SAB-

BATH before the UNIVERSE is once again REGENERATED. This CONFUSION about TIME is why many scientist have difficulty BELIEVING in the *WORD of **GOD,*** because they do not UNDERSTAND that the SIX DAYS of ***GOD'S CREATION*** simply means SIX EQUAL INCREMENTS of TIME, and not six twenty-four hour EARTH days. From what you have been TOLD thus far, you should REALIZE that the REGENERATION of the UNIVERSE takes place over a ONE TRILLION-YEAR TIME PERIOD, during ***GOD'S DAY of REST!***

As the UNIVERSE EXPANDS and slowly comes to a HALT after SIX TRILLION YEARS of EXISTENCE, it reaches its CLIMAX, and begins to ACCELERATE in the opposite direction, back towards its CENTER. The VELOCITY reached when the outer WALLS of the UNIVERSE make contact with each other is many times greater than that of the speed of light, and ALL the ENERGY within the UNIVERSE is COMPACTED into a SINGLE POINT of light, being roughly the size of a single hydrogen atom. This FOLDING BACK into ITSELF takes FORTY-NINE BILLION YEARS, thus COMPRESSING SIX TRILLION YEARS of EXISTENCE into a MOMENT!

The UNIVERSE then remains in its COMPRESSED STATE of LIGHT for another FORTY-NINE BILLION YEARS, and after that elapsed TIME, ***IXOTE AGAIN*** REGENERATES the UNIVERSE. ***HE*** does this by SPLITTING the UNIVERSAL POINT of LIGHT with a GREATER more POWERFUL ***LIGHT, ONE*** from a PURE ENERGY SOURCE (***HOLY LIGHT***). The ***HOLY LIGHT*** being INFINITELY GREATER in ENERGY than the ENERGY COMPACTING and CONTAINING the UNIVERSE STRIKES the exact center of the COMPACTED UNIVERSE on IMPACT. This DISPERSES the UNIVERSE into all directions in a SINGLE INSTANCE and the UNIVERSE is ONCE AGAIN REGENERATED. Initially the EXPANSION of the UNIVERSE is MANY TIMES GREATER than that of the SPEED of light, as WE know that speed to be TODAY, for the SPEED of LIGHT slows down as a function of TIME, coming to a HALT at the END of the LIFECYCLE of the UNIVERSE.

This phenomenon can be compared to what happens when the SPERM from a MAN penetrates and fertilizes the EGG in the WOMAN. Rapid growth immediately takes place once the two UNITE, and the RAPID GROWTH RATE DECREASES as TIME ELAPSES. This same phenomenon happens to the VELOCITY of the UNIVERSE; as does the SPERM and the EGG'S growth rate decrease with time, so does the EXPANSION RATE of the UNIVERSE DECREASE with TIME.

After the REGENERATION of the UNIVERSE has begun, it continues to EXPAND for the balance of the ONE TRILLION YEAR SABBATH. After the

ONE TRILLION-YEAR SABBATH PERIOD has ELAPSED, the STORY of CREATION and that of ADAM and EVE begin ONCE MORE, as told in the Scriptures of the HOLY BIBLE!

Chapter 24
CREATION

In all THREE BOOKS I have written for ***THE LORD*** WE have spoken a great deal about both the CREATION and the DESTRUCTION of the heavens and the EARTH, with the greater emphasis being placed on the DESTRUCTION of them. In this Chapter ***THE LORD*** wants to detail CREATION at its ONSET and EXPLAIN why ***GOD*** both CREATES and DESTROYS that which ***HE*** has CREATED, over a SPECIFIC COURSE of TIME.

THE LORD, speaking through KING SOLOMON says in Ecclesiastes 3:1, "TO EVERY THING THERE IS A SEASON, AND A TIME TO EVERY PURPOSE UNDER THE HEAVEN:" What ***THE LORD*** is EXPRESSING in this Scripture is that there are SET TIMES for all things to happen, indicating that ALL of CREATION has been SCRIPTED as to what WILL OCCUR and when it WILL HAPPEN!

As it is with a TREE, and the TIME in which it bears its FRUIT, so is it with ALL of ***GOD'S*** CREATION, for there is a TIME and a SEASON for ALL THINGS. Before ***GOD*** CREATED ANYTHING, ***HE*** SCRIPTED the DETAILS of what was to be CREATED, much like an ARCHITECT draws up his plans for the building of a STRUCTURE prior to him building it. FURTHERMORE, ***GOD*** did not omit a DETAIL in the BOOK of ***HIS CREATION,*** nor did ***HE*** omit a DETAIL regarding them who were to take part in ***HIS CREATION; ALL WAS SCRIPTED INTO THE BOOK SAITH THE LORD!***

The DETAILS of ***GOD'S CREATION*** was put into a BOOK in HEAVEN, and the BOOK is called the *WORD of* ***GOD.*** At the TIME of the SCRIPTING of the BOOK, there were JUST TWO in EXISTENCE, a ***FATHER*** and a ***SON, BOTH BEING GOD;*** and ***THEIR NAMES*** are ***YAHWEH*** and ***IXOTE;*** THE ***ALMIGHTY GOD and HIS HOLY SPIRIT.*** The SCRIPTED BOOK gave EVERY DETAIL about that which was to be CREATED. Its TIMELINE of EVENTS and LIFECYCLE; what would happen; where it would happen; when it would happen; and who would be involved with its HAPPENING! As with any BUILDER'S PLAN, a MATERIALS LIST for the CREATION was also in the BOOK, and the PRIME INGREDIENT NEEDED for the CREATION was ***LIGHT!***

SO ***THE SPIRIT of GOD, IXOTE, GAVE BIRTH TO THE LIGHT, AND THE LIGHT WAS CALLED YESHUA, THE PREEMINENT TO AN INCARNATE, CALLED:*** JESUS CHRIST. ***AND FROM THE LIGHT (YESHUA) WERE ALL THINGS MADE; THE HEAVENS, THE EARTH, AND ALL THAT WERE THEREIN, AND THE LIGHT WAS MADE FLESH TO WALK AMONG MEN.***

LET US NOW REVIEW SCRIPTURE TO SEE IF THE CLARITY OF TRUTH REVEALS THE TRUTH WITHIN THE SCRIPTURES:

> ***John 1:1*** *IN the BEGINNING was the WORD, and the WORD was with* ***GOD,*** *and the WORD was* ***GOD.***
>
> ***John 1:2*** *The SAME was in the BEGINNING with* ***GOD.***
>
> ***John 1:3*** *ALL THINGS were MADE by* ***HIM;*** *and without* ***HIM*** *was not ANY THING MADE that was MADE.*
>
> ***John 1:4*** *In* ***HIM*** *was LIFE; and the LIFE was the LIGHT of MEN.*
>
> ***John 1:5*** *And the LIGHT SHINETH in darkness; and the darkness comprehended it not.*
>
> ***John 1:14*** *And the WORD was made FLESH, and DWELT among us, (and we beheld HIS GLORY, the GLORY as of the only BEGOTTEN of* ***THE FATHER,****) FULL of GRACE and TRUTH.*

To ensure that you have GRASPED the MESSAGE WE have given thus far, let US summarize that which has been previously said. ***GOD*** SCRIPTED in a BOOK all matters concerning ***HIS CREATION*** prior to ***HIS CREATION,*** and the BOOK is CALLED the "*WORD of* ***GOD***". At the TIME of the BOOK'S SCRIPTING, there were only ***TWO*** in EXISTENCE, a ***FATHER*** and a ***SON, BOTH BEING GOD; THEREFORE IT CAN BE SAID: IN THE BEGINNING WAS THE WORD, AND THE WORD WAS WITH GOD, AND THE WORD WAS GOD.***

It can also be said, that from the WORD, (the BOOK) ALL INGREDIENTS necessary for CREATION were DETAILED, with the KEY ELEMENT for ***GOD'S CREATION*** being ***LIGHT.*** So ***IXOTE,*** THE ***HOLY SPIRIT of GOD, CREATED THAT LIGHT FOR GOD*** needed for ***GOD'S*** CREATION; and the ***LIGHT*** was called ***YESHUA.*** This is the CREATION of the ***TRINITY***, the THREE PRIMARY COLORS of LIGHT, RED, ***THE FATHER,*** GREEN, THE ***HOLY SPIRIT of GOD,*** and BLUE, ***YESHUA,*** the ***SON of IXOTE (GOD). GOD,*** being WHITE LIGHT, is COMPOSED of ALL THREE PRIMARY COLORS of LIGHT, therefore making the THREE LIGHT FORMS when COMBINED, ***GOD.*** It can further be said that the ***LIGHT*** needed for ***GOD'S*** CREATION was BLUE LIGHT, and ***YESHUA*** was that BLUE LIGHT.

The Scriptures of the GOSPEL of John also state that it was ***YAHWEH*** who was the ***AUTHOR*** and ***ARCHITECT of CREATION*** ("And the WORD was with ***GOD***") and that it was ***IXOTE*** who was the ***MASTER CRAFTSMAN*** and the ***MAKER of CREATION*** ("ALL THINGS were made by ***HIM***"). Then from the CREATION of LIGHT (***YESHUA***) came FORTH LIFE into EXISTENCE ("In ***HIM*** was LIFE; and the LIFE was the LIGHT of MEN"). The LIGHT spoken of in the Scripture was the BLUE LIGHT needed for LIFE, and the CREATION of LIVING MATTER, PHYSICAL LIFE!

ONCE the BLUE LIGHT became LIVING MATTER, there was also the need for other ELEMENTS to SUPPORT the LIFE of the LIVING MATTER, and the ELEMENTS came from the SAME BLUE LIGHT SOURCE (***YESHUA***). The BLUE LIGHT was then broken down into particles of LIGHT, and the various elements NEEDED to support LIFE was removed from the BLUE LIGHT'S COMPOSITION. Once the ELEMENTS of the BLUE LIGHT were removed, the light that REMAINED was no longer in its PUREST FORM (***HOLY LIGHT***) and it then became necessary to SEPARATE the NEW FORMS of light from the ***PURE FORM of LIGHT (RED, GREEN and BLUE LIGHT), GOD. GOD CALLED THE BLUE LIGHT MADE FROM HIS WORD, "LIVING WATERS", FOR THEY CAME OUT FROM HIS WORD AND GAVE LIFE. THE LIGHT THAT REMAINED AFTER THE GIVING BIRTH TO CREATION, HE CALLED SIMPLY "WATERS", FOR THOSE "WATERS" HAD COME FORTH FROM THE LIVING WATERS.*** Furthermore, the "WATERS" representing PHYSICAL LIFE, and the ***LIVING WATERS*** representing ***SPIRITUAL LIFE*** needed to be SEPARATED for they were different. ***SO GOD SET A BOUNDARY BETWEEN THE TWO FORMS OF LIFE (SPIRITUAL LIFE AND PHYSICAL LIFE), AND GOD CALLED THAT BOUNDARY, THE FIRMAMENT.***

> ***Genesis 1:6*** *And* ***GOD*** *said,* ***LET THERE BE A FIRMAMENT IN THE MIDST OF THE WATERS, AND LET IT DIVIDE THE WATERS FROM THE WATERS.***
>
> ***Genesis 1:7*** *And* ***GOD*** *made the FIRMAMENT, and DIVIDED the waters which were under the FIRMAMENT, from the WATERS which were ABOVE the FIRMAMENT: and it was so.*
>
> ***Genesis 1:8*** *And* ***GOD*** *called the FIRMAMENT HEAVEN. And the evening and the morning were the SECOND DAY.*

The WATERS spoken of in the Scriptures that are ABOVE the FIRMAMENT refer to the SPIRITUAL LIFE coming forth from the *WORD of* ***GOD*****,** that which was SCRIPTED into the BOOK regarding SPIRITUAL CREATION. The waters that are below the FIRMAMENT represent CARNAL LIFE (PHYSICAL Life), and the formation of the fresh and the salt waters of the EARTH. Then from the waters of the EARTH came forth the various Physical Life Forms just as the SPIRITUAL LIFE FORMS came forth from the LIVING WATERS above the FIRMAMENT.

In yet another LAYER of the same Scripture, the WATERS above the FIRMAMENT refer to the PURE BLUE LIGHT that came forth from the ***LIVING WATERS*** (*the WORD of* ***GOD***). The waters below the FIRMAMENT in that same Scriptural LAYER refer to the PARTICLES of LIGHT taken from the ORIGINAL BLUE LIGHT SOURCE. The removing of the various ELEMENTS (Particles of Light) from the BLUE LIGHT, degraded it, and the LIGHT was no longer in its PUREST FORM, therefore making the light below the FIRMAMENT, a TAINTED form of Blue Light. So ***GOD*** SEPARATED the TWO FORMS of BLUE LIGHT, the PURE (the HOLY) from the TAINTED (the Unholy), and the BOUNDARY set between the TWO was called HEAVEN (the FIRMAMENT).

The TAINTED Light

Once the essential ELEMENTS needed for PHYSICAL (CARNAL) LIFE SUPPORT are removed from the ORIGINAL BLUE LIGHT SOURCE, the light remaining is then called TAINTED LIGHT, for it has been DEGRADED by the removal of some of its critical ELEMENTS. From the TAINTED LIGHT the STARS were then CREATED and they consist of several COMPOSITE groups. The various GROUPS of STARS can be IDENTIFIED by what they lack in composition to that of their ORIGINAL BLUE LIGHT COMPOSITION.

For example, if the STAR is lacking in OXYGEN, it will be a HYDROGEN BASED STAR, or if it is lacking in HYDROGEN it will be a HELIUM BASED STAR, and so on, depending on what the STAR is lacking in when compared to its original BLUE LIGHT COMPOSITION. Differing from the STARS, PURE BLUE LIGHT (***HOLY*** LIGHT) maintains its EQUILIBRIUM in ELEMENTS and spends none of its ENERGY, therefore not producing HEAT.

All STARS are lacking in one or more of its BLUE LIGHT ELEMENTS and this causes an ongoing nuclear fusion chain reaction to occur. This continual nuclear reaction is caused by the STAR trying to equalize and balance its BLUE LIGHT ELEMENTS. The nuclear reaction goes on for the entire LIFECYCLE of the STAR, and the STAR spends all of its ELEMENTS over time to fuel the reaction; thus causing the STAR to AGE and eventually DIE. As the STAR AGES, its COMPOSITION changes by using up the ELEMENTS within itself to fuel the nuclear reaction. A very old STAR will be composed of primarily HELIUM; whereas the more middle aged STARS will consist of mostly HYDROGEN.

The light (the color bands) that the STAR EMITS can identify both its age and composition. Most of the STARS in this GALAXY (the MILKY WAY) are HYDROGEN BASED STARS that are lacking in their OXYGEN content and are middle aged. The STARS emitting a dominant BRIGHT BLUE BAND of LIGHT, are the youngest and brightest stars, and are also the stars least lacking in BLUE LIGHT ELEMENTS. As the ELEMENTS of the STAR are SPENT during its fusion process, it slowly degenerates. This degeneration of the STAR is due to its lacking in BLUE LIGHT ELEMENTS, the ELEMENTS providing Life to the STAR. As the ELEMENTS are spent in the fusion process, the STAR begins to DIM and will eventually change in color and DIE.

As the STAR ages it degrades, because it spends the elements within itself, and as the elements diminish, the fusion process slows and eventually stops. The STAR will then GLOW in a BRIGHT RED color, for RED is the PRIMARY SOURCE of LIGHT that the BLUE LIGHT ORIGINATED from. The LIGHT from the STAR will go from BRIGHT BLUE at its BIRTH, to GREEN in its declining years, and finally to RED as it begins to DIE. Once the STAR is in the form of RED LIGHT, it will start to EXPAND and shortly thereafter explode into blue gaseous particles, because the RED LIGHT by itself cannot be CONTAINED within the STAR'S ENVELOPE.

NOTE: As explained by the ***TRINITY of LIGHT,*** the RED LIGHT represents ***YAHWEH,*** the GREEN LIGHT represents ***IXOTE,*** and the BLUE LIGHT represents ***YESHUA.*** This is the BEGINNING COLOR SCHEME of LIFE from ***GOD*** in the form of LIGHT, RED, to GREEN, and then to BLUE. Therefore, in the declining LIFE of a STAR, the COLOR SCHEME of life REVERSES, and goes from BLUE, to GREEN, to RED.

It is the STAR that gives birth to the PLANET, by expelling some of its ELEMENTS from within to an orbit around itself; and the PLANET is formed by those ELEMENTS as they cool. As the PLANET'S surface cools it moves further from the STAR giving birth to it, because it grows in mass as its CORE disperses the various ELEMENTS to the PLANET'S SURFACE. As the ELEMENTS rise to the surface of the PLANET they cool, CARBONIZE, and change from a gas to a liquid, and then to a solid. The MASS of the SOLID CARBONIZED ELEMENT is significantly greater than the gas that the SOLID had originated from. It is the change in MASS of the PLANET that moves the PLANET into an outer orbit around its HOST STAR. The core of the PLANET in support of LIFE will be in the SAME COMPOSITION as the STAR providing its birth. A STAR is a form of LIVING MATTER, it experiences a TEMPORARY PHYSICAL LIFE and because it is in a TIME CONTINUUM it AGES and eventually DIES; as does all PHYSICAL LIFE.

The STAR, having life, must EXPEL ALL of its ELEMENTS in equal measure from within it to FORM a PLANET capable of LIFE. Then, as the PLANET COOLS and DISPERSES those ELEMENTS from its CORE to its SURFACE, it too can give BIRTH to PHYSICAL LIFE, providing all the ELEMENTS of the HOST STAR are present in the PLANET'S CORE. The PLANET as it COOLS provides CARBONIZATION to its rising ELEMENTS, and the STAR provides its LIGHT and its HEAT. The STAR and the PLANET can then provide the essentials for a PHYSICAL LIFE to BEGIN and live on the PLANET'S SURFACE.

If any single ELEMENT of the HOST STAR is missing from the PLANET'S CORE COMPOSITION, the PLANET will be incapable of providing LIFE or in HOSTING LIFE. ALL STARS hosting LIFE must be BLUE in COLOR at the TIME they give BIRTH to a PLANET, for it is the BLUE LIGHT that is the HOST to LIFE ITSELF. ALL LIFE comes from the BLUE LIGHT, having the ELEMENTS within it SUPPORTIVE of LIFE. Whereas BLUE LIGHT provides LIFE to ALL SPIRITUAL MATTER, TAINTED BLUE LIGHT provides the HEAT necessary to CARBONIZE the BLUE LIGHT ELEMENTS into PHYSICAL MATTER, and this process is supportive of PHYSICAL Life.

John 1:4 *In **HIM** was LIFE; and the LIFE was the LIGHT of MEN.*

SPIRITUAL LIGHT in a Physical Form

There are more STARS in the UNIVERSE hosting PLANETS with PHYSICAL LIFE than there are sands of the seas. As explained in ALL THREE BOOKS I have written for ***THE LORD,*** the GENTILE, ***GOD'S*** SIXTH DAY CREATION, has not a ***GOD GIVEN SPIRIT,*** but rather an EARTH GIVEN SPIRIT. All PLANETS providing PHYSICAL LIFE throughout the UNIVERSE do the SAME for their inhabitants as the EARTH does for the GENTILE; they as well provide a Spirit for the Physical Person they host. It is the Spirit that provides one with their IDENTITY, PERSONALITY and INDIVIDUALITY. It is also the Spirit that allows rationality in the thought process, by using logic as its guide in its decision-making.

However, only the EARTH provides a PHYSICAL LIFE FORM that is suitable to house a SPIRITUAL LIGHT BEING. All other forms of LIFE within the UNIVERSE, even though many of them are quite similar in appearance to a HUMAN BEING, cannot provide the ENVIRONMENT ESSENTIAL to support the LIFE of a SPIRITUAL LIGHT BEING. When ***GOD*** said that ***HE*** made MAN in ***HIS OWN IMAGE, HE*** was speaking more so about ***HIS SPIRITUAL IMAGE*** than about MAN'S PHYSICAL IMAGE, that of which also mimics ***GOD'S SPIRITUAL IMAGE.***

The EARTH given Spirit is the only PHYSICAL Spirit in existence that emulates the IMAGE of ***GOD'S SPIRIT,*** and, only lacks in a SOUL to be the SAME as a ***GOD*** GIVEN SPIRIT. The ***GOD*** GIVEN SPIRIT requires the EXPOSURE to both GOOD and EVIL to PROPERLY MATURE and RECEIVES an ETERNITY of LIFE after MATURITY. The Spirit given by the EARTH, like any other PLANET given Spirit, returns to the DUST of the EARTH or to the Spirit's HOST PLANET at the time of TERMINATION of PHYSICAL LIFE and does not RECEIVE ETERNITY.

However the EARTH itself as a PLANET is really quite different than all the other PLANETS hosting Life. The PLANET WE call EARTH at this TIME, is the only PLANET in EXISTENCE of its kind, and no other PLANET is like it. The EARTH is made to be a scaled down version of what HEAVEN was like at the time of the FALL of LUCIFER. And, other than it being smaller and composed of physical matter rather than LIGHT MATTER, the EARTH and the FIRST HEAVEN are unique in their likeness.

You have been told throughout this BOOK and in the other TWO BOOKS as well that the EARTH HOST'S THREE Spiritual type Entities. The SEED of the BLESSED, the ***GOD*** GIVEN SPIRIT, the SEED of the BEAST (the GENTILE) the EARTH given Spirit, and the SEED of the DAMNED, the Spirit of Lucifer. When ***GOD*** SCRIPTED CREATION and PHYSICAL LIFE, ***HE*** did not want to PENALIZE the native Spirit of the EARTH, the GENTILE, by exposing only them to EVIL. The other PLANETS hosting life haven't any EVIL in them, and the inhabitants of those PLANETS live a productive life without the complications of life as a result of EVIL. The GENTILE on the other hand was made to live amidst EVIL, so ***GOD*** gave the GENTILE the opportunity to choose between GOOD and EVIL for their DESTINY.

The GENTILE who chooses to be GOOD rather than EVIL will RECEIVE BAPTISM and a SOUL. The GENTILE choosing EVIL over GOOD receives DAMNATION and HELL FIRE along with the DAMNED; and, the GENTILE choosing neither GOOD nor EVIL as its HOST, after its brief life simply returns to the DUST of the EARTH.

LIFE in a TIME Continuum

ALL PHYSICAL LIFE in a TIME CONTINUUM ages and eventually dies! This includes the STARS and the PLANETS, the LIFE FORMS on the surfaces of the PLANETS, and even the UNIVERSE itself eventually DIES from old age.

The DIMENSION of TIME begins every SEVEN TRILLION YEARS with each and every "BIG BANG". When the BLUE LIGHT strikes the COMPRESSED LIGHT causing the COMPRESSED LIGHT to SCATTER, the UNIVERSAL CLOCK for TIME BEGINS along with the various LIFE CYCLES of that which is contained within the COMPRESSED LIGHT. The BLUE LIGHT provides the FUEL necessary to run the UNIVERSAL LIFECYCLE for the SEVEN TRILLION YEAR PERIOD, and when the FUEL is spent the UNIVERSE again FOLDS BACK into itself. It then stays in its compressed state for FORTY-NINE BILLION YEARS, and then the BLUE LIGHT once again pierces and refuels the COMPRESSED LIGHT restarting its CYCLE.

Once the CYCLE RESTARTS, the UNIVERSE over the next NINE HUNDRED and TWO BILLION YEARS expands and forms the GALAXIES and STARS to host the majority of PLANETS; some of which will host PHYSICAL LIFE. The EARTH is always the LAST PLANET to HOST Life on its surface, and the PLANET called the EARTH in the first EARTH LIFECYCLE of the NEW UNIVERSE, is always a different PLANET TYPE than those PLANETS called the EARTH thereafter. The first EARTH LIFE CYCLE in a NEW UNIVERSE is 8224 years long whereas every LIFE CYCLE thereafter is 7,000 years over the course of the UNIVERSE'S SEVEN TRILLION YEAR CYCLE.

The first PLANET Earth to host SPIRITUAL LIGHT BEINGS is not in the SIMILITUDE of OLD HEAVEN, whereas all the EARTHS succeeding the first Earth are. The reason being, Lucifer FALLS from the GRACE of ***GOD*** during the first Earth's LIFECYCLE, and only after he has FALLEN from HEAVEN are the EARTH TYPE PLANETS made in the similitude of OLD HEAVEN.

The AGE of the UNIVERSE

The measurement of the actual age of the UNIVERSE is really quite difficult for three very real reasons. The first reason is that the age of the UNIVERSE must be measured from the "BIG BANG" epicenter, and the EARTH is quite far from the epicenter. So measurements relative to the position of the EARTH can be quite deceiving for it will make the UNIVERSE appear to be much younger than it really is.

The second reason is the use of LIGHT SPEED as a standard for measuring TIME. As the UNIVERSE expands over TIME the velocity of LIGHT decreases. At the MOMENT of IMPACT with the BLUE LIGHT, LIGHT SPEED is INFINITE, and as the COMPRESSED LIGHT SCATTERS in all directions and EXPANDS it slows down. The BLUE LIGHT is what fuels the rapid expansion of the COMPRESSED LIGHT, and as the UNIVERSE EXPANDS it spends that FUEL thus changing the LIGHT PARTICLES VELOCITY as a function of TIME. Therefore, by using the velocity of LIGHT for a TIME STANDARD, the measurement of TIME will slow as the VELOCITY of LIGHT slows thus making TIME a VARIABLE consistent with the SPEED of LIGHT.

The third reason for the difficulty in the measurement of the age of the UNIVERSE is, the EXPANSION RATE of the UNIVERSE varies from its EPICENTER to its OUTER BOUNDARY (its ENVELOPE). That which is nearest to the EPICENTER moves much quicker than that which is nearest to its ENVELOPE, therefore making LIGHT SPEED VELOCITY and TIME, a variable within a variable.

The only LIGHT SOURCE that remains to be CONSTANT as a FUNCTION of TIME and EXPANSION is ***HOLY LIGHT***, PURE LIGHT, and its THREE COLOR BANDS, RED, GREEN, and BLUE LIGHT. When in their PROPER MIXTURE, the RED, GREEN, and BLUE LIGHTS form to make the PURE and ABSOLUTE ENERGY of ***WHITE LIGHT, GOD!*** PURE and AB-

SOLUTE ENERGY cannot be attenuated or dissipated in anyway, for it is INFINITE and UNCHANGEABLE in TIME!

Whereas modern scientists estimate the age of the current UNIVERSE to be between 8 and 13 billion years old, in actuality it is nearly THREE TRILLION years old and about halfway into its SEVEN TRILLION-YEAR LIFECYCLE. The reasoning behind the gross error in age approximation is in the methods of TIME measurement. The EARTH sits near to the UNIVERSE'S outermost BOUNDARY, and ALL of the LIGHT PARTICLES (STARS) created by the BIG BANG are in the shape of an expanding ring.

When looking back in time from the EARTH towards the EPICENTER of the BIG BANG, measurement of more than 25 billion light years is not practical, because there aren't any objects such as STARS to relate distance to beyond the inside of the ring. The entire width of the RING of OBJECTS created by the BIG BANG is only FORTY-NINE BILLION LIGHT YEARS in distance. Therefore, if the EARTH sat in the MIDDLE of the RING'S WIDTH (which it does not), when looking from the EARTH one could only see 24.5 billion light years in either direction.

The FORMING of GALAXIES

As a simple explanation, the UNIVERSE expands in a RING SHAPE in much the same way water moves in a pond when a stone is dropped into it. As the RING of water caused by the stone expands through the pond it spreads until it reaches its banks where the shockwave of water caused by the stone is dissipated. However, the TRUE EXPANSION of the UNIVERSE is somewhat more complicated than simply relating it to what happens when a stone is dropped into a pond.

The phenomena of the EXPANDING UNIVERSE can be more accurately related to a stone being dropped into a pond of water having an explosive charge within it; and at the exact moment the stone impacts the water the explosive charge within the stone is detonated. Now this would create a PRIMARY SHOCKWAVE in the SHAPE of a RING by the stone's impacting the water, and as well, multiple SECONDARY SHOCKWAVE RINGS caused by the particles of stone being emitted by the detonation of the explosive. To further complicate matters, the particles of stone that are scattered as a result of the explosive detonation are all different in size, and therefore each of the SECONDARY SHOCKWAVE RINGS caused by the particles of stone are also different in size. This variation in SECONDARY SHOCKWAVE RINGS is what has caused the GALAXIES to form within the UNIVERSE, with each GALAXY being like a universe within the UNIVERSE.

CARBON, the KEY to BIOLOGICAL LIFE

As explained earlier in this Chapter, a PLANET is formed by a STAR that has expelled some of its ELEMENTS into an orbit around itself, and as the PLANET cools the orbit increases due to its increasing in MASS by its changing in states. A PLANET supporting of LIFE must have all of the ELEMENTS present within the HOST STAR at its CORE. If even a single ELEMENT within the STAR is missing from the PLANET'S CORE, the PLANET will be unsuitable to create or sustain any biological forms of life on its surface. Not all STARS are suitable to create a PLANET supportive of life, for not all STARS contain the UNIQUE ELEMENTS of LIFE within them.

The STARS retaining ALL the ELEMENTS of BLUE LIGHT within them can give LIFE to a PLANET supportive of LIFE, providing all ELEMENTS of the BLUE LIGHT are present at the CORE of the PLANET. A PLANET whose CORE is consistent with the ELEMENTS essential for LIFE, as it COOLS, releases the ELEMENTS from its CORE and they begin to rise to the SURFACE of the PLANET. As all of the ELEMENTS RISE from the PLANET'S CORE to its SURFACE, some begin to CARBONIZE and move from a gaseous state to a liquid state, and then into a SOLID STATE. The ELEMENTS that RISE and stay in the gaseous state, encircle the PLANET and form its outer ATMOSPHERE. The ELEMENTS that RISE and change from a gaseous state to a liquid state, and remain in a liquid state, form its seas and fresh water. The ELEMENTS that RISE and CARBONIZE as they COOL turn into a SOLID STATE and create the PLANET'S SOIL and the SANDS of its SEAS. The CARBON molecules that collected on the ELEMENTS as they cool then act as a CATALYST for the other ELEMENTS, and they begin to attach to one another.

As the various ELEMENTS combine sharing only in their CARBON CONTENT, they become LIVING MATTER, allowing the like forms of life to reproduce and regenerate in the same form of life. It is the CARBON MOLECULES that allow the various ELEMENTS to COMBINE, for the CARBON acts as a CATALYST between the various ELEMENTS, HOLDING them together.

This begins on the PLANET'S SURFACE in a cellular form, and as the various cells reproduce, they migrate and combine with other carbonized cell forms of life on the PLANET'S SURFACE. The cell forms eventually become a species of life containing multiple cell forms of life being held together by carbon molecules. The species then adapts to the ATMOSPHERIC CONDITIONS of the PLANET and this causes the SPECIES to further MIGRATE and combine with other SPECIES. This process continues on until ALL PREDESTINED SPECIES for that PLANET have been CREATED.

GOD Determines LIFE FORMS

When ***GOD*** SCRIPTED CREATION, all the STARS and PLANETS and them who were to INHABIT the PLANETS were all predetermined, with each SPECIES serving a PURPOSE for ***GOD.*** Every DETAIL for that in EXISTENCE was SCRIPTED into the BOOK. The TIME for EXISTENCE, them in EXISTENCE, and ALL of EXISTENCE was SCRIPTED into the BOOK.

For instance, all of the PLANETS hosting life have various lower scale life forms on their SURFACES prior to the HIGHER INTELLIGENCE LIFE FORMS inhabiting them. With the exception of the first, the various PLANETS being called EARTH throughout the UNIVERSE'S LIFECYCLE initially have a population of reptiles inhabiting them. This form of reptilian life first inhabits the EARTH to provide the MAN who is to come later with a resource of fossil fuel, and all of the species that dies off prior to the coming of MAN, provide some sort of resource necessary for MAN'S survival.

GOD moves MAN throughout the UNIVERSE to inhabit the various PLANETS to be called EARTH, with each and everyone of the EARTHS having a sun for a HOST STAR, and eight or more other sister planets orbiting the HOST STAR with it. Each circumstance existing in MAN'S current world has been IDENTICALLY duplicated in each EARTH coming after it, with only the first Earth being different from all the rest.

Every EARTH CREATED by ***GOD*** sits in the SAME BOUNDARY of TIME, as TIME RELATES to the UNIVERSE. ***GOD*** does this so that the EARTH'S TIME ZONE never changes in relationship to the UNIVERSAL CLOCK'S TIME. As previously explained, the UNIVERSE is in the form of a RING, and the EARTH sits near to the outermost point of the RING. Each and every EARTH sits in the SAME TIME and DISTANCE of the UNIVERSAL RING as it relates to its EPICENTER. However each EARTH is in a different locale in relationship to the CIRCUMFERENCE of the RING.

The ONE BILLION EARTH LIFECYCLES take place in a different locale around the CIRCUMFERENCE of the UNIVERSAL RING. Each TIME the EARTH CYCLES it is REPOSITIONED about the UNIVERSAL RING by ONE ONE-BILLIONTH (1/1,000,000,000) of its CIRCUMFERENCE. At the

CONCLUSION of the SEVEN TRILLION-YEAR UNIVERSAL LIFECYCLE, the EARTH has MOVED 360 degrees around the UNIVERSAL RING, thus making one complete revolution around the UNIVERSE in ONE ONE-BILLIONTH increments.

The same physical EARTH is used for SEVEN incremental movements around the UNIVERSAL RING. The EARTH'S SURFACE is all that is DESTROYED for the first six movements around the RING'S CIRCUMFERENCE, and it is DESTROYED in its ENTIRETY at the CONCLUSION of its SEVENTH CYCLE (every 49,000 years). During those SEVEN, SEVEN-THOUSAND YEAR CYCLES a NEW EARTH has been MATURING, so each new EARTH is FORTY-NINE THOUSAND YEARS older than its PREDECESSOR. Therefore, if the current EARTH can be accurately AGED, one could tell approximately at what point in the UNIVERSAL LIFECYCLE you currently are. ALL of the NEW EARTHS were CREATED at the SAME TIME, and are located SEVEN ONE-BILLIONTHS of the CIRCUMFERENCE of UNIVERSAL RING apart from one another. Each of the NEW EARTHS is only inhabited for FORTY-NINE THOUSAND YEARS and is then DESTROYED. So when viewed from HEAVEN, the POSITION of the EARTH in relation to its POSITION on the CIRCUMFERENCE of the UNIVERSAL RING, keeps the TIME of the UNIVERSAL LIFECYCLE much like the hands do on a clock. It takes SEVEN TRILLION YEARS for the EARTH to make ONE COMPLETE UNIVERSAL CYCLE!

Chapter 25
Contradictions?

Although to the unlearned READER there appear to be CONTRADICTIONS throughout the HOLY BIBLE, they are not CONTRADICTIONS at all, but further TRUTHS pertaining to the same subject matter. In this Chapter WE will enlighten your UNDERSTANDING about the seemingly CONTRADICTORY STATEMENTS found in the BIBLE, and point out to you how the CONFUSION results from one's misinterpreting the Scriptures.

In the first five Scriptures of Chapter 7 of the GOSPEL ACCORDING to Mathew, JESUS makes it quite CLEAR that YOU should NOT JUDGE anyone other than yourself, and even that can be misleading, if one is not open to HONEST self-criticism. But yet in the 33rd Verse of the 12th Chapter of Matthew, JESUS says:

> ***Matthew 12:33 EITHER MAKE THE TREE GOOD, AND HIS FRUIT GOOD; OR ELSE MAKE THE TREE CORRUPT, AND HIS FRUIT CORRUPT: FOR THE TREE IS KNOWN BY HIS FRUIT.***

After JESUS in the 7th Chapter of Matthew had told HIS Disciples that they should not JUDGE one another, it appears in the 33rd Verse of the 12th Chapter that JESUS is giving the Disciples a GUIDELINE for JUDGMENT. Is this a CONTRADICTION in what HE had previously told HIS Disciples? It is NOT, and WE will EXPLAIN as to why it is NOT a CONTRADICTION.

In Chapter 7 of the GOSPEL of Matthew, JESUS is speaking about INTERVENING JUDGMENT, whereas in the 33rd Verse of the 12th Chapter of Matthew, JESUS speaks about JUDGMENT by OBSERVATION. INTERVENING JUDGMENT refers to when one takes it upon him or herself to criticize another and tell them where their FAULT lies based on their personal analysis and interpretation of that individual's words or actions.

JESUS says in the 7th Chapter of Matthew, that this type of INTERVENING JUDGMENT SHOULD NOT be DONE; because one must deal with their own

FAULTS FIRST, and not be JUDGMENTAL about the FAULTS they might see in another. JESUS WARNS the Disciples that whatever STANDARDS they might use to JUDGE another PERSON, ***GOD*** will JUDGE them by those very same STANDARDS. JESUS says, therefore, JUDGMENT should be left to ***GOD***, for ***GOD*** is PERFECT and can JUDGE PERFECTLY, whereas YOU are not perfect!

Furthermore, in the 33rd Verse of the 12th Chapter of Matthew, JESUS speaks about JUDGMENT by OBSERVATION, and not about INTERVENING JUDGMENT. What JESUS is saying to HIS Disciples in this Scripture, is that they should observe the actions or words coming from other people, and if they see that those words or actions are EVIL and CORRUPT, they should steer clear of them. Therefore, the JUDGMENT being provided by their OBSERVATIONS is JUDGMENT for themselves, and not for them whom they OBSERVE.

Most of the more seemingly CONTRADICTORY statements lie in the Scriptures speaking about the EARTH'S DESTRUCTION, versus them that say the EARTH remains forever. When the UNLEARNED READER reads in some Scriptures that the EARTH abides forever, and in yet other Scriptures that the EARTH is DESTROYED in its ENTIRETY, their first INCLINATION is that the HOLY BIBLE is CONTRADICTORY in its STATEMENTS.

> ***Ecclesiastes 1:4*** *One generation passeth away, and another generation cometh: but the EARTH ABIDETH FOR EVER.*

> ***Isaiah 24:20*** *The EARTH shall reel to and fro like a drunkard, and shall be REMOVED like a cottage; and the TRANSGRESSION thereof shall be heavy upon it; and it shall FALL, and NOT RISE AGAIN.*

The first Scripture cited from Ecclesiastes says that the EARTH ABIDES FOREVER, while the second Scripture taken from the Book of Isaiah says the OPPOSITE. It says that the EARTH shall FALL and NOT RISE AGAIN. So which Scripture is CORRECT, the FIRST or the SECOND?

Oddly enough BOTH Scriptures are CORRECT. The Statement made in the first Scripture refers to the EARTH being RENEWED or RECREATED after it has been DESTROYED, so that there is ALWAYS an EARTH within the UNIVERSE as long as the UNIVERSE EXISTS. WE covered this phenomenon in the last Chapter of this BOOK. When one EARTH is DESTROYED, the FACE of the EARTH is either RENEWED or a NEW EARTH is CREATED. In either case there always remains an EARTH within the UNIVERSE and while there is a PHYSICAL EXISTENCE below the FIRMAMENT there is an EARTH in that EXISTENCE. This is consistent to what SOLOMON had said in Ecclesiastes, "the EARTH ABIDETH FOR EVER".

What was discussed earlier in the last Chapter of this BOOK is also supportive of the second Scripture taken from the Book of Isaiah. This Scripture speaks about the continual movement of the EARTH about the OUTER RING of the UNIVERSE, and how when one EARTH is DESTROYED another takes its place. The Scripture says that it is MOVED around like a COTTAGE from one place to another, and it also says the EARTH is DESTROYED because of its SIN! When one EARTH is DESTROYED, another EARTH takes its place, and each NEW EARTH rotates around on the OUTER RING of the UNIVERSE.

So as YOU can SEE, even though the Scriptures appear to CONTRADICT one another, they do not, once YOU understand the phenomena relating to the LIFECYCLES of CREATION. Even in this BOOK there are many things said that could be seen as CONTRADICTORY STATEMENTS. The one thing in particular that ***THE LORD*** has pointed out to ME is that in one Chapter of this BOOK it says that the EARTH can be no older 49,000 years, while in the Chapter titled "CREATION", it says that the EARTH came into EXISTENCE at the BEGINNING of CREATION. It further says, at some point in the UNIVERSE'S LIFECYCLE, the EARTH can be over SIX TRILLION YEARS OLD. Are these CONTRADICTORY STATEMENTS?

These are really not CONTRADICTORY STATEMENTS, although they may seem to be. The first EARTH inhabited by MANKIND was most certainly older than 49,000 years, because the GENTILE inhabited the EARTH 70,000 years before the TIME of ADAM. However, the CLOCK governing the EARTH LIFECYCLES starts at the TIME of ADAM only for the first earth, and then at the TIME of NOAH entering the ARK for the REMAINING 999,999,999 EARTH LIFECYCLES.

The first Earth has a LIFECYCLE of 8224 years after the CREATION of ADAM, and each NEW EARTH thereafter has a LIFECYCLE of 7,000 years starting at the TIME when NOAH enters the ARK. At the CONCLUSION of each SEVEN THOUSAND-YEAR LIFECYCLE, either the SURFACE of the EARTH or the EARTH in its ENTIRETY is DESTROYED. The NEXT EARTH sitting SEVEN ONE-BILLIONTHS of the UNIVERSE'S CIRCUMFERENCE to the right of the previously DESTROYED EARTH, is then inhabited. This changing of one EARTH to another happens after the previous EARTH had completed SEVEN LIFECYCLES (49,000 years).

Although the PLANET called EARTH is significantly older than MANKIND (the GENTILE) or the BLESSED and DAMNED SEED that eventually inhabit it, the CLOCK starts in its LIFECYCLE at the TIME of ADAM for the FIRST CYCLE and then at the TIME of NOAH'S entering the ARK for its remaining LIFECYCLES. Each succeeding NEW EARTH is 49,000 years older than its PREDECESSOR, because ALL of the PLANETS to be CALLED EARTH came into EXISTENCE at the same TIME, as TIME relates to the UNIVERSAL CLOCK.

GOD relates the AGE of the EARTHS to the TIMES that ***HIS*** PEOPLE inhabit them, and not to the AGE of the EARTH'S GEOLOGICAL EXISTENCE. Depending on where you are at in the UNIVERSAL LIFECYCLE, the PLANET you are now on CALLED "EARTH" can be anywhere from 1.3 TRILLION years old (when the SECOND EARTH first came into EXISTENCE) to 6,999,999,999,999 years old on a GEOLOGICAL SCALE of TIME. Nothing in EXISTENCE can exceed the SEVEN TRILLION YEAR UNIVERSAL LIFECYCLE. However, after each UNIVERSAL CYCLE another CYCLE BEGINS, and this goes on and on throughout ETERNITY. Existence in itself cannot be MEASURED for only ***GOD*** KNOWS how many such EARTH or UNIVERSAL LIFECYCLES have been completed.

At the TIME the UNIVERSE reaches the END of its LIFECYCLE, its OUTER RING will be SEVEN TRILLION LIGHT YEARS away from its EPICENTER. This makes the DIAMETER of the UNIVERSE FOURTEEN TRILLION light-years in size and its CIRCUMFERENCE approximately FORTY-FOUR TRILLION light-years in time and distance. This cannot be viewed as a linear measurement, because both the SPEED of LIGHT and TIME slows as the UNIVERSE EXPANDS.

Synopsis

Whenever READING the HOLY BIBLE and finding statements by Scripture that appear to either CONTRADICT or CONFLICT with other Scriptural statements, refer to the THREE BOOKS I have WRITTEN for ***THE LORD.*** At least ONE of the THREE will contain an EXPLANATION as to the TRUTHFULNESS of the Scriptures and how ALL of the Scriptures apply, even though they might seem to be CONTRADICTORY to one another.

Life hasn't any simple EXPLANATION, and the HOLY BIBLE, that of which EXPLAINS LIFE and EXISTENCE, cannot be SIMPLY UNDERSTOOD! ***THE LORD*** has had ME write the THREE BOOKS for ***HIM*** so YOU may use them as a GUIDELINE in the INTERPRETATION of the HOLY

SCRIPTURES. The TIME of the END of the EARTH'S LIFECYCLE is NEAR; even at the DOOR; and the THREE BOOKS WRITTEN for ***THE LORD*** are done so to FULFILL END TIME PROPHECY. USE THEM AS SUCH!

> ***Revelation 10:1*** *AND I saw another* ***ANGEL*** *come down from HEAVEN, clothed with a cloud: and a RAINBOW was upon* ***HIS HEAD,*** *and* ***HIS FACE*** *was as it were the SUN, and* ***HIS FEET*** *as pillars of FIRE:*
>
> ***Revelation 10:2*** *And* ***HE*** *had in* ***HIS HAND*** *a LITTLE BOOK open: and* ***HE*** *set* ***HIS RIGHT FOOT*** *upon the sea, and* ***HIS LEFT FOOT*** *on the EARTH,*
>
> ***Revelation 10:3*** *And CRIED with a* ***LOUD VOICE****, as when a lion roareth: and when* ***HE*** *had CRIED,* ***SEVEN THUNDERS*** *uttered their* ***VOICES.***
>
> ***Revelation 10:4*** *And when the* ***SEVEN THUNDERS*** *had uttered* ***THEIR VOICES****, I was about to WRITE: and I heard a* ***VOICE*** *from HEAVEN saying unto me,* ***SEAL UP THOSE THINGS WHICH THE SEVEN THUNDERS UTTERED, AND WRITE THEM NOT.***
>
> ***Revelation 10:5*** *And the* ***ANGEL*** *which I saw STAND upon the sea and upon the EARTH LIFTED UP* ***HIS HAND*** *to HEAVEN,*
>
> ***Revelation 10:6*** *And SWARE by* ***HIM*** *that LIVETH for EVER and EVER, who CREATED HEAVEN, and the things that therein are, and the EARTH, and the things that therein are, and the SEA, and the things which are therein, that there should be TIME NO LONGER:*
>
> ***Revelation 10:7*** *But in the DAYS of the* ***VOICE*** *of the* ***SEVENTH ANGEL,*** *when* ***HE*** *shall begin to SOUND, the MYSTERY of* ***GOD*** *should be FINISHED, as* ***HE*** *hath DECLARED to* ***HIS*** *SERVANTS the PROPHETS.*

Revelation 10:8** And the **VOICE** which I heard from HEAVEN spake unto me again, and said, **GO AND TAKE THE LITTLE BOOK WHICH IS OPEN IN THE HAND OF THE ANGEL WHICH STANDETH UPON THE SEA AND UPON THE EARTH.

Revelation 10:9** And I went unto the **ANGEL**, and said unto **HIM,** GIVE ME THE LITTLE BOOK, And **HE** said unto me, **TAKE IT, AND EAT IT UP; AND IT SHALL MAKE THY BELLY BITTER, BUT IT SHALL BE IN THY MOUTH SWEET AS HONEY.

***Revelation 10:10** And I took the LITTLE BOOK out of the **ANGEL'S HAND**, and ate it up; and it was in my mouth sweet as honey: and as soon as I had eaten it, my belly was bitter.*

Revelation 10:11** And **HE** said unto me, **THOU MUST PROPHESY AGAIN BEFORE MANY PEOPLES, AND NATIONS, AND TONGUES, AND KINGS.

THESE WERE THE LAST MINUTE INSTRUCTIONS GIVEN TO THE APOSTLE JOHN; FOR IT IS JOHN WHO WILL LEAD THE TRIBULATION SAINTS!

THE END!

Reference Guide

INTRODUCTION
Introduction....................5

FOREWORD
SPIRITUAL AWAKENING....................11
Antichrist....................14
DELIVERANCE....................15
RAPTURE....................15
DESTRUCTION of the EARTH....................16
HEAVEN on EARTH....................16
The THREE BOOKS....................17

Chapter #1 The INHERITANCE
GIFTS of INHERITANCE....................21
The GIFT of the EARTH....................22
The GIFT of ABSOLUTE FREEDOM....................26
The GIFT of UNDERSTANDING and KNOWLEDGE....................27
The GIFT of ETERNAL LIGHT (LIFE)....................27
The GIFT of ETERNAL COMFORT....................28
The GIFT of TOTAL WISDOM....................29
The GIFT of HEAVENLY DOMAIN....................31
The RIGHTFUL HEIR....................31

Chapter #2 SPIRITUAL ASCENSION
SPIRITUAL AWAKENING (REBIRTH)....................33
PROTECTION....................36
Ascension Plateaus....................36
The THIRTY STEPS....................38
BAPTISM and SEALING....................39

Chapter #3 SPIRIT (IDENTITY)
Types of Spirits....................42
Spiritual DECEPTION....................45
Spiritual MASKING and DISGUISE....................47
GOOD RELATIONSHIPS versus Evil Ones....................49
Summary....................50

Chapter #4 SOUL (PURPOSE)
The Gentile and the BEGINNING....52
QUALITIES of the SOUL....55
SPIRIT and SOUL....58

Chapter #5 The ANGELS
The SWITCHING of GUARDIANS....62
SPIRITUAL IDENTIFICATION....64
The ANGEL versus MAN....65

Chapter #6 Lucifer and his Fallen Regime
Lucifer's Plan....70
The UNFORGIVABLE SIN....71
The Threat of Death, Lucifer's Ace in the hole!....73
The TEMPTER invades YOUR MIND....74
Lucifer's SEVEN HEADS....76
SIN Specialists....77
HELL OPENED....78
War of the ANGELS....79
THE METATRON are RELEASED....79

Chapter #7 SPEAKING to the SPIRIT
EMOTION from WORDS....85
Listening to the SOUL....86
EGO blocks TRUTH....87
Lost in TRANSLATION....88

Chapter #8 The FOUR SONS of GOD
The DELIVERERS....95
Bridging the GAP....97
CHRIST....98
The FOUR LIVING BEASTS (CHRIST)....100
The WRATH of the LAMB (The FOUR SERAPHIM)....101
Summary....103
LETTER and NUMBER Reference Guide....105

Chapter #9 EARTH Angels
The Beginning of EARTH Angels....108
Increasing the NUMBER of ANGELS....108
Angelic OFFSPRING and EARTHLY Marriage....109
DIVINE PURPOSE....110
UNEXPECTED HELP....112
Acts of the Earth Angel....113

Chapter #10 Gender and Sexual Behavior
Sexual Desire versus SPIRITUAL LOVE....117

Physical Attraction....118

Chapter #11 NUMBERS

The Antichrist....124
The FALSE PROPHET....124
The DEVIL and the BEAST....126
After Empowerment....127
NUMBERS of IMPORTANCE....128
TRINITY NUMBERS....130
Other TRIPLICATE NUMBERS....130
TWIN NUMBERS....130
Other IMPORTANT NUMBERS....131
Significant NUMBERS....131

Chapter #12 MIRACLES

JESUS' MIRACLES....133
GOD PERFORMS MIRACLES....134
Things Don't Just Happen!....135
MIRACLES turned to WRATH....136

Chapter #13 Welcome HOLY SPIRIT; THE DELIVERER 182

THE DELIVERER'S DESCRIPTION according to Habakkuk....140
THE DELIVERER'S DESCRIPTION according to Isaiah....149
BEAUTY and BANDS; JESUS CHRIST and THE DELIVERER 182....151
EVENTS TRIGGERED by THE DELIVERER'S PRESENCE....158

Chapter #14 Hardships

Compounding Hardships....163
TRUSTING in GOD....165
Using SCRIPTURE for GUIDANCE....165
Prepare for HARDSHIP....167

Chapter #15 COMING DOWN with VENGEANCE

Punishment LEVIED by GOD....171
Things will only WORSEN with TIME!....172
Instituting the MARK of the BEAST....173

Chapter #16 GOD'S COMMANDMENTS and LAWS

SEALING versus BAPTISM....181
GOD'S LAWS and STATUTES....182
The TEN COMMANDMENTS....183
GOD'S LAW versus Political Correctness....187

Chapter #17 The Survivors

NEW JERUSALEM....194
The World Outside of NEW JERUSALEM....196

Chapter #18 LIFE within the CITY WALLS

GOD'S PEOPLE, ISRAEL....204
The CITY'S Architecture....205
Activities within the CITY....207
The "BEHEADED SOULS" in the MILLENNIUM....208
TIME IRRELEVANCY....208
LIGHT for the CITY....210

Chapter #19 The CONCLUSION

Returning to the DUST of the EARTH....213
ENTERING IN BY THE EAST GATE....214
Communication within the HEAVENLY DOMAIN....216
The FOUR KINGDOMS....217

Chapter #20 The SCRIBE & The GUARDIAN

The SCRIBE Angel....223
The GUARDIAN Angel....223
PROTECTION for the "SAVED"....225

Chapter #21 JUDGMENT DAY!

Them of the OLD COVENANT....228
The LOT of the WORTHY....229
JUDGMENT PROCEDURE....230
Carrying OUT the SENTENCE....231

Chapter #22 HELL, An ETERNAL Reality

The world of HELL....235
The DEVIL uses YOUR MIND....237
Your Daily Meal....237
The Levels in HELL....237
HELL Resides within the EARTH....238

Chapter #23 CYCLES

HEAVEN AND HELL REMAIN....245
THE LORD'S SABBATHS, GAPS in TIME....246

Chapter #24 CREATION

The TAINTED Light....252
SPIRITUAL LIGHT in a Physical Form....255
LIFE in a TIME Continuum....256
The AGE of the UNIVERSE....257
The FORMING of GALAXIES....258
CARBON, the KEY to BIOLOGICAL LIFE....259
GOD Determines LIFE FORMS....260

Chapter #25 Contradictions?

Synopsis....266